STATE FORMATION IN THE EASTERN DECCAN

[7th Century A.D. - 13th Century A.D.]

A. ARUNA

BKP

BHARATIYA KALA PRAKASHAN
DELHI-INDIA

Published by :
C.P. Gautam
Bharatiya Kala Prakashan
Narang Colony,
3421-A IInd Fl.
Tri Nagar, Delhi-110035
Ph. 7153083

First Published : 2000

ISBN : 81-86050-37-X

Laser Typesetting by :
A-One Graphics
X-4, Gali No. 2, Brahmpuri,
Delhi-110053 Ph. : 2183470

Printed at :
Santosh Ofset Press
Delhi-110035

Dedicated

to

My Parents

Contents

PREFACE

This book is an embodiment of the dissertation submitted by the author for the M.Phil degree of the University of Hyderabad in 1997. The work was pursued under the erudite scholarly guidance of Prof. Aloka Parasher Sen to whom I owe a deep sense of gratitude. It is but for her constant pursuance and encouragement that enabled this work to take the book form.

The history of the Eastern Chālukyas is a well researched topic. Earlier scholarship provides us with rich information about the political, social, economic, and religious conditions of the period. Though much of their study was based on the information available from the inscriptional sources, however their studies garbed under conventionalism failed to understand the nature of State formation under the new ruling elites, namely the Eastern Chālukyas.

The following pages attempt to analyse the various processes of State formation in the sub-region of Eastern Deccan, during the early medieval period. This micro level study attempts to emphasize on the formation and consolidation of the Eastern Chālukyan dynasty, which controlled the entire sub-region of the Eastern Deccan for about a long span of five centuries. This was done keeping in view the dynamics of change inherent in the early medieval socio-economic structure that effected the process of State formation in almost all the major regions of the sub-continent.

For the purpose of this study, data available from the inscriptions of various Chālukyan families such as the Chālukyas of Bādāmi, Eastern Chālukyas of Vengi and the Minor Chālukyan families of Mudigonda, Jananāthapuram and Nidadavōlu were taken up for scrutiny, in order to understand various mechanisms adopted by ruling elites to integrate local polities into the larger state structure through the elements of continuity and change.

I acknowledge with deep sense of gratitude Dr. E. Siva Nagi Reddy for not only helping me with the preparation of maps but also took personal interest in getting this book published, despite his pressing official work.

I thank Prof. B.D. Chattopadhyaya and Dr. P.V. Parabrahma Sastry

Garu for rendering valuable suggestions on the topic at the time of research.

I thank Tejaswini, and Dr. Dilip M. Menon (Reader, Dept. of History, HCU) for taking the trouble of reading the proof and giving me encouragement. My sincere thanks are to Sri S.V. Rama Rao Garu (former Addl. Superintendent of Police, Orissa) who had painstakingly read the proof and provided many valuable suggestions, despite his advancing age.

I express my thanks to Librarians and staff of the State Department of Archaeology and Museums, Hyderabad, and Indira Gandhi Memorial Library, University of Hyderabad, for rendering the needed assistance.

I thank the University of Hyderabad for providing me financial assistance through MCM scholarhip for a period of ten months at the time of research, thus helping me to overcome the financial restraints.

I thank all my friends who helped me in several ways in fructifying the work. I am indebted to my beloved father Sri A.G.S. Sharma, who took pains in typing the whole manuscript, even at the oddest times on our personal computer, and the constant encouragement he gave me at all times to undertake this stupendous venture.

I cannot forget the tremendous encouragement and assistance given by my loving mother Smt. Bharati, my dear brother Vishwanath, my sister, Venkata Lakshmi and her two daughters Harita and Nikita.

I express my thanks to Sri N.S. Ramachandra Murthy Garu (Assistant Director, Dept. of Archaeology and Museums, Government of Andhra Pradesh) for kindly agreeing to write the foreword to the book, despite his busy official work.

It would be ungrateful on my part if I do not thank Shri C.P. Gautamji, of Bharatiya Kala Prakashan, who had readily accepted to publish the work.

30th May 1999
Hyderabad,

A. ARUNA

Foreword

Historical research, in recent years, has undergone a welcome change with its emphasis on understanding the various processes of state formation that were at work, at different regional and local levels. These studies attempted to examine the various mechanisms adopted by the political power to establish its authority over a large area in relation to geography and socio-economic organization and the relationship between royal political systems and local or intermediary powers. The thrust of these studies inspired mainly socio-political and socio-economic transformations from the regional perspective, which gave rise to integrative polity. To this school belong eminent scholars like B.D. Chattopadhyaya, Hermann Kulke and others. They identified major historical processes operating at the local and regional levels which led to the formation of State structures. The primary work of this kind of Chattopadhyaya's study on the state formation under theRajputs which emphasizes on the interplay of various processes like the political, economic, social, and ideological factors. These processes include the fortification of rural settlements as a political mechanism of control and consolidation, the expansion of settlements and growth of agrarian economy through assignment of land grants at the economic level. The social parameters underpinned the role played by caste or varna ideology in the fabric of the society, through the process of acculturation or allowing social mobility from tribalism to Brahmanism. At the ideological level, entering into marriage alliance with the powerful local families and finally legitimizing their rule by drawing genealogical linkages from the mythical past helped the political authority to legitimize its newly acquired political power.

The present book, **STATE FORMATION IN THE EASTERN DECCAN (7th Century A.D. - 13th Century A.D.)**, by Kum. Aruna is a welcome addition to the subject written on the above lines, the first of this kind so far as the studies on Andhra are concerned. For this she chose the State under the Eastern Chalukyas of Vengi, who exercised authority over five centuries over a most fertile and strategic area lying between the rivers Godavari and Krishna, which was considered as an "area of attraction" or nuclear zone. Earlier, traditional scholars like

N. Venkataramanayya and B.V. Krishna Rao have made an in depth study on the Eastern Chalukyan dynasty following a conventional approach. However, the present study by the author is of a novel nature, moving away from the earlier approaches. This study focused on understanding these various mechanisms adopted by the Eastern Chalukyan rulers as new comers to the land of Vengi. This kingdom, being alien to the land in the beginning, adopted certain mechanisms such as conferring land grants on the brahmaṇas, military generals, and temples, entering into marriage alliances with subordinate of feudatory families, providing for social mobility upwards, and fabricating mythical genealogies especially when its stability was under threat by internal and external forces. The author put to scrutiny, over a total of 80 inscriptions belonging to the Badami Chalukyan family, the Eastern Chalukyan family, and the Minor Chalukyan families of Mudigonda, Jananathapuram, and change and the economic, socio-ideological factors that helped in the formation and consolidation of the Eastern Chalukyan power.

The author deserves congratulations for her comprehension of the problem of study and successfully handling the sources material. According to her, the polity of the Eastern Chalukyas of Vengi was neither a centralized bureaucratic structure nor feudal. Instead it was an integrative polity wherein the State attempted to stabilize its power through creating semi-autonomous fiefdoms.

Kum. Aruna has made a discerning study of the subject and arrived at her findings supported by analytical charts. I wish her Good Luck.

N.S. Ramachandramurthy
Assistant Director
Department of Archaeology
and Museums,
Government of Andhra Pradesh

ABBREVIATIONS

AISH	*Ancient Indian Social History*
ARE	*Annual Report of Epigraphy*
BDCRI	*Bulletin of Deccan College Research Institute*
CSSH	*Comparative Studies in Society and History*
EĀ	*Epigraphia Āndhrica*
EI	*Epigraphia Indica*
IA	*Indian Antiquary*
IHR	*Indian Historical Review*
IMCDAP	*Inscriptions of Minor Chalukyan Dynasties of Andhra Pradesh*
JAHRS	*Journal of Andhra Historical Research Society*
JESHO	*Journal of Economic and Social History of the Orient*
JBORS	*Journal of Bihar-Orissa Research Society*
PAPHC	*Proceedings of Andhra Pradesh History Congress*
PIHC	*Proceedings of Indian History Congress*
MAS	*Modern Asian Studies*
SII	*South Indian Inscriptions*

LIST OF CHARTS

LIST OF APPENDIXES

LIST OF MAPS

INTRODUCTION AND SOURCES

The main aim of this study is to examine the various mechanisms adopted by a ruling elite to legitimize and consolidate power in their newly carved out kingdom during the early medieval period. The early medieval period in the Indian context presents an interesting picture in terms of socio-economic transformations seen in terms of the development of new economic relations in the form of land grant economy and change in the traditional *varṇa* structure that brought about changes in the polity in almost all the important regions of the sub-continent. These processes of change accelerated aspects of social mobility of various social groups who constantly sought to establish a new identity for themselves and this was particularly true of ruling elites. Initially, such a move was made by the members of a particular community who had gained economically by the opportunities that were offered to them through changes inherent in the land grant economy. Eventually, ruling elites emerged from within such groups by acquiring political power and authenticated their claims of legitimation and consolidation which necessarily involved ideological means. In order to do this they adopted certain mechanisms in the spheres of political, economic, social and ideological activity. The Eastern Chālukyas of Vengi have been taken up for scrutiny in this context in order to make a case study. They successfully activated and participated in the various processes that helped them to expand and consolidate their power in an alien land and to sustain their kingdom in the Andhra region for five long centuries.

In the context of this study on ruling elites it becomes essential to define the term "Ruling Elite". According to the Oxford Dictionary the term "Ruling" means "Authoritative pronouncement" and the term "Elite" stands for a select group or class advocating dominance.[1] Therefore, the term "Ruling Elite" may be understood in this respect as: "a select group or class of the society entrusted to exercise its authority or dominance over the rest of the society. In recent years studies on ruling elites became a major concern of understanding among modern social scientists. Subsequently, different definitional interpretations were put forward to understand the term *ruling elites.* Generally understood ruling elites are none other than the political elites or goverrning class of a society. While defining the term 'ruling elite' Italian Sociologist Pareto, regarded them as "Governing elites who held high status and commanded influence in the community"[2]. On the other hand, Bottomore understood the term Political elites as 'those individuals who actually exercised political power in a society at a given time'. According to him the term 'elite' stood for functional and occupational groups who enjoyed high status in society.[3]According to Nadel the governing elites are those political rulers who exercised a decisive pre-eminence over other elites, viz., social and specialised elites.[4] To Cole, the term 'elite' stood for those groups which emerged to positions of leadership and influence at every social level.[5] Thus, in all these definitions the modern scientists have over the years understood the term "Ruling elites" to undoubtedly stand for an *organized minority* exercising decisive authority over the *unorganized majority* of the population. Further, the elite in society is attributed such a status not by a single factor like birth, but due to various forces such as the possession of wealth, military prowess or status in a religious hierarchy. However, Modernity defines a political space as distinct from a religious space. This can be compared and contrasted with definition of ruling elites in the Indian source material. In contrast to these modern definitions on ruling elites, in the traditional Indian *Dharmaśāstric* texts definition of ruling elite was intrinsically embedded in the notion of *varṇa* and the ideology it was based on. Accordingly, the society was based on the fourfold division of the *varṇa* ideology representing the *brāhmaṇa*, the *kṣatriya*, the *vaiśya* and the *sūdra varṇas* along with their definite functional and hierarchical occupations. The *kṣatriya varṇa* was placed as the second order in *varṇa* hierarchy whose duties were specified as those of ruling elites.[6] In this type of social structure the elite interaction between the *brāhmaṇa* and *kṣatriya* is very significantly understood. In this sense the ruling elite from the *Dharmaśāstric* point of view cannot be postulated purely in economic or political arenas of activity. But it signifies thereligious ideology through mutual alliance between the *brāhmaṇa* and the *kṣatriya.*

Though, theoritically *varṇa* system projected itself as conservative, readings of *Dharmaśāstric* writers and thinkers constantly emphasized on the inherent flexibility of the *varṇa* system, which is explicit in the concept of *varṇaśaṃkara*. Thus, according to Kautilya ruling elites included all those rulers who discharged the duties of the *kṣatriyas*, irrespective of their origin, such as protection of people *sarva-bhūtarakshānaṃ* righteous rule *nyāyadandatvam*, patronage of learned men (*śrotriya*), living by the use of weapons and not running away from battle-field and so on.[7] Similarly, Manu *Dharmaśāstra* talks about *Vrātya Kṣatriyas* who did not rule righteously were also got accommodated into the *varṇa* hierarchy.

In order to improve their ritual status these new castes sought legitimation from a *brāhmaṇa varṇa*. Recent studies have shown that whenever a *non-kṣatriya* group acquired political power they were given validation of *kṣatriya* origin, through fabricated genealogies.[8] This was made possible with the ritually superior *brāhmaṇa varṇa*. This process helped in the social mobility of various castes which provided an opportunity for many *non-kṣatriya* castes to emerge as ruling elites.[9]

In most of the writings of the traditional historians ruling elites are regarded from the normative perspective. Therefore, in their view ruling elites are considered as belonging to the traditional unchanging *kṣatriya varṇa*. However, it is in recent scholarship that a new trend emerged in the perception of functioning and composition of the *varṇa* structure.[10] The *kṣatriya varṇa* has been understood as being nebulous during the period under study. They represented not only the aristocratic classes but was also said to include all those rulers from other *varṇas* who discharged the duties of the *kṣatriyas* irrespective of their origin. This change in the composition of the ruling elites in terms of *varṇa* status has been clearly understood by the Marxist scholars in terms of the emergence of land grant economy, which has been basically characterized as "feudal" by them.[11] Politically, this was seen as a continuous process of fragmentation and decentralization caused chiefly by the widespread practice of granting big and small territories to vassals and officials who entrenched themselves territorially and ended up as independent potentates called 'samantas'.[12] At the level of the consolidation of power by these newly emerged chiefs, it is again the system of land grants to *brāhmaṇas* that has been regarded by these scholars in providing socio-ideological support to the newly emerging states. At the economic level this is said to have led to the proliferation of settlements that helped in generating resources for the state. Although, the Marxist historiography emphasized on one single factor of land grants, they were aware of regional variations. Yet, they tended to generalize the role of land grants in defining the nature of the state for the whole of the sub-continent by characterising it through the universals of the theory of feudalism.

It is only in more recent writings that new trends emerged in understanding the socio-political and socio-economic transformations during the period under study, from the regional perspective. This new trend envisages these changes in terms of postulating an integrative polity. Unlike the Marxist historians who viewed the state in terms of fragmentation and decentralization. B.D. Chattopadhyaya and Hermann Kulke as protagonists of this new trend, have visualised the changes in the Indian polity by identifying the major historical processes in early India and examining the crystallization of these processes in their *specific temporal* and *spatial* contexts. These various societal processes have been understood by them as mechanisms of integration of historical regions through *internal processes of change.* In understanding how these distinct historical regions emerged in the early medieval perspective, B.D. Chattopadhyaya rightly emphasizes on the fact that the emergence of historical regions with distinct personalities should be comprehended: "not by being sub-merged by a single, pre-determined cultural pattern but by responding to and in turn, reshaping with a broad range of variations, an ever dynamic pattern whose dominant political, social, economic and cultural dimensions could be recognized at a pan-Indian level.[13]" The making of early medieval India was thus perceived by him in terms of the scale of fundamental movements within the regional and local levels resulting in the process of local state formations. For this, the transformation of the local economy was integral to the hereditary social groups who benefitted from it.

In this view in the context of the emergence of such new state structures it becomes essential to emphasize how these states sought to legitimize their newly acquired political power. One dimension of such legitimation was provided through the process of fabricating mythical genealogies which would help them to assert their position in the traditional *varṇa* ideology. This was not unique to any particular region or dynasty but different adaptations of this were done in the various regions. In some areas of the country according to scholars, it led to the process of transformation from tribalism to state. At the economic level, it was the entrenchment of brāhmaṇical order in the peripheral areas through the process of conferring land grants to the *brāhmaṇas* that resulted in the inner colonization of new areas, expansion of settlements and the growth of agrarian economy. At the social level, the process of caste formation became the chief mechanism through which the dominant ideology was spread. This meant incorporation of various groups especially different categories of peasants in the outlying regions into accepting the *varṇa* ideology and its hierarchical systems. The religious processes meant the integration of local cults, rituals and sacred centres into a pan-theistic supralocal structure. This mechanism of integration was possible by seeking affiliation with a deity or a sacred centre which had come to acquire supralocal significance.[14] All these processes invariably helped the state in consolidating its position at various levels. This has not been highlighted enough in the existing writings on the subject.

It is precisely in the context of understanding these processes effecting state structures and their integration at different levels that we have undertaken our study on the ruling elites with reference to the Eastern Chālukyas of Vengi. The Eastern Chālukyas of Vengi were originally an offshoot of the main branch of the Chālukyas of Bādāmi. It was under Pulakēśin II that an expedition was sent to the Eastern Deccan that resulted in the conquest of the Vengi region. Consequent to this conquest, an independent Eastern branch of the Chālukyan empire was established under Kubja Vishnuvardhana I with Vengi as its capital. The Eastern Chālukyan rulers ruled from their core area of Vengi from the 7th Century A.D. upto the 12th Century A.D. During this period the territorial extent of Vengi region included under its wider sceptre the fertile tracts of coastal Andhra country, comprising the modern districts of Srikakulam Vizianagaram, Visakhapatnam, East and West Godavari, Krishna, Guntur and Nellore regions.[15]

Thus, the broader region of study covers what can conveniently be labelled as the Eastern Deccan with a special focus on the micro-region of Vengi. The micro-region of Vengi was situated between the Krishna and the Godavari rivers. The fertile nature of this micro-region and its strategic location has particularly attracted outsiders and many rulers from the Western borders, who came and settled here from time to time. It's potentiality had still to be realized. Hence, as is well-known this region became the bone of contention for many ruling dynasties such as the Vishnukuṇḍins, the Bādāmi Chālukyas prior to the establishment of the Eastern Chālukyan kingdom in this region. From the 8th century onwards it attracted the Rāshtrakūtas, the Chālukyas of Kalyāṇi, the Chōlas and the Gaṇgas which resulted in the constant strife for the possession of this region between the Eastern Chālukyas and those other ruling dynasties that lasted for about four centuries.

Hitherto, many scholars have studied the history of the Eastern Chālukyas of Vengi. However, the writings that have been produced till recently have mainly been on dynastic lines giving a narration of major events effecting the dynasty. Even scholars who have written on the social and economic history of the period recognized change on dynastic lines. Therefore, they placed the Eastern Chālukyan rule as part of medieval India. If we give importance to the totality of historical change then we have to recognize this as an important *period of transition* and therefore accept the terminology of situating this rule during early medieval period.

Since the book aims at focussing on the changes in the evolution of genealogies of these ruling elites this helps us in characterizing the nature of state and the methods of consolidation of power adopted by them. This will necessarily involve an analysis of the land grants issued during this period. At the time when the Telugu language was still in the formative stage of development and the availability of literary sources was scanty, inscriptions have been considered to be the major source for our study on the subject. These give a clear pattern of genealogies, as no literary source of the period has much details on the ideology of ruling elites.

The science that deals with the study of inscriptions is known as '*Epigraphy*'.[16] Based on the nature and purpose of the inscriptions, they have been classified into various types. They are (a) Royal edicts, (b) Eulogistic Inscriptions, (c) Commemorative inscriptions and (d) Donative inscriptions.[17] All these types except royal edicts are available for our study. The *Praśastis* or the eulogistic records became more prominent during the early medieval period both at pan-Indian and regional levels. They are mainly written in Sanskrit language and reflects the prominent ideology of ruling elites. Since their main motivation was to gain glory they focus on the all round achievements of the ruling elites, such as their military achievements, their mythical genealogies connecting their ancestry either, to the Solar or the Lunar lineages and so on. In the present context of study, the *Praśastis* become more elaborate during the later half of the second phase of the Eastern Chālukyan rule and the same characteristics are also found in some of the minor Chālukyan inscriptions.

Based on their contents the royal charters have been generally divided into three broad sections. (A) Preamble. It generally opens with a *maṅgala* or *maṅgala ślōka*, i.e., auspicious word or verse at the beginning. The foremost part, i.e., the preamble generally comprises the place of issue, the name of the donor with his titles and the *Praśasti* of his ancestors and the address in respect of the grant. The second part is the *Notification.* Notification comprises of the specification of the gift, the name of the donee, the occassion of the grant, the purpose of the grant and the boundaries of the gift of land. The third part is the *Conclusion.* This part of the inscription contains an exhortation or admonition in respect of the grant, the names of the officials responsible for the execution of the document, and the date and the authentification of the record.[18] Therefore, in our study we have attempted to look at all these various portions of the inscriptions, while focussing mainly on the constituents in the Preamble section, i.e., the *Praśasti* portions of the ruling elites. The contents of other portions, namely, the Notification and Conclusion, were also looked at to identify the various mechanisms through which the ruling elites issued grants that consolidated their power in their newly established kingdoms.

For the purpose of this pilot study, we have made use of limited number of inscriptions, taking 10 from the Bādāmi Chālukyan dynasty, 60 from the Eastern Chālukyan dynasty and 20 from the Minor Chālukyan dynasties of Mudigonda, Jananāthapuram and Nidadavōlu. This has significantly enabled us to research into the broad trends of change envisaged in the way the *Praśastis* and other inscriptional data are organized rather than document all the exhaustive quantitative material. All these inscriptions have been found to be in Sanskrit, Kannada and Telugu Languages. Hence, we made use of the edited and translated versions which have been obtained by us from the following journals: (1) *Epigraphia Indica,* (2) *Epigraphia Āndhrica,* (3) *South Indian Inscriptions,* (4) *Indian Antiquary,* (5) *Bhārati,* (6) *Journal of Andhra Historical Research Society* and others. These inscriptions have been collected and edited since the year 1894 by eminent epigraphists and scholars such as J.F.Fleet, E. Hultzsch, Jas Burgess, V. Venkayya and others. In order to understand the terminology used in the inscriptions, D.C. Sircar's monumental *Epigraphic Glossary* (Delhi, 1966) has been consulted. Further, in order to define and get information on the physical geography of the broad region under study district Gazetteers of Andhra Pradesh, were used.

The *Praśasti* material has earlier been used by scholars in their construction of primarily political histories of the region. In this context it becomes essential to reconsider these studies to understand the various political processes that enabled the ruling elites in integrating local state structures. The inscriptional data that is available, however, does not directly describe the various processes of the state. Their purpose is entirely different. We get to know about such aspects from the changes perceived in the genealogical accounts of the *Praśasti* sections, the changes in the nature of donations of different categories of officials and peasants involved in the agrarian economy and information on deities and so on. We have analyzed these changes against the backdrop of how ruling elites perceived their political ideology in terms of the reconstruction of genealogical ancestry real or fabricated to consolidate their position in evolving a new state society under the period of our consideration.

Based on the changes reflected in the nature of inscriptional sources the study has been divided into two phases: Phase I and Phase II. Phase I covers the period between the 7th century A.D. to the 9th century A.D. and Phase II commences from the 9th century A.D. to the 12th century A.D. This division into two distinct phases has been made as these phases help us to discern the pattern in which genealogical accounts in inscriptions have been found to be different in style and description, the differences in the nature of land grants given in them and changes reflected in the socio-religious ideology of the ruling elites is evident from these epigraphic sources. In order to amplify the changes in both the phases, we have made use of nine charts entitled as :

PHASE I : *Praśastis* of Chālukyas of Bādāmi (Chart I) *Praśastis* of Chālukyas of Vengi - Phase I (7th century A.D. - 9th century A.D.) (Chart IIA)

PHASE II : *Praśastis* of Chālukyas of Vengi - Phase - II, (9th century A.D. - 12th century A.D.) (Chart IIB) *Praśastis* of Minor Chālukyan Families (9th century A.D. - 12th century A.D.) (Chart III)

Similarly the charts on grants are entitled as :

PHASE I : Nature of Grants - Phase I (7th century A.D. to 9th century A.D.) (Chart IVA)

PHASE II : Nature of Grants - Phase II (9th century A.D. to 12th century A.D.) (Chart IVB),

Nature of Grants of Chālukyas of Mudigonda (Chart Vx),

Nature of Grants of Chālukyas of Jananāthapuram (Chart Vy),

Nature of Grants of Chālukyas of Nidadavōlu (Chart Vz)

While, the *Praśasti* Charts of Chālukyas of Vengi contains columns like *Name of inscription/king* (col. I), *Dynastic Praśasti* (col. II), *Personal Praśasti* (Col. III), *Marriage alliance* (col. IV), *Titles* (col. V) *Religion/Deity* (col. VI) and a reference column, those of the minor Chālukyan families contains columns like *Name of the family/locality* (col. I), *Name of the Inscription/King/Date* (col. II), *Dynastic praśasti/linkage with Eastern Chālukyas of Vengi* (Col. III), *Titles* (Col. IV), *Political status*(col. V), *Religion/Deity* (Col. VI) and a reference column. Similarly the charts on grants contains columns like *Name of the inscription/Date* (col. I), *Donor/Status* (Col. II), *Donee/Status* (Col. III), *Nature of the grant/Location* (Col. IV), *Purpose of the grant* (Col. V), *Witnesses/Executors of the grant* (Col. VI), *Economic and Administrative immunities* (Col. VII) and a reference column.

In the context of the changes illustrated in these charts, Phase I of our study focuses mainly on the early evolution of genealogies as reflected in *Charts I & II A*.. During this phase, genealogical accounts of the Eastern Chālukyas are found to be similar with their parent branch, namely, the Bādāmi Chālukyas. In these only three generations of rulers are mentioned in the inscriptions. For this phase, with regard to the nature of land grants charted in *Chart IVA*, we find that most of the land donations were in the form of *agrahāras* or villages and the recipients were mostly the *brāhmaṇas*. As far as religion is concerned most of the early rulers of the Eastern Chālukyas were advocates of Brāhmaṇism as depicted in Column VI of Chart IIA during Phase I.

On the other hand, in Phase II based on *Charts IIB, IVB, Vx, y, z*, we find a different picture. Now no longer were the genealogies short pedigrees, but a long list of the chronological orders of kings were given starting from the founder of the dynasty of the eastern branch to that of the donor of the branch. Further still, in the later half of the second phase, we find the evolution of lengthy Paurāṇic or legendary genealogies which are neither found in the genealogical section of the inscriptions of their parent branch namely, the Bādāmi Chālukyas, nor, in those of the early rulers of the eastern branch. Similarly, the nature of land grants appeared to be more secular as seen in *Charts IV & Vx, y, z*. Most of the land grants during this phase were in small pieces of land, instead of villages and the recipients mostly belonged either, to the military class and merchant class or, they were given to the temples. As far as religion is concerned as revealed in column VI of *Chart IIB* we find the emergence of new religious sects during this phase, such as the Kālāmukha sect of Śaktism gaining prominence in the region. This marks a shift in the form of patronization from Brāhmaṇism in Phase I to other ideologies based on Purāṇic religion in Phase II.

By analyzing the various inscriptions in this manner an attempt has been made in this book to integrate political, economic, social and ideological aspects in understanding the superstructure of the polity under the Eastern Chālukyan rulers. In this process it has been understood that the various processes of State formation in the Eastern Deccan during the early medieval period were integral to the concerns of the ruling elite to establish their suzerainity in a new territory. The present book has been divided into five Chapters, prefaced and suffixed by an *INTRODUCTION* and *CONCLUSION* respectively.

In *CHAPTER-I* entitled : "*HISTORIOGRAPHY*" the various conceptual and ideological approaches that historians in the past have used to study the formation of ruling elites in the broader context of various regions of the country as a whole are highlighted. These historiographical approaches have been focussed on four major spheres of activity - the political, social, economic and ideological and divided into Orientalists and Imperialists endeavours, the Nationalist efforts and their impact on regional history writing, the Socialist and Marxist writings besides those recent scholars who emphasized on the broad social history framework. Further the various definitions of the term "Ruling Elites", particularly those who emerged in the early medieval, such as *Brahma-Kśatriyas,* the *Rājaputras,* the *Sat-Kṣatriyas* and *Asat-Kṣatriyas* are highlighted upon.

In *CHAPTER II* entitled: "*GEO-POLITICAL BACKGROUND*", our study was focussed first and foremost on the geographical significance and the historical evolution of the micro-region of Vengi. This enabled us to highlight the reasons of the conquest of this micro-region by the Bādāmi Chālukyas and installing one of their family members as an independant ruler, thus starting a new branch of the Chālukyan empire, namely, the Eastern Chālukyas of Vengi. Further, in this Chapter we also discussed the political and military history of the Chālukyas of Vengi in relationship with their predecessors and their successors in two different phases. This again explains the process for consolidating their power in an alien land. The nature of polity under the Eastern Chālukyas is highlighted upon in two Phases of our study.

CHAPTER III entitled : "*GENEALOGY AND MARRIAGE NETWORKS*" has been divided into two parts. In Part I we have attempted to show the changes discerned in the pattern of how the genealogies of these ruling elites evolved in the inscriptions in two distinct phases. In this chapter we also analyzed how the Eastern Chālukyan rulers tried to assert their *kṣatriya* hood first by seeking *brahma-kṣatra* identity and later, through fabrication of genealogies, to the mythical past. At the same time they maintained the genealogical linkages with their parent branch namely, the Bādāmi Chālukyas. Similarly, we have also focussed on the Minor Chālukyan inscriptions, to analyze how they tried to establish genealogical linkages with the Eastern Chālukyas. This is to ultimately understand the nature of the relationship between these three families to finally identify the complex process of consolidation of power by the Eastern Chālukyas. In the latter half of Chapter III, we discussed the marriage networks established between the main ruling family of the Eastern Chālukyas with other contemporary rulers and also with the local chiefs as furnished by the inscriptions which is again seen as an important mechanism of the consolidation of power.

CHAPTER IV entitled : "*ECONOMIC LINKAGES*", intends to study and highlight the nature of grants issued by the Eastern Chālukyan family and contrasted these with those of the three minor Chālukyan families of Mudigonda, Jananāthapuram and Nidadavōlu. This information has been collected through main part of the inscriptions and has been categorized in the form of Charts IVA, IVB and Vx, y, z. This classification of the information helped us in understanding the important changes perceived in the nature of donations of land and other economic resources in the form of grants to various religious and secular authorities such as the priests, military chiefs, merchants, temple centred organizations in two phases of our study. Also attempts are made to analyse the other means of resource mobilization of the State. This primarily focuses on the study of the nature of settlement patterns, as a means of acculturating new lands which also includes pasturages. This gives an idea of the nature of ownership patterns. Further, study of the temple centred settlements in Phase II helped us in understanding the development of trade and commerce particularly in some areas. All these changes not only yielded resource base for the state, but also acted as an important process for the stabilization of power through economic means.

In *CHAPTER V* entitled : "*socio-ideological parameters*", we intend to focus on how ruling elites tried to control society through socio-ideological variables. The essence of social variable has been identified by the use of *varṅa* ideology as a means of understanding the proliferation of castes and *jātis* through horizontal and vertical mobility. In this context an attempt has been made to study the nature of patronization extended by ruling elites to various caste groups in two phases. Similarly, the ideological processes shall focus on the emergence of various religious sects such as Śaivism, Vaiṣṇavism, Śaktism, etc. In Phase I, the dominant religious ideology of the ruling elites was Brāhmaṇism. During this phase many *brāhmaṇas* of various *gōtras* were patronized through the process of conferring land grants. In Phase II, the ruling elites patronized not only the *brāhmaṇas*, but also people belonging to other *varṅas* such as the *vaiśyas* and *śūdras*. This phase also witnessed construction of temples such as Śaivite temples of the Kālāmukha sect, at places like Drākshārāmam, Bheemēśvaram, Vijayawāda, etc. Also, *bhakti* as an ideology emerges during this time which is centred around temples. This explains the ideological base sought by the ruling elites through patronage of temple construction of dominant religious sects prevailing during that period.

Finally, in the *CONCLUSION* an overall picture of what has been discussed is provided in understanding the various processes adopted by the ruling elites in the formation of new regional state structures and also the various mechanisms such as the political, the social, the economic and the ideological variables undergoing changes as was seen in the inscriptions which helped in integrating various forces that provided the base for the consolidation of the power of the Eastern Chālukyas.

References

1. Lesly Brown, *The New Shorter Oxford English Dictionary*, vol. I & II. 1993, p. 800.
2. R.C. Swarankar, *Political Elite*, Jaipur, 1988, pp. 3-4.
3. *Ibid*, p. 6.
4. *Ibid*, p. 7.
5. *Ibid*, p. 8.
6. Romila Thapar, "Social Mobility In Ancient India With Special Reference To Elite Groups" in *Ancient Indian Social History,* henceforth (*AISH*), New Delhi, 1978, p. 133.
7. Om Prakash, *Religion and Society in Ancient India,* New Delhi, 1985, p. 128.
8. Romila Thapar, *Op.Cit.*, 1978, p. 136.
9. *Ibid*, p. 138-139.

10. Suvira Jaiswal, "Varna Ideology and Social Change", *Social Scientist,* vol. 19, p. 41.
11. R.S. Sharma, *Social Change in Early Medieval India (circa A.D. 500-1200),* 1969, (Rpt) 1987, pp. 6-10.
12. Hermann Kulke, *State in India* (A.D. 1000-1700), New Delhi, 1995, p. 9.
13. B.D. Chattopadhyaya, *The Making of Early Medieval India,* New Delhi, 1994, pp. 16-17.
14. B.D. Chattopadhyaya, "Political Processes and Structure of Polity in Early Medieval India: Problems of Perspective", *Social Scientist,* 1985, vol. 13, pp. 6-11.
15. B.V. Krishna Rao, *The Eastern Chalukyas of Vengi,* Hyderabad, 1973, p. 47.
16. D.C. Sircar, *Indian Epigraphy,* Delhi, 1965, p. 1.
17. *Ibid,* p. 126.
18. N.R. Vijaya, "Evolution of *Praśasti* in the Inscriptions of the Eastern Chalukyas", *PAPHC,* Warangal, 1990, pp. 76-77.

Chapter-I

HISTORIOGRAPHY

The main thrust of our study in this chapter is to comprehend the conceptual and ideological approaches of historians in trying to understand the formation and consolidation of ruling elites and the various structural models of State formation in the early medieval Indian Kingdoms. However, we have also made an attempt to analyse these historiographical trends as they effected four major spheres of activity - the political, social, economic and ideological. According to their date of origin, these trends have been characterized as the Imperialist and Orientalist endeavours, the Nationalists efforts and their impact on regional history writing, the Socialist and Marxist writings and those scholars emphasizing on the broad social history frame work. In the following pages an in depth analysis will be made on how these earlier historians have viewed the formation of ruling elites and understood various processes of state formation, in the broader context of the region as a whole, the terminologies they have used in describing the early medieval period and their overall characterization of the social, economic and ideological spheres of activity.

The study of the nature of ruling elites and various mechanisms they had adopted in the formation of new states has in recent years became one of the most concerned subject of research in the scholarly world. The beginnings in this direction were made by the European scholars who were known as Imperialist historians and Orientalists. By applying the scientific positivist method and using the various ancient Indian literary texts that were extant, such as the *Manu Smṛthi*, the *Dharmaśāstras* and the *Upaṇiśads* as their major source material they evolved the concepts of *Oriental Despotism* and *Asiatic Mode of Production*, in describing the nature of state and society in ancient India.[1]

The interpretations of the Indian philosophical and literary texts by the early scholars of Europe had aroused two schools of thought within the Orientalist discourse. One was led by cynical Utilitarians. The other was the sympathetic *Romanticists*, led by William Jones, Max Muller and others.[2] The *Romanticists* discovered in Indian culture and religion, non-modern, non-utilitarian aspects which are highly acclaimed and praised. India has been described by these idealists as the land of spirituality, a distant Utopia, thus, giving a spiritual character to the Indian society and culture.[3]

On the other hand, the Utilitarian views which are dominated in the Imperialist and Administrative writings of Mill[4] and Smith[5] characterised Indian State as a monarchical institution with a hierarchical bureaucracy. Yet, the power was rarely concentrated at the centre. In this type of State everyone exercised absolute authority in their own way. Therefore, the whole system of functioning of the government in ancient India was regarded by them as barbaric and rude.[6] These scholars have understood the Indian political, economic and social system as dominated by the ideology of caste and religion. These writings in general projected Indian society and culture as engulfed in the concept of 'caste' with its supporting institution of religion, namely Hinduism. In this representation of caste dominated society, the *brāhmaṇas*, priests and ascetics and the principle of purity and hierarchy took precedence over kings and the state. Caste was further associated with race and occupation, religion and status, land control and psychic security with birth and death, marriage and education.[7] Thus, through their interpretations the early Imperialist scholars projected a picture of socio-ideological factors as impending any progress or change in Indian society. For Mill, the principal value of a culture was the degree to which it contributed to the furtherance of rationalism and individualism. He saw neither of these two values in Hindu civilization and therefore, condemned it severely.[8] However, Smith does not appear as blunt as Mill in characterizing Indian state and culture. With his great fascination towards classical Greek and Roman histories, he wrote about Indian history with the usage of concepts like the '*age of heroes*' and the '*age of empires*'. Though much has been written on the *theory* of the state, kingship and administration, little analytical study was devoted to the *actual structure* of the late and early medieval kingdom.[9]

The periodization on which the Imperialist and Orientalist scholars constructed Indian history, was predominantly marked by major shifts in the dynasties and religion. Thus, while Mill's periodization of Indian history was categorised into Hindu, Muslim and British,[10] on the other hand, Smith adopted a periodization of Ancient, Medieval and Modern. However, even in his writings Ancient came to be equated with Hindu period and Medieval with Muslim period.[11] The early medieval was regarded by him as a period of darkness, as there was an absence of the empire based kingdom during this period. Therefore, it was given a marginal attention.[12]

The writings of the Imperialists took shape in the concept of *Oriental Despotism*. The concept of *Oriental Despotism* and its characterization of early Indian State and society were also found in Marx's model of Asiatic Mode of Production. Marx conceptualized Indian State as a strange hermphrodite juxtoposing of an unchanging State, dominated by self sufficient village economies, communal ownership of land and internal exploitation of the village communities. In this view, in order to increase agrarian surplus the central bureaucracy took charge of large-scale irrigation projects. Marx's model of Asiatic mode of production, clearly reflect the strong prejudice held by the Occidentalists towards the Orient.[13]

The Imperialist and Administrator historians wrote about India as if South did not exist. They identified the '*age of heroes*' and '*age of empire*' mainly with the North Indian dynasties. Even the periodization they had set up was mainly based on keeping in view the major dynastic changes that ruled in the North. In this regard the history of South India and those particularly of Andhra received only peripheral attention highlighting only on the major dynasties that ruled the region. In this regard the history of the Eastern Chālukyan dynasty did not attract their attention. The changing topography of South India appeared as a more complex structure permitting less political uniformity than the less complex structure of the northern plains.[14] Hence, the history of the South was marginalized in their writings.

The study on the South received its attention in the 19th century mainly from the Christian missionaries and some of the enthusiastic British administrators who were posted in the South. Unlike the Utilitarians, the missionaries did not focus on State but carried on a tirade against the inherent backwardness of Indian society which was rooted in its religion.[15] Thus, they attempted to expose the weakness of Indian religion in their writings. The most important writings of the missionaries in the Deccan and Madras Presidency were those of Abbe Dubious, Caldwell, among many others. Abbe Dubious, work on *Hindu Manners customs and ceremonies*, was one of the earliest accounts on society in South India. Similarly, administrators like Col. Mackenzie H.H. Wilson, C.P. Brown, and others did pioneering work related to South India and the Deccan. Mackenzie and Brown collected and preserved local village accounts which are popularly known as *Mackenzies' Kaifiyats.*[16] However, the accounts of the administrators and missionaries was mainly an atempt to create source material rather than to write the history of South India. Many of these early surveys nonetheless laid the foundations for the later interpretations.

Thus, views of the Imperialists and Orientalists and much of the writings of the Missionaries entail the belief that the Indian State was represented by despotic rulers controlled by irrational agencies of caste and religion. In this State all the land belonged to the king, who ruled over servile population and exploited them at his will. The economy of the Indian sub-continent was characterised as largely self-sufficient in this perception. Thus, in this view, the economic, social and political setting in India, since the Ancient times is said to have remained unchanged.

The intellectual and technological advancement in the scientific study of European history made its impact on India in the late 19th century. Consequently, new disciplines such as Archaeology, Epigraphy, Numismatics were developed, providing a new outlook to the study of history as a whole. The decipherment of the *brahmi* script by James Princep in 1837 opened up the study of epigraphical sources.[17] Eminent epigraphists such as Rev. Thomas Foulke, G. Buhler, Sir Walter Elliot, Robert Sewel, E. Hultzsch, Jas Burgess, J.F. Fleet and others undertook an arduous task in deciphering, editing, interpreting and publishing number of inscriptions which were discovered in the various regions of Indian sub-continent.[18] The intensive study of inscriptions yielded more insights into the early phases of political institutions and ideas. Further, it gave a new focus to the study of regional and local histories. Eminent epigraphists like J.F. Fleet, E. Hultzsch and others have unearthed a great number of inscriptions belonging to the Eastern Chālukyan dynasty. However, they in general devoted all their attention mainly to the problems of solving the chronology of the Eastern Chālukyan dynasty rather than on studying the various aspects of society, economy, the nature of political elites, state etc., as was reflected in various epigraphical sources.

These early interpretations of Indian history by the British and European scholars had its impact on the Indian historians, writing during the late 19th and early 20th centuries. Most of their writings during this period came to be termed as the *Indian Historiographical School*[19] or the *Nationalist* school. Two trends prevailed within this school. While the adherents of the first trend of the Nationalist School have written basically with elitist perspective following the Orientalist method and approach[20], the second major trend in this school emerged as a reaction against Orientalist and Imperialist writings on Indian History. Most of the Indian Historian's writings during the early 20th century were influenced by the concept of nationalism and national movement.

Subsequently, they unashamedly glorified the ancient Indian past. They depicted the early medieval ('Hindu') State and the post 1200 A.D. late medieval ('Muslim') State likewise as polities headed by a strong ruler, equipped with an efficient and hierarchically organized central administration based on a religiously legitimated monopoly of coercion in a clearly defined territory.[21] The concept of the "*Golden Ages*" of ancient India which Kulke calls as the "Imperial Model"[22] emerged particularly during the time of the Indian freedom movement at the height of the British Imperialism. It was emphasized in their writings that classical Indian culture and civilization had produced political and social institutions which were equal if not superior to those of their imperial masters.

The most prominent historians who belonged to the Nationalist school of Indian Historiography were H.C. Ray Chaudhari, K.P. Jayaswal, R.C. Majumdar, R.K. Mookerjee and H.C. Ojha among many others. Irrespective of their ideological moorings, in terms of glorification of Indian past, these scholars, could not evolve new methodological patterns in history writing. Thus, most of their writings were concentrated on political and dynastic history of the major dynasties that ruled primarily Northern India. At the same time, they even accepted the periodization and methodology that had been adopted by the Imperialists and Orientalists.

The discovery of *Arthaśāstra* in 1905, and its publication by Shama Sastry in 1909, provided new material foundations to the study of Indian state and polity.[23] In this regard K.P. Jayaswal's *Hindu Polity*, became a classic work on Hindu political thought for Indian nationalists. In his book Jayaswal highlighted the aspects of constitutional monarchy, republican institutions, corporated economic practices, and several principles of modern polity to demonstrate the fitness of Indians for self government disproving the generalizations of British administrators and the Christian missionaries. The early medieval period was regarded by him as a period of darkness and disruption. Hence, during this period popular institutions of polity decayed and Hindu traditions dwindled.[24] The major concern of the historians during this period was to draw similarities between classical Greek and ancient Indian civilizations. Thus, Jayaswal maintained that the political life of the ancient Indian republics had been based on the concepts of democrary and representative government as had the political life of the Greek city-states.

Another important work on Indian State and government in the same vein but which comes chronologically much later was A.S. Altekar's *State and Government in Ancient India.* This book succintly explains the Hindu political ideas and theories that prevailed in ancient Indian state system and its administration. Regarding South Indian administration, he attempted to show the influence of North on the South[25] and therefore gave little importance, to South Indian history.

The nationalist writers in the early 20th century attempted to establish the monolithic edifice of Indian State which was said to be characterized with a strong unitary, centralized bureaucracy, headed by a strong monarch. Similarly, the Indian social system was represented by caste which was based on the bibliocentric description of the four fold *varṇa* system with its hierarchical gradation of the *brāhmaṇa* at the apex and the *sūdra* at the bottom. Further, ancient Indian economy was characterised as a self sufficient economy with the existence of the private ownership of land. Discussion on religion was associated with the presence and descriptions of major religions and their sects. In their obsession with nationalism they attempted to glorify all these aspects of the Indian past. Since the main concern of the Nationalist historians was to construct detailed dynastic and political histories under whom prosperity in all fields was visualised, they tended to focus on those dynasties which are categorised as 'Golden Ages' in Indian history. Most of the historical writings of this school were confined to the descriptions of political and dynastic histories with the parcelling off social, economic, cultural history simply as important fringes for understanding the totality of the historical past. They have failed to see the formation of state by the ruling elites through an integrated approach of all these processes of the social, the economic and the cultural as important mechanisms. Also, those books written exclusively with '*State*' in their titles regarded the 'State' as a separate entity which was strong and powerful and as though its activities were mainly related to administrative aspects. Hence, their discourses lack relevant discussion of the social base of the ruling elites that made possible the emergence of states in the early and late medieval India.

Further, they attempted to glorify the Indian past within a limited geographical boundary pertaining mostly to the Indo-Gangetic plains of the north, and conceptualized the whole thing from the pan-Indian perspective. In this respect, south Indian kingdoms and those particularly of Andhra got accommodated only in a corner in most of their writings. Thus, as Settar rightly postulates, "the 19th and early 20th century historians, who were used to the '*Age of Empire*' were more easily attracted to the North than to the South, which (with its changing topography caused by mountain, plateau and river valleys), permitted less political uniformity than the north". This according to him was the main reason for the negligence of the South for those periods when it too could boast of empires.[26]

However, the writings of the nationalist historians with focus on ancient political and dynastic history soon necessiated the study of social and economic history as well as studies in regional histories that emerged as distinct branches or sub-disciplines of history. In fact, the study of regional histories emerged as a valuable offshoot of nationalist school. Studies of regional histories of small geographical areas and States such as histories of Bengal, Maharashtra and various parts of the peninsula became common towards the mid twentieth century.

Geographically, the peninsular region appeared as a more complex structure to be studied. With its diverse topographical variations, it emerged as a complicated phenomenon for the historians to define the land south of Vindhyas. Until almost the middle of the century, some historians identified the peninsula into two distinct units of study (1) the "Deccan" and (2) "South India".[26] Eminent scholars such as R.G. Bhandarkar, D.C. Sircar, G. Yazdani among others have identified the Deccan with the upper unit of the peninsula. According to them, Deccan is a land lying between the Vindhyas and the Krishna-Tungabhadra deltas.[27] On the other hand, South India was identified with the land south of the Krishna-Tungabhadra region and was broadly confined within the territorial boundaries of the present day linguistic States of Tamilnadu and Kerala.[28]

The first Indian historian to write on the peninsular India with "Dekkan" as its title, in the late 19th century was R.G. Bhandarkar. In his study Deccan was indentified as a land mainly confined to the present day Maharastra region. His text is largely based on the literary sources located in Northern India. In his text, the definition of the early historical phase of the Deccan was concerned, prior to the coming of the Aryans. Since his book concentrated mainly on Maharastra region, the development of historical phase in the Eastern Deccan was given a corner place of study.[29]

Several years later there emerged another important work on the Deccan in the form of Yazdani's edited work entitled *Early History of the Deccan*. In this book 'Deccan' was defined by the scholar keeping in view its relatively specific and political boundaries, that coincided with the erstwhile Nizam's dominions of Hyderabad State. In his definition, Deccan is described as "a land stretching from the Sahyadri Parvat and Mahendragiri ranges and the Mahanadi and the Godavari rivers in the north, to the Krishna and the Tungabhadra rivers in the south. Towards the West and East of the Deccan comprised the Arabian sea and the Bay of Bengal" respectively.[30] Thus, Deccan in his definition comprised major parts of the present day States of Maharashtra, Karnataka, and Andhra Pradesh. In this respect, therefore, the dynasties that ruled the Andhra region were also focussed. Being an edited work, there are several contributions of well-known scholars. In this book the chapter on the Eastern Chālukyas of Vengi was contributed by K.A.N. Sastry and N. Venkataramanayya. However the main concern of these scholars was to discuss the political history of the dynasty and therefore little analytical study was made to comprehend the various processes of the Eastern Chālukyan polity.

Simultaneously, in South India the research of European scholars found its expression in the pioneering studies in South Indian history by scholars like V. Kanakasabhi, Swaminatha Iyer, Nilakanta Sastry and few others. These scholars envisaged the south Indian Tamil polity as a centralised bureaucracy. Nilakanta Sastri's work on the *Cōlās* was full of idealization and glorification of the Cōlā kings. He emphasized that in its administrative system and in its literary and artistic achievements, Tamil civilisation attained its high watermark under the Cōlās.[31] Further, in his work on *History of South India* he concentrated on those dynasties of the South under whom the all round prosperity was envisaged in terms of progress in trade and commerce, evolution of new cultural patterns in art, architecture, literature and sculpture. Sastri had therefore, though not consciously, but because his vantage point is the extreme South, treated the history of Andhra in a peripheral manner that came to prominent light only during the early period under the Satavahanas and during later times under the Vijayanagar rulers.[32] In this regard focus on the Eastern Chālukyas was marginalised in his writings.

The biased attitude of the early Tamil Brahmin scholars and the arbitrary administrative policies of the British Government, developed a feeling of regionalism among various States. The British government's proposal in 1905 to merge the Telugu speaking Ganjam and Visakhapatnam areas with the proposed Oriya territory and the subsequent rise of *Vandemataram* and *Swadeshi* movements had awakened the Andhra sentiments. As a result, the Andhras attempted to resuscitate their identity. This was done with the help of history to create their own historical identity. It began with the publication of the *History of the Andhras* by the *Vignana Chandrika Mandali* in 1910.

In 1925, as an attempt to give fillip to further research on Andhra History, the *Andhra Historical Research Society* was founded. The prominent members of this society such as, Chilikuri Veerabhadra Rao, K. Lakshmana Rao, Mallampalli Somasekhara Sarma, B.V. Krishna Rao, and other scholars, toiled hard to unearth the chronicles of Telugu civilization through the ages. Consequently, many monographs on the Eastern Chālukyas, the Kākatīyas, and the Reddi kingdoms were brought out by the society during the first two decades of its inception. Thus, under their eminent scholarship, a solid foundation was laid for the edifice of Andhra History. The main concern of these earlier scholars was to construct the chronological and dynastic histories of the dynasties that ruled the Andhra region based on various inscriptional sources.

The post-independent era witnessed the further development of regional histories within the framework of the present day linguistic States of the Indian Union. The main concern of the scholars writing during this time was to focus on the dynasties of a particular region. Hence, their works largely came to be identified with the dynasties, areas and people. For the present, we shall focus on those scholars writing on the early medieval period and those on the Eastern Chālukyas in particular. In this respect, scholars like N. Venkataramanayya, B.V. Krishna Rao, N. Ramesan, M. Krishnakumari, K. Suryanarayana among many others have made valuable contributions to the study of the history of the Eastern Chālukyan dynasty.

N. Venkataramanayya's the *Eastern Chalukyas of Vengi* (1950) was the earliest work on the dynasty. This book has dealt largely with aspects such as the origin, chronology, genealogy, caste of this dynasty. Further, major emphasis was made on the political history and military conquests of the Eastern Chālukyan rulers. However, the author tries to create the general impression that the Eastern Chālukyan period is a period of general peace and prosperity which led to the development of vernacular literature, art and architecture. Similarly, B.V. Krishna Rao[33] wrote a voluminous and comprehensive book on the Eastern Chālukyan dynasty. In this book the scholar mostly concentrated on the problem of solving chronology of the dynasty. Major part of the discussion of this work was dealt with the chronological succession of ruling elites with emphasis on their military conquests in a narrative form. He also discussed aspects such as the geography of the region, the Eastern Chālukyan attempts to consolidate and expand their power, the growth of the minor Chālukyan families. However, these scholars do not characterize the nature of their polity or highlight the processes of state formation that were underlying the transition from the ancient to the early medieval period in Andhra History.

At the other level we have works of M. Krishna Kumari[34] and K. Suryanarayana[35] that dealt with the micro level study of the minor Chālukyan families. Their works reflects the importance of the minor regional powers as local potentates in exercising influence and power within their limited geographical boundaries. Krishna Kumari regards the rule of the Chālukya-Chōlas in Andhradēsa as a transition period between the Chālukyas of Vengi and the Kākatīyas of Warangal. Similarly, K. Suryanarayana acclaims the role of the various minor Chālukyan families and the feudatories of the Eastern Chālukyans. It is postulated by these scholars that the stability of the Eastern Chālukyan kingdom was perpetuated with the great role of the feudatories and minor Chālukyan ruling families in various geographical localities.

As the dominant area of investigation for these historians being political history, they followed the positivist methodological framework. They further attempted to reconstruct genealogical tables with the primary epigraphic, numismatic and literary sources. Thus, there was a tendency to dynasticize regional history by mainly focussing on the political ascendancy of the various ruling elites that were powerful. Inspite of this, these scholars did not completely ignore the socio-economic and cultural aspects which were included as an addendum in one or two chapters at the end. There was, however, no attempt to relate these socio-economic changes with the understanding of the nature of polity in the period under discussion.

With regard to the periodization of Andhra history these scholars expressed difficulty in fixing the chronological frameworks of the Andhra history. Therefore, they have adopted the pan-Indian perspective in defining chronology. Thus in their writings Ancient period ended with the Vishnukundins around 7th century A.D., and the Eastern Chālukyan period was identified with the beginnings of the Medieval period. The same periodization is adopted even till today without much questioning.

As an alternative to the imperialist, orientalist, nationalist and much of the regional history based on these methodological paradigms, there emerged in the post independent period a new trend in the form of Marxist influenced historical writings. Influenced in some cases by vague socialist thinking and in others by ideas of the materialist interpretation of history, and by giving a new 'socio-economic orientation' to the study of Indian history, the prominent writings of D.D. Kosambi, R.S. Sharma, B.N.S. Yadava, Romila Thapar, D.N. Jha, Suvira Jaiswal and others began to emerge. They exploded the myth of "Unchangeableness" of Indian State and society as was expounded in the AMP model of Marx. As an alternative to the AMP Model, some of the afore mentioned scholars evolved the concept of Indian Feudalism to understand the early medieval period. The "Indian Feudalism Model" emphasised on the economic changes that took place during the early centuries of the Christian era. These changes, according to them, had corroded the strong edifice of central bureaucracy through the processes of decentralization and fragmentation of political power. Similarly, they rejected the earlier chronological lables set up by the conventional historiography to demarcate periodization in Indian history and in its place began to accept the socio-economic changes as a criteria for marking periodization. The early medieval period was seen in the context of the development of feudalistic tendencies from 600 A.D. onwards, which is said to have given an impetus for the emergence of new ruling elites at the regional level.

D.D. Kosambi, in his famous book entitled *An Introduction to the study of Indian History* had staged a two-fold theory of feudalism, namely, 'Feudalism from Above' and 'Feudalism from Below'. The working of these two paradigms seem to have developed over the period, a class of landowners within the village. They acted as important levels between the State and the peasantry and gradually wielded armed power on the local population.[37]

Similarly, R.S. Sharma, B.N.S. Yadava and Romila Thapar have attempted to explain the development of feudalism in terms of major economic changes that occured during the early historical period. R.S. Sharma attributed external factors to the emergence of feudalism, such as the decline in inter-regional and international trade and commerce, paucity in metallic currency and the subsequent decline in urban centres that, necessitated the ruling elites during this period to evolve a new mechanism of exploitation for surpus generation and tax collection. It is in this context that the emergence of large scale donations of land to *brāhmaṇa* and religious institutions and later, to the government officials, can be explained according to him. This process has been explained by Sharma as the prelude to the development of feudalism in terms of decentralization and fragmentation of political power. This ultimately led to the rise of new ruling elites.[38]

On the other hand B.N.S. Yadava had explained the emergence of feudalism through emphasizing on the breakdown of the Chaturvarṇa system as was explicitly stated in the Kali age texts. For him the term *sāmanta* which is identified with 'vassal' or 'tributary chief' became the key word of Indian feudalism.[39] He sees the emergence of the *sāmantas* to political prominence mainly through their economic and military power.

Similarly, Romila Thapar observes the rise of new class of ruling elites in the context of social mobility created through the process of land donations to both religious and secular officials in the early medieval period. In order to raise their status to *kṣatriya* hood these ruling elites fabricated genealogies connecting their ancestry either to Solar or Lunar race. Subsequently they emerged as ruling elites with proper ideological legitimation.[40]

On the other hand, Suvira Jaiswal understands the whole phenomenon of social mobility and the emergence of new ruling elites under feudalism through explicating the social and material aspects of caste system. She argues that it is because of the flexible and assimilative nature of the caste system determined by changing economic and political changes embedded in its ritual aspects of purity and impurity that led to the multiplication of ruling elites who were drawn from various *varṇa* categories. She concludes by saying that it is the economic position, that is, the possession of private property either in terms of land or wealth that determined the social status of the *varṇa* based society.[41]

Thus, these scholars, while discussing the various factors for the growth of feudalism emphasized on the break down of the centralised state structures that led to the emergence of new ruling elites. However, with their main focus on land grant economy they identified change in class/caste relationships of the new ruling elites. The Indian Marxist historians did recognise regional variations in the development of Feudalism in different parts of the country. In this context we have studies of scholars like R.N. Nandi, K. Satyanarayana, M.G.S. Narayanan and Kesavan Veluthat who have attempted to study the development of feudalism in different regions of South India.

R.N. Nandi, applying the major props of Sharma's theory, studied the process of the development of feudalism in the Karnataka region. He argues that the decentralization of political power at the central level led to the emergence of local landed intermediaries who subsequently came to wield political power. To stabilize their power, these new ruling elites in turn had evolved various mechanisms which are seen as developmental processes for the resurgence of urban economy.[42] On the other hand, K. Satyanarayana, adopting Kosambi's method and approach, regarded the history of the Andhras as a process of change and progression in terms of changes perceived in social production. The Eastern Chālukyan rule in Andhra Country is seen as a crucial period since the traces of feudalism were taking a permanent shape during this period according to him. Feudalism during this period was explained by this scholar in terms of the large scale donations made to *brāhmaṇa* and secular officials which saw the emergence of a new class of land owners in the villages. They acted as intermediaries between the state and the peasantry.[43] Similarly, M.G.S. Narayanan and Kesavan Veluthat have studied the development of feudalism in the region of Kerala and Tamilnadu. They explained the concept of feudalism as coeval to the Tamil *bhakti* idealogy in the early medieval period which provided sanction and legitimization to the development of feudalism.[44]

The socio-economic perspective of the Marxists scholars opened new avenues for the regional historians writing on socio-economic histories. In this regard we have the works of Suravaram Pratapa Reddy,[45] and B.N. Sastry[46] at the social level and that of R. Narasimha Rao,[47] K. Sundaram,[48] and Alladi Vaidehi[49] at the socio-economic level. While the social historians emphasised on the history of people rather than on the dominant classes or political elites in general. Their study was mainly pertained to the descriptions of dress, food habits, amusements, economy and such other aspects that were prevalent during the Eastern Chālukyan Period. On the other hand scholars like Narasimha Rao and Sundaram have dealt with the various economic activities and social groups who involved in trade and commerce. Therefore, they generally discussed aspects dealing with corporate bodies such as the pekkandru, the nakaramu, the telki, the artisans, the traders etc. Since their main concern was to study these various trading groups, they gave little attention to understand the role of ruling elites in these various activities. Similarly, Vaidehi's *Social and Economic conditions in Eastern Deccan,* dealt primarily with caste system, position of women, occupations of various social groups, education, dress, ornaments, games, sports, religion and temples under the Eastern Chālukyan period.

At the level of art and architecture, we have the works of M. Rama Rao,[50] B. Rajendra Prasad,[51] A. Surya Kumari[52] and others. They have surveyed the various art and architectural forms evolved during the Eastern Chālukyan period. The main focus of these scholars was on the study of classification of art styles, measurement of structures, indexing and decipherment of inscriptions without understanding the major role played by the temple as an economic and ideological institution that provided legitimation to the new ruling elites in the early medieval context. However, all these scholars considered the political history of the period as an essential background to their study. Hence the approach and methodology of some of them is traditional. Though, they have not treated social, economic and religious aspects as separate compartments yet, they have failed to theoretically establish the linkages of these aspects which played an important role in state formation.

The construct of Indian Feudalism provided by the Marxist historians, based on the European model, has been refuted by scholars such as Burton Stein, Harbans Mukhia, B.D. Chattopadhyaya and others.

While criticizing the idea of feudalism in South India, Burton Stein applies the model of Segmentary state in understanding the political changes during the early medieval Tamil country. Influenced by much of Southall's study on the Allūr society and also by the concepts of ethnic and nuclear areas of attractions, Stein elaborates his concept of nuclear areas of corporate institutions which became a basic element of his interpretation of south Indian history. While distinguishing between the three levels of 'zones' (i.e.) the central, the intermediate and the peripheral, Stein reiterates that it is only at the central zone, which constituted the 'core domain of the Cholas' that inter-relationship between these three cultural zones is understood in terms of *ritual sovereignity* rather than the actual political centre. However, it is established that the persons who were distributing the royal message viz. the *brāhmaṇas* in terms of ritual sovereignity converted a congeries of local political systems into a segmentary state. Further, acculturation of Śaiva cults by royalty is considered by Stein as an over reaching ideological element which makes these units segmentary as a whole. Another important feature of the segmentary state according to him is found in the *brāhmaṇa peasant* alliance.[53] Stein's concept of segmentary model has aroused vehement criticism from all quarters by Indian historians. While refuting much of Stein's concept of segmentary state Champakalakshmi emphasizes on political and ideological factors which worked for political centralisation of Chola power. She also argues that several economic changes led to the break down of the insulated body and thus considerable social change took place.[54]

Besides these major concepts of the State in pre-modern India within the contemporary historiography, there exists a considerable number of 'non-aligned'[55] contributions. The scholars of this school followed the social history framework in their method and approach. The emphasis that state formation should be studied not by applying certain models but by understanding the various processes of change that envisaged state formation in various regions was expanded. This method of studying state formation is reflected in the writings of Hermann Kulke, B.D. Chattopadhyaya and others. Hermann Kulke, while studying the process of state formation in early medieval Orissa envisages an integrative polity. According to him various processes such as donating land to *brāhmaṇas* in the peripheral areas, *kṣatriyization* of tribal chiefs, acculturation of tribal cults by the ruling elites were all seen as major processes in consolidating the power of the ruling elites and the formation of states[56] in Orissa.

Similarly, B.D. Chattopadhyaya studied the process of state formation with reference to the emergence of various Rajaput clans to political prominence, in the present day State of Rajasthan. He observed that various political, economic, socio-ideological processes of the ruling elites, which are explained in terms of the fortification of rural settlements, assignment of land grants, maintaining horizontal marriage networks and finally, legitimization of their rule by establishing genealogical linkages with the *kṣatriya* line of the mythical past have helped the ruling elites in Rajasthan to consolidate their power in the early medieval period.[57] All these mechanisms have been understood by the scholar as important through which new state structures emerged and consolidated their power in the early medieval period. Thus, while the models of Indian Feudalism and the segmentary state restricted political change mainly to the aspects of fragmentation and the segmentation of political authority, those who adopted a new trend in history writing based on a new social history approach have perceived political changes through the process of centralization and integration rather than fragmentation and decentralization.

Significantly, all the three models, namely Indian Marxist school, the Segmentary school and the non-aligned school have envisaged the early medieval period as a period of transition, between the early historic and the medieval period. It is perceived that the political, economic and social changes during this period underwent a process of metamorphosis which ultimately led to the formation of new ruling elites along with the formation of new states in almost all parts of the country. All the recent theoretical models on state, as had been explained above, reveal the existence of large scale social mobility during the early medieval periods, which is assigned to the development of new economic relations in the form of land grants and transformation of the traditional *varṇa* structure. These processes of change saw the emergence of large number of ruling elites such as the various Rājput clans in Northern India, the Pallavas, the Chōlas in Tamilnadu, the various families of the Chālukyas in the Deccan, the Pālās, and Sēnas in Bengal and many other ruling elites. It has been further noticed that there was a constant attempt by the ruling elites to assume new *varṇa* identity either, by claiming traditional kṣatriyahood as was done by the Rajput families or, by adopting *brahma-kṣatra* identity as in the case of the Pallavas, or claiming the status of Rājaputras which is explained as process of Rajputization. This was followed by the local ruling chiefs in North India and Bengal. These processes, it has been regarded by scholars, helped the ruling elites, who emerged cutting across *varṇa* identity, to legitimize their role as rulers in the newly emerging regional kingdoms that were being established all over the country.

As the conventional historigraphy represented by the imperialists, Orientalists and the Nationalists did not envisage any change in the early medieval Indian society, they have understood the emergence of the ruling elites during the early medieval period on the basis of the *varṇa* ideology as was propounded in the normative view of traditional *Dharmaśāstra* texts. According to the traditional view of the *varṇa*, the society was supposed to function on the basis of hierarchical gradation of the fourfold *varṇa* order which constituted the *brāhmaṇas*, the *kṣatriya*, the *vaiśya* and the *sūdra*. The functions of these four castes as has been stated in the first *maṇdala* of the *Ṛgvēda* were based on their divine creation. Accordingly, the functions of the *kṣatriyas* were explained in terms of military rulership qualities as they were created from the arms of the Great God Prajāpati.[58] Thus, theoritically , the corpus of ruling elites supposed to be mainly drawn from the *kṣatriya varṇa*.

However, the scholars representing recent historigraphy such as R.S. Sharma, B.N.S. Yadava, B.D. Chattopadhyaya, Kesavan Veluthat, Kameswara Rao, R.N. Nandi, and many others have observed that a new trend emerges in the functioning and composition of the *varṇa* structure in the early medieval period. *Kṣatriya varṇa* being nebulous, represented not only the aristocratic classes, but also included all those rulers who discharged the duties of the *kṣatriyas* irrespective of their origin, such as the Abhiras,[59] the Rājputs[60] in Northern India, the Kādambas in Karnataka,[61] the Pallavas[62] in Tamilnadu, the Chaturthakulajas[63] in Andhra etc. The origin of these ruling elites were seen by the scholars in terms of social mobility that was prevalent during the early medieval period. Thus, by this time, many ruling elites emerged mainly on the basis of their functions rather than on their birth, thus cutting across both caste and class lines of distinction.

In defining the changes in *kṣatriya varṇa* during the early medieval period, divergent opinions have been expressed by the historians following both the conventional and more recent approaches on the subject. Thus, while discussing how the *kṣatriya varṇa* got a *brahma-kṣatriya* identity during this period, Bhandarkar explains this phenomenon through a change of occupation by a *brāhmaṇa* to a traditional occupation of a *kṣatriya*, i.e., adopting rulership, leads to a permanent change in his status.[64] On the other hand, Sarkar argues that *brahma-kṣatriyas* orginated as a result of mixed marriage alliances between the *kṣatriyas* and the *brāhmaṇas.*[65] Sankaranarayanan, while supporting the claim of the *Vishnukundins* of *brahma-kṣatra* origin by seeking their descent from the Puru dynasty, explains that a *brāhmaṇa* could assume kṣatriyahood by performing various *vēdic* sacrifices such as *Mārutstoma* sacrifice, thus becoming a *brahma-kṣatriya.*[66] On the other hand, Kesavan Veluthat regards the origin of the *brahma-kṣatriyas* by adopting the *Bharadvāja gōtra.* For instance, the Pallavas of South India, regarded themselves as *brahma-kṣatriyas* by adopting the *Bharadvāja gōtra.*[67]

On the other hand, scholars such as B.N.S. Yadava, and B.D. Chattopadhyaya connect the origin of *brahma-kṣatriyas,* with the growth of feudal tendencies in the early medieval period, in terms of landed property, martial qualities and regalian rights which emerged as the chief basis of the determination of status and social privilege, which in turn attracted members of *brāhmana varṇa* also. These *brāhmaṇas* further attempted to exchange their priestly duties for martial ones and ultimately, became *kṣatriyas.*[68] B.D. Chattopadhyaya regards *brahma-kṣatriya* as an intermediary status, seized upon by the new royal families before they could formulate a claim to a pure *kṣatriya* origin. For example, the Guhilas, the Cahamanas were originally *brāhmaṇas* but later they assumed *brahma-kṣatriya* lineage to legitimize their new *kṣatriya* role.[69] Thus, both these scholars, Yadava and Chattopadhyaya, consider "*brahma-kṣatriya*" as transitional status from *brāhmaṇa* to *kṣatriya* status.[70]

The second view in defining the *kṣatriya varṇa* in the early medieval period was observed in terms of *sat-kṣatriya* and the *asat kṣatriya varṇa.* Based on Ibn Khurdadbha's categorization of *kṣatriya varṇa* into two broad divisions of Sabkufriya or Sakriya and Kataria or Kastaria, Altekar identifies the former with the *sat-kṣatriyas* and the latter with ordinary *kṣatriyas.*[71] Similarly, C.V. Vaidya regarded the Subkufriya *kṣatriyas* as ruling *kṣatriyas* and the kataria *kṣatriyas* as agriculturists.[72].

The *third view* in defining the *kṣatriya varṇa* has been expressed, while discussing mainly the emergence of Rājaputras to political prominence during the early medieval period. Scholars like Vincent Smith, Todd and others have regarded the Rājputs as foreigners. On the other hand, C.V. Vaidya regards them as descendants of Indo-Aryan race, as they exhibited the chivalrous qualities of warfare. B.D. Chattopadhyaya had shown that by the early medieval period, the Rājputs included various military clans and numerous petty chiefs, holding villages, who largely constituted the ruling landed aristocracy. According to him Rajputs constituted a "mixed caste".[73] B.N.S. Yadava observes that by the twelfth century A.D., even the traditional *kṣatriyas* came to be represented as Rājputs. This explains to us the widely prevalent process of "Rājaputization" which has been recognized as a channel of transition from tribal to state polity.[74].

The *fourth view* in defining the ruling elites was identified as dominant peasantry and dependent peasantry. Especially in South India, Burton Stein while explaining these terms says that the dominant peasantry were regarded as the powerful ruling elites as they exercised both administrative and military functions. Thus, the ruling elites in South India, in the words of Stein emerged in terms of power and status within the agrarian structure.

It is in the context of these various definitions in defining the ruling elites in the early medieval period which are assigned to various political, social and economic changes, makes an interesting topic of research the study of Eastern Chālukyas as belonging to the *kṣaytriya varṇa.* Hitherto, divergent opinions have been expressed by scholars with regard to the caste of the Eastern Chālukyas. Based on the information available from literary and inscriptional sources, most of the scholars regarded Chālukyas as belonging to the traditional *kṣaytriya varṇa.* However, scholars like Suravaram Pratapa Reddy, regarded them as *śūdras*, as they had emerged from the feet of Brahma.[75]

Though the Imperialists, Orientalist historians and most of the nationalists historians regarded the ruling elites as mainly constituting the traditional *kṣaytriya varṇa* without perceiving any change at social, economic levels, others suggest that the emergence of ruling elites from other *varṇa* categories, occurred due to the various changes in socio-economic milieu, and this led to the emergence of new ruling elites cutting across both caste and class lines. These changes perceived in the recent historigraphical tradition at the pan-Indian level was also reflected in the writings of some of the Andhra historians, too. In this regard we have in more recent years the works of Y. Balarama Murthy, B.S.L. Hanumantha Rao, K.S. Kameswara Rao, Y. Kumara Swamy among others. These works give an indepth insight into the various aspects of political, social, economic, and ideological processes of the ruling elites during the Eastern Chālukyan period. Thus eminent scholars like Balarama Murthy,[76] B.S.L. Hanumantha Rao[77] and Kameswara Rao[78] discussed at great length the social mobility of the various *brāhmaṇa* groups, bōya tribes and Chaturthakulajas during the Eastern Chālukyan period. Their mobility according to these scholars was effected due to the changes perceived in the royal patronization of various social groups and the adoption of the practice of land donations. Similarly, Kumara Swamy's[79] study brings out the prominent features of feudalism during the Eastern Chālukyan period. However, all these studies lacked integrated approach in understanding the various aspects as important mechanisms adopted by the ruling elites in the formation of new regional state forms.

Therefore, an attempt has been made to study these various political, social, economic and ideological processes of the ruling elites for the defined region of study, namely, the Eastern Deccan in the following chapters.

References

1. Romila Thapar, *AISH*, New Delhi, 1978, p. 2.
2. Ronald Inden "Orientalist Construction of India" *MAS*, 20,3,1986, pp. 430-31.
3. *Ibid*, pp. 430-31.
4. James Mill, *History of British India,* New Delhi, 1817.
5. Vincent Smith, *The Oxford History of India*, Delhi, 1919.
6. James Mill, *Op.Cit.*, 1871, p. 160.
7. Ronald Inden, *Op.cit.*, 1986, p. 409.
8. Romila Thapar, *Op.Cit.*, 1978, p. 4.

9. Hermann Kulke, "Fragmentation and Segmentation versus Integration and the Segmentary State in Indian History, *Studies in History*, vol. IV, No. 2, 1982, p. 3.
10. Ronald Inden, *Op.Cit.*, 1986, pp. 417-418.
11. *Ibid*, p. 418.
12. Vincent Smith, *Op.Cit.*, p. 190.
13. Hermann Kulke, *The State in India, 1000-1700 A.D.*, New Delhi, 1995, pp. 2-3.
14. S. Settar, 'Twentieth Century in Ancient India', Presidential Address, *PIHC*, 43rd ss, 1982, p. 58.
15. M. Pattabhirama Reddy 'Some Thoughts on Historiography today', Presidential Address, *PAPHC*, Vijayawada, 1978, p. 143.
16. *Ibid*, p. 146.
17. Romila Thapar, *Op.Cit.*, 1978, p. 10.
18. Kesavan Veluthat, *The Political Structure of Early Medieval South India*, New Delhi, 1993, p. 2.
19. Herman Kulke, *Op.cit.*, 1995, p. 2.
20. Romila Thapar, *Op.cit.*, 1978, p. 11.
21. Hermann Kulke, *Op.Cit.*, 1995, p. 4.
22. *Ibid*, p. 4.
23. M. Pattabhirama Reddy, *Op.cit.*, 1978, pp. 1445-145.
24. K.P. Jayaswal, *Hindu Polity*, Bangalore, 1924, p. 351.
25. A.S. Altekar, *State and Government in Ancient India*, Delhi, 1958, pp. 370-76.
26. S. Settar, *Op.cit.*, 1982, p. 58.
27. *Ibid*, p. 59.
28. *Ibid*, p. 59.
29. R.G. Bhandarkar, *Early History of the Dekkan*, New Delhi, 1985 (First published in 1892).
30. G. Yazdani, *The Early History of the Deccan*, New Delhi, 1982, (Rp.) Part - I - IV, p. 3.
31. Kesavan Veluthat, *Op.cit.*, 1993, p. 7.
32. Aloka Parasher 'Early History of Andhra - Some Interpretations *PAPHC*, 9th session, Kurnool, 1985, p. 187.
33. B.V. Krishna Rao, *History of the Eastern Chālukyas of Vengi (A.D. 610-1210)*, Hyderabad, 1973.
34. M. Krishna Kumari, *The Rule of the Chālukya-Cholas in Andhra Desa*, Delhi, 1985, p. 1.
35. K. Suryanarayana, *History of the Minor Chalukya Families in Medieval Andhra Desa*, Delhi, 1986 and also *Feudatories Under Eastern Chalukyas (History and Culture of Andhras)*, Delhi, 1987, p. 59.

36. Aloka Parasher, *Op.Cit.*, 1985, p. 186.
37. D.D. Kosambi, *An Introduction to the study of Indian History*, Bombay, (First published 1956) (Rpt.) 1990, p. 295.
38. R.S. Sharma *Indian Feudalism (C.A.D. 300-1200)*, Delhi 1965, also 'Indian Feudalism Retouched' *IHR* vol. I, 1974, pp. 320-330.
39. B.N.S. Yadava, *Society and Culture in North India, (In the 12th Century A.D.)*, Allahabad, 1973.
40. Romila Thapar, *Op.cit.*, 1978, pp. 132-134.
41. Suvira Jaiswal 'Varna and Indeology' *Social Scientist*, vol. 19, 1991, p. 49.
42. R.N. Nandi 'Growth of Rural Economy in Early Feudal India, *PIHC*, 1984, pp. 1-72.
43. K. Satyanarayana, *A study of the History and Culture of the Andhras*, New Delhi, 1975, p. xvi.
44. M.G.S. Narayanan and Kesavan Veluthat, 'Bhakti Movement in South India' in D.N. Jha (ed) *Feudal Social Formations in Early India*, Delhi, 1989, pp. 358-368.
45. Suravaram Pratapa Reddy, *Andhrula Sanghika Charitra*, 1992, (First published 1950) pp. 1-14.
46. B.N. Sastry, *Social History of Andhras*, Hyderabad, 1975, pp. 256-263.
47. R. Narasimha Rao, *Corporate Life in Medieval Andhra desa*, 1967.
48. K. Sundaram, *Studies in Economic and Social Conditions of Medieval Andhra (A.D. 1000-1600)* Madras, 1968.
49. Alladi Vaidehi Krishnamurthy, *Social and Economic Conditions in Eastern Deccan (A.D. 1000-1250)*, Madras, 1970.
50. M. Rama Rao, *Select Andhra Temples*, also *Early Chalukyan Temples of Andhra Desa*, Hyderabad, 1970.
51. B. Rajendra Prasad, *Chalukyan Temples of Andhra desa*, New Delhi, 1983.
52. A Surya Kumari, *Temples in Andhra desa*, Delhi, 1988.
53. Burton Stein, 'Segmentary State Interim Reflections', in Hermann Kulke (ed) *Op.cit.*, Delhi, 1995, pp. 138-139.
54. R. Champaka Lakshmi, 'The State in Medieval South India -Emerging Perspectives' *PAPHC*, Srisailam, p.7
55. Hermann Kulke, *Op.cit.*, Delhi, 1995, p. 40.
56. Hermann Kulke, 'The Early and the Imperial Kingdom: A Processural Model of Integrative State Formation in Early Medieval India', (ed) by Hermann Kulke *Op.cit.*, Delhi, 1995, pp. 233-235.
57. B.D. Chattopadhyaya 'Political Processes and structure of Polity in

Early Medieval India: Problems and Perspectives' *Social Scientist*, vol. 13, 1985, p. 11.

58. Romila Thapar, 'Social Mobility in Ancient India - with Special Reference to Elite Groups in *AISH*', New Delhi, 1978, p. 138.
59. R.S. Sharma, *Social Change in Early Medieval India*, (circa A.D. 500-1201), New Delhi, 1969, pp. 23-24.
60. B.D. Chattopadhyaya 'Origin of Rajput: The Political, Economic and Social Processes in Early Medieval Rajasthan', *IHR*, Vol. 112, No. 2, July 1976, pp. 43-58.
61. R.N. Nandi, 'Clan Names and Social Mobility in the Deccan' *PIHC*, 33rd sesson, 1973, pp. 111-113.
62. Kesavan Veluthat, *The Political Structure of Early Medieval South India*, New Delhi, 1973, p. 31.
63. K.S. Kameswara Rao, 'Social Structure of Medieval Andhra - Emergence of New Political Elites', *PAPHC*, Nellore, 1991, pp. 80-82.
64. Suvira Jaiswal, 'Studies in Early Indian Social History: Trends and Possibilities', *IHR*, 1979-80, vol. 6, p. 32.
65. *Ibid*, p. 32.
66. S. Sankaranarayanan, *The Vishnukundins and Their Times*, Delhi, 1977, p. 25.
67. Kesavan Veluthat, *Op.cit.*, 1993, p. 31.
68. B.N.S. Yadava, *Op.cit.*, 1973, pp. 20-22.
69. B.D. Chattopadhyaya, *Op.cit.*, 1976, p. 61.
70. *Ibid*, p. 61.
71. B.N.S. Yadava, *Op.cit.*, 1973, p. 35.
72. *Ibid*, p. 35.
73. B.D. Chattopadhyaya, *Op.Cit.*, 1976, pp. 60-61.
74. Suvaram Pratapa Reddy, *Op.cit.*, 1992, pp. 1-2.
76. Y. Balaramamurthy, 'Social Mobility - Horizontal and Vertical' *PAPHC*, Nagaram, 1987-88, pp. 166-167.
77. B.S.L. Hanumantha Rao, *Social Mobility in Medieval Andhra*, Hyderabad, 1995, pp. 76-92.
78. K.S. Kameswara Rao, 'Social formation during Eastern Chalukyan Period' - *PAPHC* Nagaram, 1987-88, pp. 59-63, also 'Social Structure of Medieval Andhra - Emergence of New Political Elites', *PAPHC*, Nellore, 1991, pp. 80-83.
79. Y. Kumara Swamy 'Traces of Feudalism during the Eastern Chalukyan Period', *PAPHC*, Warangal, 1983, pp. 30-36.

Chapter-II

GEO-POLITICAL BACKGROUND

It is a well understood fact that geographical knowledge becomes rudimentary for the study of political and military history.[1] Highlighting the importance of geography for the study of history, eminent historian, Mischelet had stated in the Preface to his *Histoire de France* that history in essence was founded upon geography. He further asserted that 'without geographical basis, the people, the makers of history, are seen to be walking on air, as those Chinese pictures where the ground is wanting. The soil, too, must not be looked upon only as the scene of action. Its influence appears in a hundred ways, such as food, climate etc."[2] Therefore, the historical transformations and the social changes within a specific time and space have to be understood in terms of man's interaction with his geographical environment. While discussing the seminal role played by geographical factors in determining the political, economic, social and cultural developments within specific localities, Subba Rao quotes E.W. Gilbert to the effect that "Geography is the art of recognizing and describing the personalities of region".[3] Therefore, in this respect, it becomes important to comprehend the crucial role played by small localities such as Vengi to understand the historical development of the broader region in its totality.

Recognizing the importance of geography to understand historical change of a specific region has meant that first a study of its geographical features has to be made. It would be pertinent to point out here that since the micro-region of Vengi, which forms the main focus of attention and has invariably been treated as part of the sub-region of Krishna-Godavari basin, it becomes crucial to get an understanding of the geography of this sub-region first.

In historical terms, the sub-region of the Krishna-Godavari basin can be seen as a part of Eastern Deccan. It forms one of the three basic sub-regions of the present day linguistic state of Andhra Pradesh. The other two regions being, the Hyderabad-Telengana region and the southern peneplains of the Rayalaseema region. According to some scholars, "Eastern Deccan covers the coastal portions of Modern Andhra and

MAP I
AREA OF STUDY

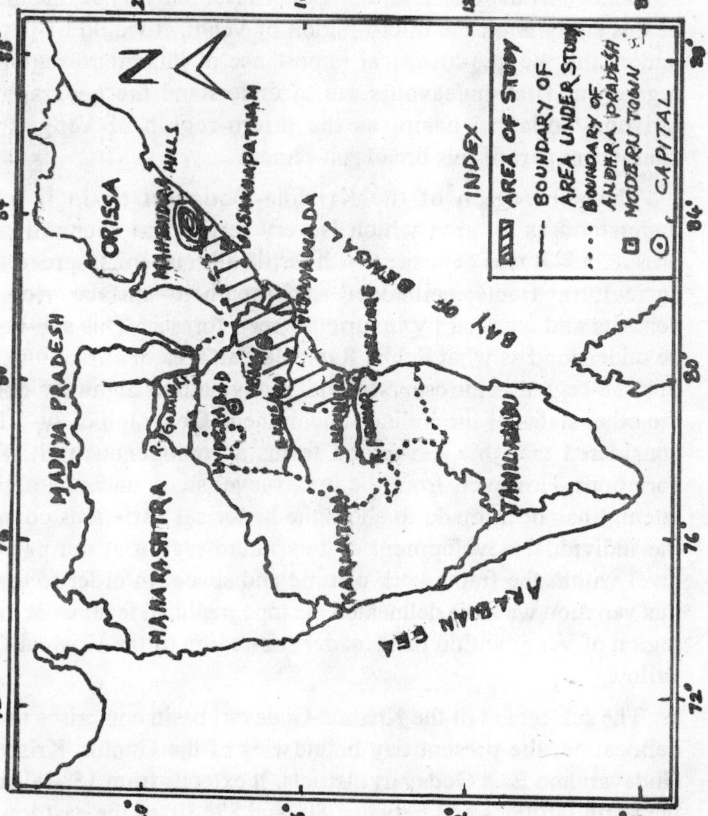

extends from Ganjam to Nellore.[4] The present study is to focus on the micro region of Vengi. Though at the time of its conquest, Vengi region constituted only few areas that surrounded this micro-region, however the extent of the kingdom in the period of our study covered all those areas spanning the Mahēndra mountains in the North to the river Manneru in the South (MAP-I). Therefore, our area of study covers what scholars generally called as the "Eastern Deccan". Since, the main focus of this study is on the micro-region of Vengi, it would be pertinent to understand the geo-historical importance of this micro region. In this regard our first endeavours are to understand the geography of the Krishna-Godavari basin, as the micro-region of Vengi formed a component part of this broad sub-region.

The sub-region of the Krishna-Godavari basin is generally understood as an area which is very fertile and economically very prosperous. It was deposited with fertile alluvial soils, spread with vast agricultural tracts, embedded underneath its surface, rich mineral deposits and covered by luxurious green forests.[5] This sub-region can be understood as what Subba Rao calls "an area of attraction". Further, this sub-region is intrespersed with many natural highways connecting the other states of the Indian subcontinent. Geographically, it has been considered that this sub-region forms a homogenous unit with little variations. However, from the micro-level study undertaken by us, an attempt has been made to show the historical variations connected to the individual development of this micro-region at the pan-regional level within the framework of time and space. In order to understand this variation we have delineated the topographical features of the micro-region of Vengi within the broader sub-region of the Krishna-Godavari valley.

The sub-region of the Krishna-Godavari basin comprises in its broad delineation, the present day boundaries of the Guntur, Krishna, West Godavari and East Godavari districts. It extends from 15^0 18' and 18^0 of the north latitudes and between 80^0 and 82^0 30' of the east longitudes.[6] This sub-region as the very name suggests, is watered by two major rivers, namely, the Krishna and the Godavari and their tributaries. These two rivers made the region the nucleus of agricultural production and commercial activity. The area of our study, namely the micro-region of Vengi which forms an integral part of this broad sub-region is situated at the very heart of these two river valleys. Physiographically, the micro-region of Vengi lies between 16^0 48' of the north latitudes and 81^0 07' of the east longitudes. It is presently identified as Peda Vegi and China

Vegi which are situated about 11.3 kilometres from modern day Eluru, within the present day boundaries of the West Godavari District.[7]

The northern part of the Krishna-Godavari sub-region presents three types of physiographical units namely (1) the deltaic region, (2) the upland regions and (3) the agency tracts forested on the western and north-western areas.[8]

The deltaic region which is very fertile is watered by the river Godavari and its tributaries. The rich mineral wealth brought by the inflow of these rivers makes the region the agricultural nucleus by producing a variety of crops such as paddy, sugarcane, tobacco etc. The upland area lies between the delta and the Agency areas. It consists of an undulating plain broken by low ranges of hills.

On the other hand, the Agency tracts are covered with forests. The area that covers the forests according to the recent statistics is about 11.3% of the total land area. However, it can be assumed that during the period of our study, it must have been undoubtedly constituted more than what it has been today. This area is predominantly a hilly region traversed by the broken ranges of the Eastern Ghats. They form the Papikonda range of hills. The hills also flank the main ridges and spurs rising from the lower uplands. These hills are supported by thick forests which are classified into four types.[9] The Southern thorn shrub forests are found on the plain areas of Peda Vegi region, which is a part of the vast delta formed by the Krishna and the Godavari rivers.[10] These forests bear wide variety of flora and fauna. The type of soil which predominates the major part of this region is the riverine alluvium. This is found on the lower courses of the valleys of most rivers in the deltaic region. The exceptionally fertile nature of these soils proved conducive for agricultural production, especially paddy cultivation. The other important soils are laterites which are formed by decomposition of gneiss.

The richness of the soils and their high yielding capacity in this micro-region can be attributed to the riverine systems. The major and the most important river that wets this region is the river Godavari. This river takes its birth in the hills behind Triambak in the Nasik district. It runs a course of 900 miles and drains an area of 1,12,000 square miles. After it enters Andhra Pradesh, it runs placidly in the Telengana region, and then forces its way across the Eastern Ghats through a deep and narrow gorge barely 200 yards wide. Once across the ghats, the river opens out again and forms a series of broad ridges dotted with low alluvial islands called the *Lankas.* At Vijjeswaram, the river breaks itself into two branches namely the Gautami Godavari which constitutes the Eastern branch and the Vasista Godavari comprising the Western branch, of the Godavari District. At Antervedi, the river merges itself into the sea.[11] The other minor rivers that feed the upland areas of the micro-region include the *Tamilēru* flowing along the Western boundary of Chintalapudi and Eluru taluks, the *Yerrakālva*, flowing in the Northern portion of Chintalapudi taluk and along the Western border of Kovvur taluk, the *Bynēru*, the *Kovvada kālva* and the *Jụlēru* flows in the Polavaram taluk. The *Rallamadugu* and the *Gundēru* rivers flow through the Kovvuru and Eluru taluks respectively.[12]

Apart from these vast riverine beds, the Kolleru Lake forms an extensive shallow depression towards the south of the Eluru taluk and the West of the Tadepalligudem and Bheemavaram taluks. This lake is created by the gradual rise in the level of the country on either side by alluvial deposits from the two big rivers, the Godavari and the Krishna. It has an outlet to the sea by means of the upputeru and it serves as a good fishing ground.[13]

The configuration of the micro-region is further characterised by its geological rock formations. The oldest rock formations of the micro-region are the Archaeans, followed by the lower and upper Gondwana types. The gneisses together with the quartzite and the calc silicate rocks belong to the Archaean type. The other types are the granitic type made of quartz and felspar. These are found around the Eluru taluk. The magnetite, Sillimanite, Cordierite and Gneiss are found in the hill ranges of the Eastern Ghats. The metamorphic rocks occur in the valley areas. The gondwana systems are represented by the Chintalapudi Sandstone, Gollapalli Sandstone, Raghavapuram shales and Tirupati Sandstone.[14]

Along with these various geographical features, the climate of the region also played its due role in determining the nature of settlements in this region. Situated close to the Tropic of Cancer, the climate of the region exhibited moderate variations. Though summers proved oppressive, the region did receive good average rainfall during both the south-west and post-monsoon seasons. These favourable geographical and climatic conditions proved conducive for good economic subsistence and continuous human habitation.[15]

Due to these factors this micro-region has become the nucleus for agrarian production and commercial activities. Hence, this micro-region can be rightly termed as what Subba Rao calls as an "*area of attraction.*"[16]

In this way the geographical features of this micro-region can be understood to have exercised a tremendous influence on the soil, the vegetation, food, land, economic life of the people inhabiting the area. However, Subba Rao pertinently points out that it should be remembered that "ancient boundaries are not simple linear boundaries around natural division which coincide with the familiar geographical sense of the term".[17] Therefore, he goes on to explain that apart from the consideration of the climate, geology and soil, most important are the historic and social traditions. In other words, the historical origin and development of a micro-region or a locality can be better understood in terms of the interaction of geography and material culture with human agency that then helps to identify historical transformations and social changes over historical time.[18]

The earliest inhabitants referred to generally by term Āndhra as people or tribe was made in the *Aiṭarēya Brāhmaṇa*. It mentions the Āndhras as the exiled sons of Viśvāmitra. Further, it refers to the Āndhra people along with the Puṇḍras, the Śabaras, the Pulindas and the Mūtibas who were all described as dāsyus living on the borders of civilised life. They were also characterized as a tribe who took to dog's meat.[19] The inscriptions of Asōka mention Āndhras along with Pulindas as border peoples.[20] The *Rāmāyana* and the *Mahābhārata* speak of the Āndhras along with Cōḷas, Cēras and Pāṇḍyas.[21] The *Purāṇas* refer to the *Āndhra Jātiyas* who enjoyed the same political status as Kāmbōjas, Yavanas and Gandhāras in the north.[22] Pliny refers to the Āndhras as a powerful tribe who possessed numerous villages and thirty well-fortified towns. They had under their control a huge army consisting of an infantry one lakh strong, a two thousand strong cavalry and one thousand strong elephant force.[23] The *Bṛihatsamhita* a fifth century A.D. text, on the other hand, continues to describe tribes of the Āndhras as *Cheñchukas*, identified with modern Chenchus who lived on hunting.[24] From these early references, it can be understood that the Āndhras were referred to in the earliest sources, not as a territorial entity but as people or tribe inhabiting some part of the present day Andhra Pradesh region. The region derived its name from the inhabitants. According to Gopalachari, Andhra People were a tribal group most of whom had settled down in the valleys of the river Krishna and Godavari.[25] It can be suggested that based on ancient literary works and their interpretation by modern scholars, the geo-cultural aspects of the micro-region of Vengi can be understood in three distinct historical phases of its origin, its rise and its decline as an important micro-region upto early medieval times.

Archaeologically, the micro-region of *Vengi* did not evince any pre-historic settlements. However, inorder to understand the origin of Vengi in the historical period and its rise as an epicentre implies that first we must get an idea of the pre-historic settlements around the micro-region. In this context, it has been rightly pointed out that the origin of the very idea of the city/town is inevitably linked with the nature and character of the earlier cultures,[26] since as pointed out by Lewis Munford, "Before the city there was the hamlet, and shrine and the village; before the village, the camp, the cache, the cave, the cairn-and without these 'the larger urban community would have lacked an essential base for physical permanence and social continuity'.[27] Therefore, in this context, it is imperative for us to understand the earliest settlements around this micro-region, covering broadly the sub-region of the Krishna-Godavari valley.

Recent archaeological excavations have shown that the sub-region of the Krishna-Godavari valley had the existence of stone age cultures. It has been observed that the area lying around the Krishna valley exhibited more numerous pre-historic settlements than the area surrounded by Godavari Valley. The reasons for the absence of large-scale stone age settlements around the Godavari basin according to B.R. Subramanyam was due to the environmental conditions of this sub-region. It has been shown that the two tributaries of the river Godavari frequently changed their courses. This rendered the area as a vast marshy land making it unsuitable for sustained human habitation.[28] On the other hand, the Krishna basin, with its strategic position, rendered favourable conditions for the earliest human habitation possible.

The earliest pre-historic cultural settlements of the sub-region can be traced back from the Palaeolithic and the Mesolithic phases around 4000 B.C. These settlements occured on the red sandy, clayey and black soils. This phase has been identified by the discovery of tools and weapons used by the earliest man. The next phase of human-habitation namely, the Neolithic-Chalcolithic phase dated around 2000-1000 B.C. in the sub-region has been identified with the presence of pottery assemblages, with craft specialization and rudimentary trade. The pottery of the Neolithic-Chalcolithic phases of this sub-region comprises greyware, burnished ware, red ware, black ware, reddish brown ware. They represent a predominantly hand-made traits of the pottery. Kesarapalli and Nagarjunakonda exhibit the artefacts belonging to this phase.[29]

The Chalcolithic phase was intruded upon by the Megalithic phase around 1000 B.C. The megalithic settlements are found at sights like Amarāvati, Dharanikōta, Jaggayyapēta, Kēsarapalli, Nāgarjunakonda among other sites. The megalithic cultures have largely been identified in these sub-regions by the evidence of the occurence of ceramic sherds of the Black and Red-ware and Red and black ware along with the occurence of iron objects. The use and proliferation of the iron objects of Megalithic cultures over the Neolithic-chalcolithic sites suggests a demographic expansion in Andhra during the post-fifth century B.C. Consequently, we witness the spread of settlements from the highland peripheral areas to the deltaic plains of the nuclear areas. Further, this movement transformed the hitherto pastoral-cum-subsistence economy to a primarily agrarian one.[30] This phase also suggests the acculturation of those areas which were hitherto uninhabited.

All these changes were witnessed on a large scale around the Krishna basin. However, the recent excavations carried out around the area south of the river Godavari also revealed sites of earlier settlements patterns. Sites like Jami, Elamanchili, Yellavaram, etc., have yielded ground stone tool types and pottery of Neolithic assemblages as well.

It has been noted that most of the early stone age settlements were found in the Krishna basin rather than in the Godavari basin. However, the Megalithic settlements revealing the demographic expansion and proliferation of iron implements helped in the gradual process of acculturating the most fertile and thickly forested tracts of the Godavari basin. It is in this context that we have attempted to comprehend the emergence of the micro-region of Vengi to its geo-historical importance and its significant role in determining the destinies of many ruling families that have ruled the Andhra region for centuries. It has been argued by us that though the micro-region of Vengi did not evince any traits of stone age settlements, its gradual rise can be evident from the Buddhistic and early historic periods, marked predominantly by Buddhist monuments.

The period spanning from 200 B.C. to 200 A.D. can be regarded as an important phase in the history of the Andhra region when the cities and towns began to emerge around the micro-region of Vengi. This period is generally regarded by scholars as a period of urbanization the phenomenon that has been evidenced at the pan - Indian level. Most of the urban centres that emerged during this period were concentrated around the Buddhist centres. Some of the famous Buddhist sites in Andhra region can be noted as Amaravati, Bhattiprolu, Ghantasala,

Nagarjunakonda, Jaggayyapeta and others. Most of these sites however, have been found to be concentrated in the Krishna region. The emergence of these cities and their important role as commercial centres can be buttressed from the existence of institutions such as *Goshthi* and *nigama* during this period.[31] However, the growth of towns did not depend on any centralised adminsitration. They had their growth due to the interaction of various economic and social factors. The favourable geographical situations helped these regions as flourishing centres of agriculture and trade. Consequently, this paved way for permanent settlements in these regions. The micro-region of Vengi comes to lime light during this period as an important area of communication connecting these commercial centres and port-towns with the rest of the Indian sub-continent.

From the third century A.D. there was relative decline in trade and commerce all over the sub-continent. This, according to the Marxist scholars was due to the absence of metallic currency. This period also witnessed the revival of brāhmanical religion and the decline of Buddhism. These factors resulted in the gradual dwindling of the Buddhist sites. Thus, by the 3rd-4th century A.D. the above mentioned Buddhist centres were relegated towards background. However, the favourable strategic position of the micro-region of Vengi as a nucleus connecting various parts of the country started attracting political attention from this period onwards.

The historical geography of the micro-region of Vengi has been viewed by scholars as constantly shifting at successive periods of human habitation. Similarly, the historical understanding of the micro-region of Vengi also has changed according to the conceptual limitations of the historians. The earliest reference to Vengi is made in the early historic period. During this period the region of Vengi acted as a natural highway converging five great routes of Kalinga, Drāvida, Karnataka, Maharashtra and Dakṣhina Kōsala.[33] In the 2nd century A.D. Ptolemy refers to the region of Vengi pura. He called it as 'Benagouron' which was located in the country of the Śālakenoi (Śalankāyana).[34] The first epigraphic reference to the region of Vengi as an important region is found in the Mayidavōlu inscription of the 4th century A.D. In this inscription, the area of Vengi has been identified as a country lying between the river Godavari and the Krishna.[35] In the 5th and 6th centuries A.D. the Pallava charters refer to the conquest of Vaingēyakas, who ruled over Vengo Rāstra or Veṇgi Dēśa. Vengi Rāshtra, during this time corresponded to the Reṇd-ēṛu-lu-nadimi-vishaya or Sindhuyug Māntara-dēśa which when literally translated meant "Two rivers-middle district".[36] This clearly suggests to the land lying between the Godavari and the Krishna, rivers which possessed all kinds of grain and an abundance of fruit. In the seventh century A.D. Yuan Chwang, the Chinese pilgrim regarded Vengi and Andhra as identical, as he makes a mention of Ping-Ki-lo which has been identified as Vengipura and known as the capital of An-to-lo (Andhra).[37] In the 8th century A.D. the eastern boundary of Vengi-maṇḍala seems to have extended to the confluence of the Krishna verna or Krishna and the Musi which flows past Hyderabad.[35] In the tenth, eleventh centuries, the Vengi Kingdom stood at its zenith under the Eastern Chālukyan rulers. During the period, the kingdom included under its wider sceptre the fertile tracts of coastal Andhra country, comprising the modern districts of Srikakulam, Visakhapatnam, East and West Godavari, Krishna, Guntur and Nellore regions. The kingdom of Vengi is regarded as a land embracing the rich rice-producing deltas of Krishna and Godavari and having command over a long sea board.[39] Some of the modern scholars have gone to the extent of identifying Vengi synonymously with the entire coastal Andhra region.[40]

From these various references to Vengi in both the literary and eipgraphic sources such as *Veṇgi-nādu, vengi-pura, Veṇgi-maṇḍala, Veṇgi-dēśa, Veṇgi-mahi, Veṇgi-bhūmi* and *Vengi-mahā-rājyam* suggests the changing position of Vengi region from the lowest position of *Vengi-nādu* to its gradual elevation to the status of *Vengi-mahā-rājyam i.e.*, "the Great kingdom of Vengi" under the Eastern Chālukyan rulers.[41] This further explains the significance of the micro-region of Vengi as one of the agriculturally nucleated region or the "area of attraction". In course of its long history, the Vengi region acted as the political, economic and cultural matrix of the Krishna-Godavari basin. It attracted various centripetal and centrifugal forces, thus becoming a bone of contention between various ruling families.

The first political power that brought the micro-region of Vengi under its control were the Mauryas. After the decline of the Mauryan authority, it was noticed that there was a political vacuum in Andhra for about three centuries. This political vacuum is said to have been caused due to the absence of kings with dynastic appelations or extent of territorial authority.[43] However, it cannot be denied that there were many local chiefs ruling different localities, preceding the conquest of the Andhra region by the Sātavāhanās. From the Bhaṭṭiprōlu relic casket inscription of the 3rd century B.C. we come to know about one Kubirak rāja who is understood to have emerged as a ruler in the deltaic Andhra sometime during the close of the second century B.C.[44] Similarly, the Vaddamānu inscription found near Amarāvati mentions one Somakarāja, who is said to have ruled around 2nd century B.C. Further the Velpuru epigraph found in the Amarāvati museum refers to one Aira Mana Sada and Ayira Siri Sāka Sada who exercised political authority in the Krishna valley preceding the Sātavāhana conquest.[45] Their rule was described by scholars as a locality rule that corresponded to the gana-saṁgha or gana-rājya system that existed in the north India.[46] When the Sātavāhanas conquered the Eastern Deccan around 2nd century A.D., these local chiefs accepted their sovereignty. However, they remained semi-independent through out the Sātavāhana period. The Sātavāhana expansion towards the Eastern Deccan was the result of the new economic policy initiated by them, namely, the land grant economy. The donation of large scale agrahāra land in the peripheral areas to *brāhmaṇa* and Buddhist ideologues, explains the process of acculturation. The use of the feudatory titles such as *Mahārāthis, Mahābhōjas,* and *Mahāsēnapatis* appointed in the peripheral areas by conferring upon them semi-independent or feudatory status.[47] When the Sātavāhana power declined in the 3rd century A.D. some of these local chiefs and semi-independent rulers declared independence and emerged as independent rulers in the coastal region.[48] The Ikṣvākus and the Bṛhatpālāyanas who held such semi-independent status under the Sātavāhanas, soon came into political prominence with the dwindling of the Sātavāhana power in this region. The Ikṣvāku dominions extended into the present day Guntur-Nellore District with Vijayapuri as their capital. They became prominent more by virtue of their patronage of Buddhism.[49] However, their polity was similar to that of the Sātavāhanās. The contemporaries of the Ikṣvākus in the north were the Bṛhatpālāyanas. They ruled over an area which extended upto the Kollēru lake in the north and covered the northern half of the present day Guntur districts and South of Kudura with modern Guduru as their capital.[50] The Bṛhatpālāyanas were succeeded by the Sālankāyanas. They were also called as Vaingēyakas. They, ruled over the micro-region of Vengi. It was first under them that the micro-region of Vengi emerged as an important political centre.[51] Contemporaneous to the Sālankāyanas were the Ānanda Gōtrins. They are also known as Kandaras and they controlled the northern part of the Guntur district in the 4th century A.D.[52] The decline of the Sālankāyanas paved way for the emergence of the Vishṇukundins to the throne of Vengi around 5th century A.D.[53]

Thus, it was under the rule of the Sālankāyanas and the Vishṇukundins that the micro-region of Vengi first came into political prominence. Its strategic position and its growing importance as the nucleus of political activity started attracting many ruling families from the West by the early medieval period. First it were the Chālukyas of Bādāmi, who conquered the micro-region of Vengi. As the Bādāmi Chālukyan kingdom was located in the arid dry and rugged zone of the South Western Deccan, they were easily attracted by the rich and abundant resources produced by the micro-region Vengi. Subsequently, coupled with his two fold desire to establish a 'great empire' over the whole of the Deccan and to manipulate the vast economic resources of the micro region of Vengi, Pulakēśin II conquered Vengi around 611 A.D., after defeating Mahendravarman III of the Vishṇukundin dynasty. The Aihōle inscription of Pulakēśin I describes his various military conquests which includes the conquest of the Lātās, the Mauryas of Konkan, the Mālavas and the Gūrjaras etc. before his conquest of Vengi.[54] For reasons of political strategy and to perpetuate his control over the coastal region, Pulakēśin II evolved a viable administrative unit and deputed his brother Kubja Vishnuvardhana as ruler of Vengi.[55] This kingdom hence forward came to be known as the Eastern Chālukyan kingdom or Vengi kingdom. The Eastern Chālukyas held their sway over Vengi for five long centuries. During their rule the micro-region of Vengi started attracting rulers from the West once again from mid ninth century A.D. For reasons of geo-political interests, the Rāshtrakūtas of Malkhed and later the Eastern Chālukyas of Kalyani waged constant wars against Vengi. It was under these circumstances that the Eastern Chālukyas had to shift their capital from Vengi to Rājahmahēndravaram around eleventh century A.D. The shift in capital simultaneously resulted in the gradual decline of the Vengi region. From this brief outline of political history it has been manifested that a small locality such as Vengi, because of its favourable geographical location emerged as an important super structure and decided the destinies of various contending political powers of the Deccan over the years.

Since the Eastern Chālukyas of Vengi formed the main subject of our study, we have attempted in this part to study the nature of polity under the Eastern Chālukyan rulers. This study has been undertaken in two different phases.

MAP II
PHYSIOGRAPHIC FEATURES
AND EXTENT OF EASTERN
CHALUKYAN KINGDOM PHASE I

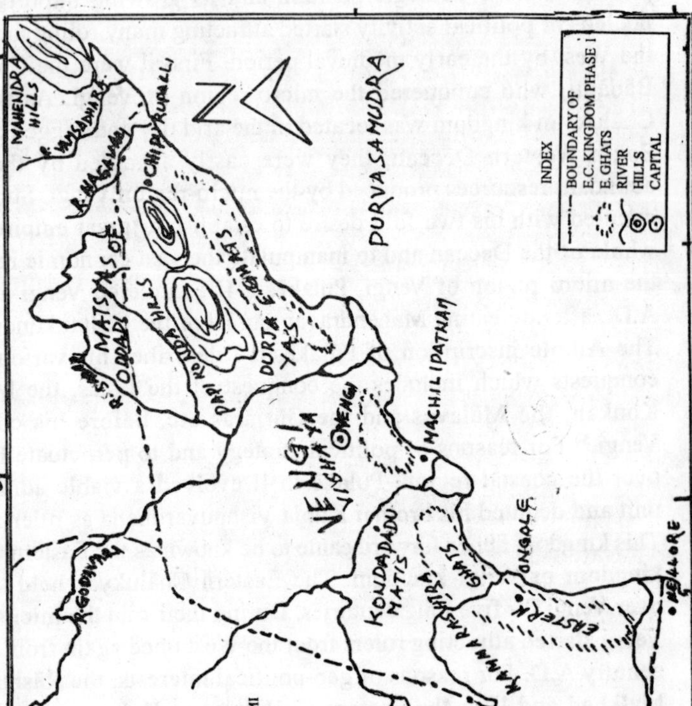

The first phase begins from the 7th century A.D. and extends upto the 9th century A.D. In this phase as new comers to an alien land the Eastern Chālukyan rulers adopted certain political mechanisms to stabilize their power. When Kubja Vishnuvardhana who was the earliest ruler of this dynasty was made the ruler of Vengi region, by his brother Pulakēsin II, he was still ranked as a *Yuvarāja.*[56] This was obviously because the conquest of the territory was still fresh and perhaps incomplete. There were many local chieftains who were still to be conquerred and subdued. Therefore, the new ruling elites had initiated the policy of expansion which was made possible through conquests. This is known from the inscriptions where the ruling elites were described as successfully humbled the circle of all vassals. Further the assumption of titles such as *Vishamasiddhi, Sarvasiddhi,* and *Vijayasiddhi* (Chart IIA, v, 1-5, 7,8,13,15,18) are explained as those who have obtained success in impossible straits, on land, on sea, in the woods and on the hills. On the other hand some of the powerful local chiefs were reconciled and made loyal firstly, through the process of conferring land grants to them and secondly by recruiting some of the powerful chiefs into the higher positions in bureaucracy and at the same time allowing them to enjoy certain autonomy within their localities. Some of such local chiefs who were made loyal through these mechanisms were the Pattavardhanis, the Kondapadamatis, the Dūrjayas of Giripaschima-seema, and the Mastyas of Oddadi (MAP-II). Similarly some of the powerful tribal chiefs like the Bōyas were reconciled through granting large scale land donations and placating them as buffers between the Pallava kottams and the Eastern Chālukyan kingdom. All these local chiefs helped the ruling elites in Phase I in their struggle against their hereditary enemies namely, the Gaṇgas of Kalinga and the Pallavas of Kanchi. They also contributed to the physical extension of the Eastern Chālukyan kingdom. Thus, during this phase the boundaries of the Eastern Chālukyan kingdom included Chipurupalli taluk in the North-east, along the river Nāgavali in the Visakhapatnam District. On the south of the kingdom included the Karmarāshtra or Kammanādu, bounded by river Mannēru in the Nellore district. On the west it included a country known as Telangana in the modern times (MAP-II). Presumably, thus the whole of modern Andhra except the Southern districts formed the part of Vengi kingdom.[58] These boundaries of the kingdom were kept intact by the other rulers in succession (APPENDIX I). Thus, it is through the mechanisms of conquest and reconciliation that the ruling elites, in phase I attempted to expand and consolidate their power through integrating various local chiefs into the newly emerging state structure.

It is interesting to state that though the Eastern Chālukyan rulers were instated as independent sovereigns of Vengi kingdom, yet they remained as subordinates to their parent branch of Bādāmi Chālukyan Dynasty. This is inferred from the fact that the Vengi rulers during this phase did not even adopt on their seals the boar symbol namely, *Varaha-lāñchana* the emblem of the Chālukyan imperial authority.[59] Further, the assumption of simple titles such as *Mahārāja*, (Chart IIA, v, 1,3,5-10,13) by the early rulers revealed their loyalty and subordination to their parent branch. However, it has been noticed that from the end of this phase, i.e., around last half of the 8th century a new trend in terms of assuming titles is perceptible. The rulers of this dynasty starting from Vijayāditya I onwards assumed high sounding imperial titles such as *Samastabhuvanāśraya, Mahārājādhirāja, Chakravarthi* (Chart IIA, v, 17-20). This suggests to us the declaration of complete independence by the Eastern Chālukyan branch. The reasons for this change are attributed to the downfall of the Chālukyan power at Bādāmi. In this regard Vijayāditya I's reign can be marked as a period of transition from the first phase of consolidation and subordination to their kinsmen at Bādāmi and to their emergence as supreme sovereigns in the second phase.

The process of expansion and consolidation continued throughout the Eastern Chālukyan rule but taking different stand from time to time. While in the first phase integration of local chiefs was made through conquests and land donations, in Phase II we find the nature of polity under the ruling elites to be different. Phase II of our study commences from the 9th century A.D. upto the 12th century A.D. By this phase there was total eclipse of the Bādāmi Chālukyan dynasty. This phase also synchronises with the rise of many hostile powers such as the Rāshtrakūtas of Malkhed, the Gaṅgas of Kaliṅga and later the Western Chālukyas of Kalyani. The hostile kingdoms posed a great threat to the stability of the Eastern Chālukyan kingdom at Vengi. Further, the weak successions and the incessant family feuds weakened the authority of the Eastern Chālukyan rulers during this phase. It is pertinent to state here that some of the members of the main family of the Eastern Chālukyan dynasty broke away from its parent branch and established Minor Chālukyan kingdoms in different localities. In this regard mention has to be made about the Chālukyas of Mudigonda, Jananāthapuram and Nidadavōlu, as the rule of these minor Chālukyan dynasties synchronize with our period of study. The Chālukyas of Mudigonda ruled over the areas surrounding Mudigonda and Koravi which corresponded to the present parts of Khammam and Warangal Districts (MAP-III). Chālukyas of Jananāthapuram controlled the areas of Rājahmundry, Pithāpuram and Drākshārāmam, with Jananāthapuram as their capital (MAP III). On the other hand the Chālukyas of Nidadavōlu ruled over places like Bezawāda, Dendalūru and other places (MAP III). All these minor Chālukyan rulers maintained their affiliation towards their parent branch which is prominently manifested in their *Praśastis*[60] (APPENDIX IIA, IIB, IIC)

Another prominent feature of this phase is the emergence of many local chiefs within the Eastern Chālukyan kingdom, such as the Chōdas of Velanādu, the Kondapaḍamati chiefs of Nādendla, the Pārichchedis of Omgerumārga and the Kōtā chiefs of Dharanikōta (MAP III). Thus, we find that during phase II, the Eastern Chālukyan kingdom was parcelled off among various local ruling families who attempted to assert their independence during this period.

In the circumstances of the emergence of such fissiparious tendencies within the kingdom and the rise of hostile powers outside the kingdom, who posed a threat to the Eastern Chālukyan power, it became necessary for the ruling elites to adopt new mechanisms for the sustenance of the kingdom. These mechanisms are to be seen in the form of maintaining matrimonial alliances with the Rāshtrakūtas, the Gaṇgas and later with the Chōlas. Further, the assumption of high sounding titles mentioned earlier in phase I became more prominent during this phase. This is important as this would establish the superior authority of the ruling elites over the increasing power of local chieftains.

In the later half of the second phase, a new trend is discernible. The political vacuum caused in the Chōla kingdom started a new regime of Chālukya-Chōlas in Vengi region. During the time Kulōttunga I, many local chieftains were being conferred with the insignia of royalty, with the intention that these local chiefs might buffer the position of viceroys with their own might.[61] By this time the Vengi kingdom was parcelled off among various local chiefs. Thus, there is a significant change in the nature of polity in both the phases.

This type of polity has been postulated by the conventional historiography as a centralised bureaucracy. On the other hand the Marxist historians regarded it as the development of a new phenomenon that started developing from the 3rd century A.D. all over the Indian sub-continent. This was represented by the donation of land grants as a mode of payment to officials and religious beneficiaries. The initiative in this regard was made by the Sātavāhana rulers under whom for the first time the administrative and judicial powers were transferred along with the land grants made to Buddhist monks and *brāhmaṇas.* The beginnings of this process has been seen mainly due to the decline in trade and commerce and decay of towns which is indicated by the paucity of coins. According to Sharma, this necessiated the ruling elites to make large scale donations of land in the peripheral areas, so as to yield economic resources.[62] Such a mechanism of transferring of both the administrative and judicial powers by the centralised monarchy is postulated by Marxist scholars as fragmentation and decentralisation of political power. According to B.N.S. Yadava this led to the rise of a '*sāmanta*' which became the key word in defining Indian Feudalism.[63] The beginnings of feudal polity was suggested by the Marxist scholars on the basis of the usage of designations such as *Mahāsēnapati, Mahārathi, Mahābhōja, Mahātalvara,* etc., which are considered as epithets used for the feudatories serving under the Sātavāhanas and their successors in the Andhra region.[64] Thus, the Marxist historians regarded the nature of polity under the Sātavāhanas, the Iksvākus, the Viṣṇukundins and the Eastern Chālukyas as a decentralised polity where the State was seen as parting away with its administrative powers. On the other hand scholars like B.D. Chattopadhyaya and Kulke postulates it as an integrative polity, where the state was seen as making constant attempts to integrate various local polities into the larger processes of state structure. In this regard the nature of polity under the Eastern Chālukyas can be regarded as an integrative polity, where the state attempted to mediate its political authority and consolidation of power through creating semi-independent localities held by local chieftains and the Minor Chālukyan families who provided political stabilization to the Eastern Chālukyan kingdom in both the phases.

From the above discussion, we conclude that the history of a broader region can be better understood by placing the history of a micro-region within the context of studying the history against its general geographical setting. It has been shown that the micro-region of Vengi which forms a small part in the larger entity of the sub-region of the Krishna-Godavari basin, had contributed its share in the evolution of civilization in the region of coastal Āndhra as a whole. Though this region revealed total absence of pre-historic settlements, its strategic

MAP III
EXTENT OF EASTERN CHALUKYAN KINGDOM AND MINOR CHALUKYAN KINGDOMS PHASE II

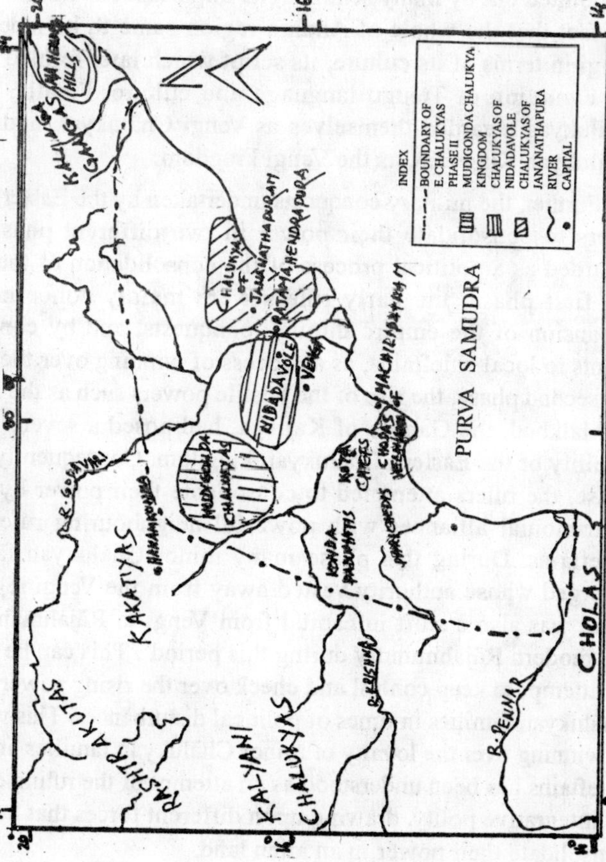

location, however did attract the immigrants from the period when Buddhism was popular in coastal Āndhra. Though, initially the micro-region formed a politically peripheral zone under the Mauryans, the Sātavāhanas and the Ikṣvākus it subsequently emerged as an important centre of political power during the transition to early medieval period. As pointed out by many scholars, its importance is further affirmed by the fact that the whole of Andhra region came to be indentified with Vengi in terms of its culture, its script which later formed the base for the evolution of Telugu language and culture. Finally, the Eastern Chālukyas regarded themselves as Vengi Chālukyas, and the Eastern Chālukyan Kingdom, as the Vengi kingdom.

Further, the military conquests undertaken by the Eastern Chālukyan rulers to consolidate their power in two different phases has been regarded as a political process of the consolidation of their power. In the first phase, the early rulers were mainly concerned with the expansion of the empire through conquests, and by conferring land grants to local chieftains, as a process of winning over their loyalty. In the second phase, the rise of the hostile powers such as the Rāshtrakūtas of Malkhed, the Gaṇgas of Kalinga, had posed a severe threat to the stability of the Eastern Chālukyan kingdom. Consequently, during this phase, the rulers attempted to consolidate their power by getting into matrimonial alliances with powerful neighbouring rulers and local chieftains. During this phase many minor Chālukyan families have emerged whose authority vested away from the Vengi region. In fact, there was also a shift in capital from Vengi to Rājahmahēndravaram, i.e. modern Rājahmundry during this period . This can be explained as an attempt to keep control and check over the rising power of the minor Chālukyan families in times of political disturbances. This whole process of winning over the loyalty of minor Chālukyan families and other local chieftains has been understood as an attempt of the ruling elites to build an integrative polity, drawing upon different forces that helped them to consolidate their power in an alien land.

References

1. Arthur Marwick, *Nature of History,* London, 1970, p. 109.
2. *Ibid*, p. 109.
3. B. Subba Rao, *Personality of India, Pre and Proto-Historic foundations of India and Pakistan,* Baroda, 1958, p. 14.

4. Alladi Vaidehi Krishna Murthy, *Social and Economic conditions in Eastern Deccan (A.D. 1000-1250)* Madras, 1970, p. ix.
5. Amita Ray, *Life and Art of Early Andhradesa,* Delhi, 1983, p.1.
6. N. Ramesan, *Andhra Pradesh District Gazetteers of Guntur, Krishna, West Godavari and East Godavari Districts,* Hyderabad, 1979.
7. N. Ramesan - *Andhra Pradesh District Gazetteers of West Godavari District,* Hyderabd, 1979, p. 231.
8. *Ibid,* pp. 3-4.
9. *Ibid,* p. 4.
10. *Ibid,* p. 15.
11. *Ibid,* p. 4.
12. *Ibid,* p. 4.
13. *Ibid,* p. 4.
14. *Ibid,* p. 6.
15. *Ibid,* pp. 16-17.
16. B. Subba Rao, *Op.cit.,* 1958, p. 85.
17. B. Subba Rao, 'The Geographical Factor in Andhra and Archaeology,' *BDCRI,* vol. IX, No. 1-2, Poona, 1948, pp. 169-171.
18. *Ibid,* pp. 169-171.
19. Amita Ray, *Op.cit,* 1983, p. 3.
20. K. Gopalachari, *Early History of the Andhra Country,* Madras, 1976, p. 1.
21. *Ibid,* pp. 1-2.
22. *Ibid,* pp. 1-2.
23. Amita Ray, *Op.cit.,* 1983, p. 4.
24. *Ibid,* p. 3.
25. K. Gopalachari, *Op.cit,* 1976, p. 3.
26. Aloka Parasher, "Early Settlement patterns in the Deccan and the study of Regional History", *PAPHC,* 1993, Warangal, p.15.
27. *Ibid,* p. 5.
28. B.R. Subramanyam, "Ancient History and Archaeology", Presidential Address, *PAPHC,* 7th session, Warangal, 1983, p. 11.
29. N. Ramesan, *Op.cit.,* 1979, p. 19.
30. Aloka Parasher, "Small Localities and the writing of Regional History", *PAPHC,* 1996, pp. 17-18.
31. H. Sarkar, "Growth of cities in Andhradesa (200 BC. to A.D. 300) *PAPHC,* 10th Session, Guntur, 1986, p. 4.
32. B.V. Krishna Rao, *The Eastern Chalukyas of Vengi,* Hyderabad, 1973, p. 47.

33. R. Ramanathan, 'Vengi', *JAHRS*, vol. XX, p. 8.
34. G. Yazdani, *Early History of the Deccan*, vol. I, 1982, p. 30.
35. K. Gopalachari, *Op.cit.*, 1976, p. 2.
36. G. Yazdani, *Op.cit.*, 1982, p. 30.
37. *Ibid*, p. 30.
38. *Ibid*, p. 30.
39. B.V. Krishna Rao, *Op.cit.*, 1973, p. 47.
40. K. Sundaran, *Studies in Economic and Social conditions of Medieval Andhra (A.D. 1000-1600)* Madras, 1968, p.1.
41. B.V. Krishna Rao, *Op.cit.*, 1978, pp. 47-48.
42. B.D. Chattopadhyaya, 'Political Processes and structure of Polity in Early Medieval India: Problems and Perspectives.' *Social Scientist* vol. 13, 1985, p. 4.
43. P.V. Parabrashma Sastry, 'Political system in Early Coastal Andhra', in Devendra Handa (ed) *AJAYA SRI*, vol. I, Delhi, 1989, p. 71.
44. B.D. Chattopadhyaya, 'Transition to the Early Historical Phase in the Deccan: A Note' in B.M. Pande and B.D. Chattopadhyaya (ed) *Archaeology and History*, vol. II, Delhi, 1987, p. 728.
45. P.V. Parabrahma Sastry, *Op.cit.*, 1989, p. 71.
46. *Ibid*, pp. 71-72.
47. *Ibid*, pp. 72-73.
48. *Ibid*, p. 73.
49. *Ibid*, p. 73.
50. K. Gopalachari, *Op.cit.*, 1976, p. 158.
51. *Ibid*, pp. 158-159.
52. *Ibid*, pp. 165-167.
53. *Ibid*, pp. 185-187.
54. *Ibid*, pp. 185-187.
54. *EI*, vol. VI, p. 1.
55. K.V. Ramesh, *Chalukyas of Vatapi*, Delhi, 1984. pp. 83-84.
56. *Ibid*, p. 84.
57. B.S.L. Hanumantha Rao, *Social Mobility in Medieval Andhra*, Hyderabad, 1995, p. 37.
58. B.V. Krishna Rao, *Op.cit.*, 1973, pp. 48-49

59. P.V. Parabrahma Sastry, *Op.cit.*, 1989, p. 74.
60. K. Suryanarayana, *History of the Minor Chalukyan Families in Medieval Andhra Desa*, Delhi, 1986, pp. 41ff.
61. K. Sundaram, *Op.cit.*, 1968, pp. 7-8.
62. R.S. Sharma, "Problem of Transition from Ancient To Medieval Indian History, *IHR*, no. 1, 1974, p. 5.
63. B.N.S. Yadava, *Society and Culture in North India in the 12th century A.D.*, Allahabad, 1973, p. 136.
64. R.S. Sharma, *Aspects of Political Ideas and Institutions in Ancient India*, Delhi, 1991, p. 284.

Chapter-III

GENEALOGY AND MARRIAGE NETWORKS

The early medieval period in Indian History has been characterised by some scholars in recent years by the absence of strong centralized monarchical kingdoms. In this view the socio-political and economic metamorphosis the society was undergoing during this period provided a nebulous picture of the political structure of these new regional states. These kingdoms had to resort to the various mechanisms in order to consolidate and sustain their power. These mechanisms have been explained by B.D. Chattopadhyaya as political, economic, social and ideological variables that ignited the processes of state formation and later led to its consolidation. Politically, it is postulated that the ruling elites first tried to establish themselves by subordinating the local chieftains and other neighbouring kings through military conquests. Having conquered large territories, economic processes became important and these involved the practice of donating land grants to both religious and secular personnel in order to consolidate the fiscal basis of the state. Socially, consolidation of power was considered desirable and this was done by maintaining cross regional marriage alliances with powerful ruling dynasties of the period. Finally, through ideological processes namely, the process of legitimization of establishing genealogical linkages with the *kṣatriya* line and by concocting mythical genealogies the new ruling elites were able to assert their power and, in a regional context this meant establishing pan-Indian linkages.[1] This hypothesis is developed as against the views expressed by traditional scholars who described genealogies and marriage networks to "dynasticize" the history of the ruling elites.

This CHAPTER on *GENEALOGY AND MARRIAGE NETWORKS'* focuses on the ideological and social variables evolved by the new ruling elites called the Eastern Chālukyas to stabilize their power in the Eastern Deccan. This is discussed in relation with their parent branch, the Bādāmi Chālukyas and their collateral branches, namely, the Minor

Chālukyan families of Mudigonda, Jananāthapuram and Nidadavōlu, and also other comtemporary ruling dynasties. These two variables, namely, the ideological and social variables are discussed in two different parts. Part I deals with the ideological variables which involves the study and analysis of genealogical linkages established between the Bādāmi Chālukyas and the Vengi Chālukyas on the one hand and on the other, with the minor Chālukyan families, in two distinct chronological phases. Part II of this chapter deals with the study of the social variable, namely, the marriage alliances maintained between the main ruling family that is the Eastern Chālukyas and the other contemporary ruling dynasties and local chiefs.

The study of genealogies to understand a major process in fabricating the political and social history of the ruling elites has gained momentum in recent historical writings. Genealogies are described as records related to the past where the history of the lineages of different groups are preserved.[2] The core of a genealogy consists of the succession lists or the lists of descent groups which, Romila Thapar calls as *The fixed tradition*'.[3]

The tradition of formulating genealogies goes back to early centuries when the tribal communities were gradually transforming into pristine state structures. The earliest composers of this tradition were the *sūtas* and *māgadas.* They acted as royal panegyrists, glorifying the gods, the *ṛṣis*, and the kings. The genealogies thus composed were transmitted through oral tradition.[4] However, by the early centuries of the christian era, the oral tradition of transmitting genealogies was replaced by the written tradition of the *itihāsa-purāṇa.* The *itihāsa-purāṇa* literally means `thus it was'. The composers of the *itihāsa-purāṇa* tradition now had been appropriated by the literate *brāhmaṇas.* The *Purāṇas* and epics became the major source of preserving the genealogies in the form of written tradition.

Pargiter, one of the pioneers to study the political content of the *Purāṇas* suggests, that there were two major and important genealogical traditions embedded in the *itihāsa-purāṇa* tradition which were adopted by the new ruling elites to trace their lineages. They were the *Suryavaṃśa* tradition and the *Caṅdravaṃśa* tradition.[5] The *Suryavaṃśis* were supposed to be the descendants of the *Ikṣvāku* lineage. *Ikṣvāku* was the son of Manu and the progenitor of the *Suryavaṃśa* lineage in direct line of descent from Aditi and Sūrya.[6] The heroes of the epic *Rāmāyaṇa* were regarded as descendants of *Ikṣvāku* and hence, they belonged to the *Suryavaṃśa* tradition. On the other hand the *Caṅdravaṁśa* lineage presents a different pattern of descent. The *Candravaṁśa* lineage is said to have descended from the daughter of Manu, Ilā, who is said to have given birth to a son through Budha, the son of the Moon deity, Sōma. The main line was from Āyus to his eldest son Nahusa and further, to his eldest son and so on. The main focus of the *Candravaṁśi* genealogy or Aila lineage is found in the other important epic of India, namely, the *Mahābhārata.*[7] This is how the ancient *kṣatriya* lineages were explained in the literary tradition.

From the early medieval period, the formality of claiming *kṣatriya* status as embodied in the *itihāsa-purāṇa* tradition became more apparent in the various inscriptions. The changing political, social and economic scenario at the pan-Indian level during this period emphasised the need to fabricate new genealogies connected to the mythical past. This has been seen as a *legitimation*[8] process by the newly emerging state societies in different regions of India. In the words of B.D. Chattapodhayaya, "One dimension of the presence of trans-political ideology in all state systems was the need for constant validation of power, which was made possible by establishing linkage with a respectable *kṣatriya* ancestry or by underlining its local roots".[9] In this context, the *itihāsa-purāṇa* tradition became one of the means of legitimizing the newly acquired *Kṣatriya* status by the new ruling elites as an effective means of consolidating political power. This was done with the help of the sacred domain, namely, the *brāhmaṇas,* who were well versed in the *itihāsic* and *purāṇic* lore preserved in the tradition. The study of genealogies for this period as records of social relations[10] and also as records emphasising on the 'legitimation' process of ruling elites in comprehending the social and political history of the period is very essential in order to lay bare the intricacies of the socio-political formation of early medieval times.

The study of ruling elites as central to the political system has been emphasised in various historiographical traditions. The two basic conventional historiographical traditions, namely, the monoliths of the Oriental Despotism and its Marxist variant, the Asiatic Mode of Production and secondly, the natonalist historians of India have comprehended the emergence of ruling elites in the frame work of the traditional *varṇa* ideology as emphasised in the *Dharmaśāstra* texts. Therefore, according to them the ruling elites were mainly drawn from the traditional *kṣatriya varṇa* thus underlining the idea of a changeless socio-political system. On the other hand we have regional historians who did recognised change in *varṇa* status of the ruling elites. However, since their main interest is to construct elaborate dynastic history of the region, the study of change in the *varṇa* status of the ruling elites was given marginal importance. These constructs, however, have been questioned in recent years, which have enlarged the scope to study the emergence of various ruling elites and underline the processes they have adopted in validating and consolidating their power in early medieval states. In their attempts to comprehend the changes that took place in the early medieval period, eminent scholars representing the recent historiographical schools such as Romila Thapar, B.N.S. Yadava, Suvira Jaiswal, B.D. Chattopadhyaya, among many others, have studied the emergence of ruling elites and their attempts to fabricate mythical genealogies as a method of consolidating power of the newly emerging state structure in the early medieval period.

In the views of Romila Thapar the political decentralization in the post-Gupta period, as a result of large scale land grants to non-religious donees all over India, witnessed the accentuating power of the *sāmantas* of the country. The social insecurity experienced by these *sāmanta* chiefs in the new lands aroused the need to record genealogies in order to validate their family connections and legitimize the new royalty that they had acquired. Subsequently, these ruling elites had to collate various genealogical fragments, as embodied in the *itihāsa-purāṇa* traditions as a process of the assertion of power and acquisition of social status by them. Therefore, the genealogies have been seen as constructs providing *kṣatriya* status to large number of tribes or castes who had produced ruling families. Thus, according to Thapar, "the genealogies should be seen as an attempt to plot the settling of lineages in various areas at a point in time, when they were moving towards forming states".[11]

On the other hand, B.N.S. Yadava, apart from discussing the economic factor, underlines the social factor also as explicated in the passages ostensibly meant as predictions of the Kali Age.[12] According to him the emergence of new ruling landed aristocracy were drawn first and foremost from the new land grant economy with its emphasis on agraian and local character. Secondly, in northern India the new ruling elites were drawn from foreign stock who incessantly invaded the country in the pre-Gupta and the post-Gupta periods. A section of outlandish people as ruling aristocracy had to be assimilated into the already shaken *caturvarṇa* system. Thus, according to Yadava, the ruling elites in the early medieval period were drawn from all sections of the *varṇa* ideology. On the basis of determination of status and social privilege, he has argued that they had to resort to the fabrication of new genealogies, namely, that of *brahma-kṣatra.*[13]

Similarly, scholars like Suvira Jaiswal postulates that the new system of land grant economy acculturated many tribal priests into the *varṇa* based society. These tribal priests subsequently acquired political power and played a significant role in state formation. It is precisely in this context that the attempts of these tribal groups to trace *brāhmaṇa* or *brahma-kṣatra* ancestry, to derive a respectable *kṣatriya* ranking has been understood by the scholar.[14]

Therefore, in the light of some of the views enumeratd above for primarily northern India, the study of the evolution of genealogies in different stages helps us to understand that constant endeavours were made on the part of the ruling elites to fabricate the *kṣatriya* and the *brahma-kṣatra* genealogies to legitimize their newly acquired political status. The study of the latter becomes more significant as it particularly emerged during the early medieval period and was used prolifically by dynasties located in the Deccan and South India. This validation of power by the temporal authority became possible through the "spiritual" authority exercised by the *brāhmaṇas* who were the chief ideologues of the time and also the group that engineered the writing of the *Praśastis.* The need for both the temporal and spiritual authority to work in unison was reciprocal, as the latter required sustenance from the temporal power and the former needed their ideological support.[15]

For North India, the case study of the emergence of various Rajput clans who were drawn from different strata of the indigenous population such as the *kṣatriyas,* the *brāhmaṇas*, some aboriginal tribal groups and foreign invaders who had settled here and got assimilated in the Indian social systems,[16] has attracted the attention of many historians in recent times. Eminent historians like B.N.S. Yadava, Surajit Sinha, B.D. Chatopadhyaya and others have done scholarly research on the history of the Rajput clans which has brought to light various processes adopted by these ruling elites to establish their states and adopt mechanisms for the consolidation of their newly political acquired status.

The growth of feudal tendencies such as the acquisition of landed property, martial qualities and regalian rights, in the early medieval period had evolved a wide spread tendency among many Rajput ruling families to make claims to traditional '*kṣatriya*' status.[17] Such claims were regarded by B.D. Chattopadhyaya as attempts made by these Rajput chiefs to get away from their original ancestry which was not the *kṣatriya* lineage. This, they did by acquiring various symbols for the legitimation of their newly acquired political power thus underlining the particular nature of their polity.[18] However, in course of time, the term '*rājaputra*' like the traditional *varṇa* categories came to be synonymously used to represent the *kṣatriya* caste.[19] This has been regarded as assimilative in space and time, wherein the transformation from tribe to state structure had facilitated the upper heirarchies of the tribal groups to attain Rajput status.[20] Thus, these scholars have seen the fabrication of the genealogies in the context of the changing social, political and economic relations as a process of legitimisation of power.

The pan-Indian phenomenon of inventing mythical genealogies in the early medieval period can be seen in South India and Deccan as well. In fact the Deccan region saw some of the first early medieval kings resort to claim the *brahma-kṣatra* ancestry. In recent years attempts have been made by scholars such as Sankaranarayanan, M.G.S. Narayanan, Suvira Jaiswal, Kesavan Veluthat and others to study the origin of the *brahma-kṣatra* ancestry. According to Sankaranarayanan the *brahma-kṣatriyas* traced their descent from the Puru dynasty. In this context the Viṣṇukundins were regarded by the scholar as the first kings of the Andhra region who had claimed the *brahma-kṣatra* origin by seeking their descent from the Puru dynasty.[21] On thc other hand historians on South Indian history observed that the increasing economic power of the *brāhmaṇa varṇa*, as a result of increasing practice of land grants and extension of patronage by the royal power to the *brāhmaṇas* created inner social contradictions among the tribal communities. Consequently, there was a tendency in early medieval South India, among the priestly class of a different origin to acquire political power by claiming *brāhmaṇa* ancestry or *brahma-kṣatra* status through the process of fabricating genealogies.[22] The aquisitions of such high status of *brahma-kṣatra* lineage was made possible by performing rituals such as *hiraṇyagarbha, tulābhāra* or *tulāpurusadāna*, or, by performing sacrifices such as *Aśvamēdha* sacrifice. They also did this by suffixing the *varman* title to their names as for instance, Mahendra *varman* of Pallava dynasty and by confering more and more privileges on the *brāhmaṇa* groups.[23] In this way the ruling elites were able to seek legitimacy and retain their power through the sacred domain of the *brāhmaṇical* groups which explains the nature of relationship between the temporal and the sacred domains. In detailing the views of the above mentioned scholars we have emphasised the importance of the study of genealogies as a source for comprehending the social and political ideology of the ruling elites in consolidating their power.

As discussed in Chapter II, the period between A.D. 600 to A.D. 1200 in the history of the Eastern Deccan and Andhra country in particular was dominated by the rule of the Eastern Chālukyan dynasty. Their inscriptions which were both in Sanskrit and Telugu were prefaced with long *Praśastis,* which in a majority of cases were written in the Sanskrit language. Several eminent scholars like N. Venkataramanayya, B.V. Krishna Rao and N. Ramesan have attempted to write exclusively on the history of the Eastern Chālukyan dynasty. Their pioneering work which was done through the information collected from various inscriptional and literary sources was basically focused on giving a dynastic account of the Eastern Chālukyan history. In their obsession with political history, they naturally attempted to reconstruct the stereotypes of political history of the dynasty as was reflected in their eulogistic epigraphs. They primarily focussed their study in tracing the origin of the family, chronology, caste, at the same time enumerating various political activities such as wars, conquests and alliances. With regard to the caste of the Eastern Chālukyan rulers, scholars like N. Venkataramanayya and N. Ramesan attributed *kṣatriya* status to them.[24] However, B.V. Krishna Rao regarded them as belonging to the brāhmaṇical creed.[25] On the other hand scholars like Suravaram Pratapa Reddy identified Eastern Chālukyas with *sūdra varṇa*. This, he inferred from the phrase where the Chālukyas describe themselves as being born from the feet of Brahma.[26] Though these scholars have unanimously agreed that there exist three stages in the pattern of the evolution of the Eastern Chālukyan *Praśastis* which, they consider is unique to the dynasty when compared with the Bādāmi Chālukyan inscriptions. However, they paid very little attention to particularly understand the political and ideological underpinnings of the evolution of long mythical genealogies embedded in the *Praśastis.* In these sections attempt has been made by the ruling elites to connect the origin of the family to a mythical past, which can be seen as a clear indication of asserting their *kṣatriya-hood* first by seeking *brahma-kṣatra* identity and latter through fabricating mythical genealogies, especially when their real origins were blurred. Further this can also be understood as an attempt for legitimization of power by the new ruling elites in regions where they did not have their original roots. Recent writings discussed above have emphasised the need to look into the mythical portions of genealogies within the frame work of a new perspective, in order to explicate the processes of state formation in the early medieval period. Therefore, following the methodology and framework as against that followed by traditional scholars, we argue below that the genealogies provide us a scope to probe into this matter at some depth to understand the ideological influences on the ruling elites which enabled a process of consolidation and legitimization of their power.

For elaborating these points, for the present study the period between the seventh century A.D. to the twelfth century A.D. has been taken as a broad period covering the entire span of the early medieval period signified primarily by Eastern Chālukyan rule. However, for highlighting the above processes two different phases of change with regard to how the genealogies of kings were given have been emphasised. It would be pertinent to state here that the Eastern Chālukyan inscriptions, unlike the Bādāmi Chālukyan records, show definite stages in the evolution of *praśastis*. *Praśastis* which are otherwise called as *Meykīrtis* or eulogistic compositions, are of two types, namely, the dynastic *praśastis* and the personal *praśastis*.[27] The former describe the genealogy, religious customs, origin of the family, titles and achievements of the ancestors of the donor from the establishment of the kingdom, and the latter describe the greatness, titles and qualifications of the donor.[28]

In Phase I which covers the period from the 7th century A.D. to the 9th century A.D. an attempt has been made to analyse and highlight the changes found in the Eastern Chālukyan inscriptions and to establish linkages between the Bādāmi Chālukyas and the Vengi Chālukyas on one hand, and the Eastern Chālukyan and minor Chālukyan families on the other. Data about genealogies from inscriptional sources belonging to these three families has been collected. The information thus collected has been placed in the form the *Charts* I, IIA, IIB, and III) which have been appended to this chapter.

In Phase I, an attempt has been made to look at the link between *Praśasti* sections of the Bādāmi Chālukyan family and the Eastern Chālukyan family (Charts I and IIA) as this phase indicates the continuity of relationship between the two families. During this phase, it has been noted that the records of the two families bear only names of three generations, i.e., the names of the donor of the grant, his father and grand father apart from mentioning their descent and *gōtra* (Chart I and IIA, Column II). Similarly, personal *praśastis* and titles (Chart I Column III and IV, Chart IIA, columns III and V) of this phase also evince a close relationship maintained between the two branches of the Bādāmi Chālukyas and the Eastern Chālukyas as they reveal similarities in their descriptions. The early rulers of these families adopted to claim a genealogy in a high *gōtra* so that their real origins remain blurred.

In the early medieval period it has been observed that there was a tendency among the ruling elites to belong to a high *brāhmaṇa gōtra* status. Over a period of time these ruling elites came to political prominence as a result of their military strength. It has further been pertinently pointed out that during this period there was also an attempt among non*brāhmaṇa* families and groups to adopt traditional *brāhmaṇic gōtras* to gain social prestige[29] and in this context *gōtra*[30] had become a useful tool of social mobility. In Phase I we find that the early Chālukyan rulers consistently described themselves as being of high *gōtra* status of *brāhmaṇical* lineage. In the *praśastis* of both the Bādāmi Chālukyan rulers and the Eastern Chālukyas (Chart I and IIA, col. III), it has been variedly mentioned that the Chālukyas were descendants of Hariti, that they belong to the Mānavya *gōtra*, that they were nourished by the Saptamātrikas or Seven mothers of Mankind, and that they had acquired uninterrupted continuity of prosperity through the favour and protection of Karttikēya and so on. Here, the mention to a *brāhmaṇic gōtra* namely, the Mānavya *gōtra* by the early Chālukyas is considered as an attempt by these ruling elites to gain social prestige. It should be noted here that even before the Chālukyas, the Chutus and the *brāhmaṇa* dynasty of the Kādambas also called themselves as *Haritipūtras* of the Mānavya *gōtra*.[31] Harita is stated in the *Vāyu Purāṇa* as the son of Yuvanaśa of the Ikṣhvāku lineage of the Gangetic-north. The sons of Harita were adopted by Angiras of spiritual lineage and hence they came to be regarded as *brāhmaṇas* but endowed with *kṣatriya* like heroic prowess.[32] It is for this reason that the descendants of Harita came to be recognized with double *gōtra* and double *varṇa* status of *brahma-kṣatra*. Equally important to mention here is the origin of the Mānavya *gōtra*. In the inscriptions of the Western Chālukyan dynasty Mānavya *gōtra* has been regarded as taken from an eponymous sage Mānavya/Māndavya. It has been stated in these inscriptions that Mānavya/Māndavya was the son of Svayambhu-Manu who was in turn was born to Brahman. Mānavya's son is said to be Harita. His son was Panchasikhi Hariti, and the son of the latter was Chālukya from whom sprang the race of the Chālukyas. It has thus been suggested that the Chālukyas adopted the Mānavya *gōtra* from Māndavya who was an eponymous *brāhmaṇa* sage.[33]

Besides the mention of this family *praśasti,* which is commonly found in all the inscriptions belonging to the Chālukyan dynasties

(Chart I, IIA) the dynastic *praśastis* also enumerate the names of three generations of rulers found during this phase. The British Museum plates[34] of Pulakēśi I (543-567 A.D.) who is regarded as the founder of the Bādāmi Chālukyan dynasty in the sixth century A.D., records the earliest members of the Chālukyan family as Jayasimha and Raṇarāga who was the grand father and father of the king respectively. It is interesting to note here that in all the other records of the Bādāmi Chālukyas (Chart I, Col. II, Nos. 2-10) the genealogy begins from Pulakēśi I. A similar pattern of enumerating the names of three generations of rulers has been followed by the early rulers of the Eastern Chālukyan dynasty. Interestingly, in the inscriptions from the reign of Kubja Vishnuvardhana up to Vishnuvardhana II (Chart IIA, Col. II, Nos. 1-12) we find reference to the Bādāmi Chālukyan rulers in terms of the paternal relations existing between them either, as great grand father, grand father or, father of the king. For instance, in the Timmapuram plates[35] Kubja Vishnuvardhana mentions the names of Raṇarāga, Raṇavikrama, Kīrtivarman and Pulakēśin II of the Bādāmi Chālukyan dynasty. This indicates that even though Pulikēśin II had made Kubja Vishnuvardhana I and his successors as independent rulers of the Eastern branch of their kingdom yet, the Vengi Chālukyas constantly referred their parentage to the Bādāmi Chālukyas. This reflects the continuity of relationship that had existed between these two branches. Interestingly, however, in the records of Vishnuvardhana II's successors, i.e., from Mangi Yuvarāja to Vijayāditya II (Charts IIA, Col. II and III, Nos. 13-21), we do not find any reference to the Bādāmi Chālukyan rulers. This we presume to be mainly because of the weak succession and the declining political power of the Bādāmi Chālukyas.

However, this does not imply that the Eastern Chālukyas have completely broken their linkages with their parent branch. This can be seen in the personal *Praśasti* and the titles. Almost all the Eastern Chālukyan rulers in phase I, upto Vijayāditya I (753-770 A.D.), assumed ordinary titles such as *Mahārāja, Vishmasiddhi*, and *Vijayasiddhi* (Chart IIA, Col. V, Nos. 1-16) which only indicates their military achievements as conquerors. It also indicates their being still subordinates of the Bādāmi Chālukyas inspite of their being regarded as independant rulers of a newly established kingdom. However, significantly, it is from the reign of Vijayaditya I (753-770 A.D.) that, for the first time, an attempt has been made by the Eastern Chālukyan rulers to assume high sounding titles. The Alluvālu grant[36] and the two copper plate grants of this ruler calls him by epithets *Samastabhuvanāśraya, Mahārājādhirāja,*

Paramēśvara, Bhaṭṭāraka, Chakravarti, Paramabrāhmaṇya, Parama Mahēśvara, Vijayasiddhi, Vikramarāma, Tribhuvanaṁkuśa. A similar attempt has been made by the other rulers of the dynasty during this phase. (Chart IIA, Col. V, Nos. 18-20). P.V. Parabrahma Sastry opinionates that the assumption of such high sounding titles by Vijayāditya I may be regarded as the declaration of his independence indicating his supreme sovereignty which could have been done after the total eclipse of the Bādāmi Chālukyan monarchy in 757 A.D.[37], that coincides with the succession to power by Vijayāditya I to the Vengi kingdom.

Thus, in Phase I, the Eastern Chālukyan rulers largely maintained their linkage with the Bādāmi Chālukyas as their off shoots in the Eastern Deccan. First this was made through adopting a similar family *praśasti*. It has been observed that during this phase, the early Chālukyas, sought legitimation to their power by linking up their descent to old *kṣatriya* families, namely, to that of Harita and secondly, by adopting a *brāhmaṇic gōtra*, namely the Mānavya *gōtra*. This meant imbibing in their dynastic tradition both the *brāhmaṇa* and *kṣatriya* lineages, and clearly adopting a *brahma-kṣatra* lineage though their inscriptions do not explicitly describe them as *brāhma-kṣatras*. The *brahma-kṣatra* lineage is described as a brāhmaṇical lineage yielding the powers adjunct to *kṣatriyas*.[38]

This process of claiming a *brahma-kṣatra* status is widely prevalent in early medieval South India. Earlier in Chapter I, we have discussed in detail how different scholars have regarded the origin of the *brahma-kṣatra* genealogy.

Therefore, in the context of these various theories on the origin of *brahma-kṣatra* we argue that though the Chālukyas do not describe themselves as *brahma-kṣatriyas*, their attempts to adopt a *brāhmaṇa gōtra* namely the Mānavya *gōtra* and secondly claiming their descent from the sons of Hariti (*Haritiputrānam*) who are shown by us as *brāhmaṇas*, endowed with martial qualities, surely indicates that the Chālukyas were *brahma-kṣatriyas*.

In phase II of our study commencing from the 9th century A.D. to the 12th century A.D., we have taken up the study of genealogies belonging to the later half of the Eastern Chālukyan dynasty and its collateral branches, namely, the Minor Chālukyan families of Mudigonda, Jananāthapuram and Nidadavōlu. This phase is crucial as it reflects changes in the pattern of genealogical accounts in inscriptions which have been found to be different in style and description. During this phase it has been perceived that the genealogies, unlike in phase I, were no longer short pedigrees, but give a long list of the chronological orders of kings starting from the founder of the dynasty of the Eastern branch to that of the donor. (Chart IIB, column III). It is chiefly in the later half of the second phase (11th century A.D.) of our study that we find the evolution of lengthy *paurānic* or legendary genealogies in accordance with the *itihāsa-purāṇa* tradition of North India. These were neither found in the genealogical sections of inscriptions of their parent branch, namely, the Chālukyas of Bādāmi nor in those of the early rulers of the Eastern branch. This phase is in fact concommitant with the emergence of Minor Chālukyan families as semi-independent states. A similar attempt was made by the latter to trace mythical genealogies, as was found in the records of the later Eastern Chālukyan rulers (Chart III).

In the first half of Phase II, that is, starting from the reign of Gunaga Vijayāditya III (844-888 A.D.) to that of Danarnava (970 A.D.) Chart IIB, Nos. 22-42), we find the dynastic *praśasti* of these rulers being similar to that of Phase I, namely, that the Chālukyas were descendants of Hariti, belonging to the Mānavya *gōtra*, nourished by *Saptamātrikas*, and so on. However, it is in referring to the names of the family members that a change has been perceived. It is in the records of Gunaga Vijayāditya III who reigned from 844-888 A.D. that a new type of *Praśasti* emergeṣ. He introduces for the first time in his grants long pedigrees of Eastern Chālukyan rulers, tracing the ancestry of the Eastern Chālukyan branch only from Kubja Vishnuvardhana I, who was regarded as the founder of the Eastern branch of the Chālukyan rule in the Vengi region to that of the donor of the grant. This was given in a chronological order mentioned along with the reign of each ruler (Chart IIB Col. II, Nos. 22-42). For instance, in the Chimbullur grant[43] of Gunaga Viyajāditya III, it has been described that Kubja Vishnuvardhana who was the brother of Satyaśraya Vallabha, adorned the glorious race of the Chālukyas, who belonged to the Mānavya *gōtra* and were descendants of Hariti, has ruled for 18 years, his son Jayasimha for 33 years, Vishnuvardhana, the son of his younger brother Indra-rāja for 9 years and so on. This eulogy continued upto the reign of Guṇaga Vijayāditya in whose reign this record was written.

However, it is in the later half of this phase, i.e., from the 11th century A.D. onwards that a new trend in the description of dynastic *praśasti* emerged. During this period there was a constant attempt on the part of the court poets, with the consent of their masters, to invent mythical genealogies linking up with the *itihāsa-purāṇa* tradition known from earlier times in north India. This mythical origin formed part of the *Praśastis.* They contain, in most cases, an elaborate account of the *Sūryavaṁśa* lineage upto an eponymous founder of the dynasty. This is followed by historically known figures, down to the contemporary ruler who made the grant. In the Eastern Chālukyan grants starting from the reign of Vimalāditya onwards (A.D. 1011-1018) there was a conscious attempt on the part of the ruling elites to concoct new mythical genealogies by claiming their descent from *Caṅdravaṃśa* lineage (Chart IIB, Col. III, Nos. 43-50). Thus, for instance, the Ranastipundi grant[44] of this period trace the origin of the Chālukyas from the lotus in Lord Nārāyana (i.e. Viṣṇu), through Brahma, Ātri and the Moon (see Appendix-I) up to the reign of Udayāna the ruler of Magadha. Further, the grant goes on to describe that "with him, fiftynine emperors whose successors were uninterrupted and who sat on the throne of Ayodhya, had passed away". It is also explained that Vijayāditya, who belonged to this race, went to the Dekkhan to conquer it. In this process he is said to have come into conflict with Trilōchana Pallava and by illfate had lost his life. However, his widowed queen Mahādēvi who was pregnant during this time had been rescued by Viṣhṇubhattasōmayājin, a *brāhmaṇa* saint. Under his parental care, she gave birth to a son named Vishnuvardhana, who assumed descent from the double gotra of Mānavya and the sons of Hariti. The son of this king was Vijayāditya, born through his great queen who belonged to the Pallava race. His son was Pulakēśi Vallabha followed by his son Kīrtivarman and so on. After this, the grant proceeds to give the genealogy of the Eastern branch of the Chālukyan rulers commencing from the reign of Kubja Vishnuvardhana to Danarnava.

Similar attempts were made by the Minor Chālukyan families who owed their origin and allegiance to the Eastern Chālukyas. This can be inferred from a study of inscriptions belonging to these families. In this chapter, we have taken the sample study of inscriptions belonging to three Minor Chālukyan families of Mudigonda, Jananāthapuram and Nidadavōlu. We have deliberately left out the other Minor Chālukyan families of Elamanchili, Srikūrmam etc. as they do not synchronise with the chronology of our study though these families also owed their allegiance to the Vengi Chālukyas.

Taking the examples from five inscriptions belonging to the three families of Mudigonda, Jananāthapuram and Nidadavōlu, we have attempted to study the genealogical sections of these families which enabled us to establish the ideological linkages between the Eastern Chālukyas and these collateral branches of the Chālukyan family. Thus, we have the Krivvaka grant (Chart III, II, 2) of the Mudigonda Chālukyan family that claims its descent from Viṣṇu through Brahma. The genealogy commences from Kariya Goṇaga, the eighth ruler of the Eastern Chālukyan dynasty and ends with the donor of the grant Kusumāditya. Similarly, the Edaṛupalli re-issued grant (Chart III, ii, 3) dated to 1179 A.D. of Vishṇuvardhana, belonging to the Chālukyan family of Jananāthapuram, begins with the Paurāṇic and mythical genealogies of the family clearly identical with that of the later inscriptions of the Eastern Chālukyas of Vengi. On the other hand, the Ganapavaram inscription (Chart III, ii, 5) of Gōkarāja who belonged to the Chālukyan family of Nidadavōlu describes the king as belonging to the lunar race, of the Mānavya *gōtra,* without mentioning the mythical origin of the family.

Significantly, the invention of mythical genealogies by these minor Chālukyan families emulating the trend set by the Eastern Chālukyas shows that these families, as the subordinates of the main family of the Vengi Chālukyas, began to seek ideological support to their kingdoms from the dominant rulers of the region, namely, the Eastern Chālukyas of Vengi. Further, the support and allegiance the Eastern Chālukyas got through the affiliation of these minor Chālukyan families can be established by the emulation of the genealogies by the latter. This helped in asserting the political and ideological strength of the Eastern Chālukyas.

Similarly, the personal *praśastis* and titles during this phase became more elaborate enumerating the virtuous qualities not only of the king but also of his predecessors. This was done by often drawing analogies from the heroes of the *Mahābhārata*. The elaborate military conquests of the rulers are given after describing the ruler as the destroyer of his enemies through his personal valour (Chart IIB, Col. III, Nos. 22-50). Equally important are the titles given to describe these rulers such as *Rājamārtānda* (Chart IIB, v, 34), *Birudānka Bhīma, Tribhuvanaṁkuśa, Mummadi Bhīma, Bhūpa Mahēndra* (Chart IIB, v, 43). During this period it has been noticed that the ruling elites assumed high sounding titles similar to that of the Vijayāditya I's records of Phase I. Titles such as *Mahārājādhirāja, Samastabhuvanāśraya, Sarvalōkāśraya,* ostensibly indicates the soverign power of the ruling elites during this period. On the other hand, titles such as *Paramēśvara, Parama-bhaṭṭāraka, Parama Mahēśvara, Paramabrāhmaṇya* indicates their consideration towards their religion and *varṇa*. Some of the titles during this period describes the personal qualities such as *Manjuprākāra, Parāchakrarāma* etc. (Chart IIB, Col. v. No. 22-48).

Thus, in Phase II the origin myths of the *itihāsa-purāṇa* type suggesting a pan-Indian tradition of the origin of dynasties, seeking legitimation by claiming *kṣatriya* status was conspicuous. This points to the commonness of the political ideology that was evolving in early medieval India, which sought legitimacy through what Romila Thapar calls legitimation by fabricated descent.[45] This necessity may be explained in terms of political instability caused due to incessant wars of succession. This emasculated the Eastern Chālukyan polity. Added to this was the social crisis which was created through large scale social mobility that shattered the claims of *varṇa* based *brāhmaṇical* ideology. Therefore, it was considered by the rulers during this period that in order to assert their political power in the days of turmoil and secondly, to revive the *varṇa based* brāhmaṇical ideology, tracing the genealogy to the *Caṅdravaṃśa* lineage has been regarded by rulers as a necessity to legitimize their power.[46] They also patronized *brāhmaṇa* poets who in turn wrote long eulogies about their patron's ancestry. The claim to higher status was not only due to their increasing military and economic power but to assert themselves and consolidate their political stability in weak periods of rule. This, further explains to why we do not find in the first phase the fabrication of mythical genealogies. Therefore, this phenomenon of adopting new mythical genealogies by the latter rulers was consciously a political ideology to consolidate their own power in the kingdom at a time when fissiparous tendencies were emerging. Such tendencies to fabricate mythical genealogies by making claims to being *kṣatriya* or *brahma-kṣatriya* becomes even more crucial in a situation of competition for status, which was maintained through horizontal marriage alliances among the "new" *kṣatriya* or *brahma-kṣatriyas.*[47]

II

In the early medieval period, marriages into other established *kṣatriya* families were regarded as important since the ruling elites considered that it was only through matrimonial links that claims to higher *varṇa* status could be recognised.[48]

Not much study has been undertaken so far to understand the politico-social significance of marriage networks, among various ruling families. This absence has been mainly due to the lack of information furnished in the inscriptions of the ruling elites in the early medieval period. However, despite the meagre information that was available through inscriptional sources eminent scholars, such as B.D. Chattopadhyaya and Surajit Sinha have attempted to study the marriage networks that were established among various Rajput clans. Chattopadhyaya postulates that the main intention of the ruling elites in recording the marriage alliance becomes significant as it underlines the political implications for the family. He had perceived a change in the marriage network pattern as a development towards an understandable pattern of interclan relationship. According to Chattopadhyaya this pattern of marriage networks was secured as essentially political as it provided social legitimacy to such groups who had acquired sufficient political power during the early medieval period. Secondly, he explains the interclan marriage relationships as a process of social and political activity to maintain kinship relations.[49]

Similarly, Surajit Sinha observes that there was a tendency among the Rajput families to attain higher social recognition which could be possible through marriage alliances. He argues that rather than ritual purification, the crucial factors in social upgrading were the setting up of characteristic social relations. This was done firstly by getting the service of a *brāhmaṇa* and secondly by marriage affiliation with a recognized Rajput family. Both of these are said to be attainable with persistent effort and with the backing of economic and political power. Thus, marriage alliance with a strong political power was necessary in getting legitimization to their *kṣatriyahood* and secondly to maintain kinship relations. Kinship relations are said to be maintained through genealogical connections of a kin's father and mother. It has been pointed out that marriage networks were crucial for engendering power relations of various ruling families.[50]

Hence, considering marriage networks as a necessary adjunct for consolidation of political power, and secondly to maintain kinship relations, which helped in the legitimazation of their *kṣatriya* status, an attempt has been made in this chapter to see the marriage networks as a significant social variable in consolidation of political power by the Eastern Chālukyan rulers. This study was made possible from rather limited information available from the inscriptional sources. Earlier, the authorities on Andhra history have seen the marriage alliances between various ruling families only as a political mechanism with no underlying social purpose.

In Phase I the inscriptions belonging to the Eastern Chālukyan rulers are completely silent about marriage alliances (Chart IIA, Column IV).

However, the only reference that has been made with regard to marriage alliance is found in the Ipur plates[51] of Vishnuvardhana III (A.D. 709-746) Chart IIA, Col.IV, No.16). This grant mentions the name of Prithivipōti. She was the daughter of Maghīnduvarāja of the Pallava dynasty. She was given in marriage to Vishnuvardhana III of the Eastern Chālukyan dynasty. The Pallavas had called themselves as *brahma-kṣatriyas* of the *Bharadvāja gōtra*.[52] During this period (i.e. about 717 A.D.) the Pallava power was completely crushed on account of their incessant warfare with the Bādāmi Chālukyas. Vishnuvardhana III is said to have vanquished the Pallava power in Kanchi. The latter in turn had compromised by giving his daughter in marriage to the Chālukyan ruler. This not only explains the marriage alliance between the two powerful ruling families of the time as a political ideology but if caste considerations are taken into account it also explains the social factor of aligning with a powerful member of the *brahma-kṣatra* lineage.

On the other hand, in Phase II the information on marriage alliances is more frequent. During this phase, the Eastern Chālukyan rulers got into marriage alliance with the powerful neigbouring rulers of the time. Thus, attempts were made by these rulers to maintain marriage relations with the Rāstrakūtas of Malkhed, the Chōlas of Tanjore, the Gaṇgas of Kalinga and even the powerful locality chiefs such as the Pattavardhanis. In the early reign of Gunaga Vijayāditya III, the Rāshtrakūtas who claimed to belong to the *kṣatriya varṇa* emerged as a strong political force in the Deccan often posing a great threat to the stability of the Eastern Chālukyan rulers. This was to some extent controlled by marrying the princesses of the family (Chart IIB, Col. IV, nos. 1-2). The Kākumrānu grant[53] of Chālukya Bhīma I mentions a certain queen by name Gāmakāmba. She is described as the mother of Chālukya Bhīma I, and wife of Vikramāditya. She is mentioned as daughter of Nissannabhūpāla of the Pattavardhan family. Pattavardhanis were the powerful military chiefs, who rendered loyal services to the royal family. Aligning with powerful military chiefs, through marriage alliance who are non-*kṣatriyas*,[54] reveals that the Chālukyas did not give much consideration to caste. This suggests that the main ideology of the ruling elites during this phase was to seek support from powerful clans through marriage networks who could provide sustenance to their power (Chart IIB, Col.IV, Nos. 26, 36).

In the later half of the second phase, i.e., from the eleventh century A.D. we find the emergence of the Chōla power in South India and the Gaṇgas in the North. The Chōlas regarded themselves as *kṣatriyas* of the *Suryavaṁśa* lineage.[55] The inscriptions of Eastern Chālukyan dynasty continuously made references to Chōla princesses who were married into the Chālukyan family (Charts IIB, Col. IV, Nos. 43-47, 49-50).

Thus, from the information found in the inscriptions on various marriage alliances established by the Eastern Chālukyan rulers we can explain the phenomenon that there were marriage networks establishing social relations between various ruling families. In the first phase, the Eastern Chālukyas, asserted their *kṣatriya* status by aligning with powerful families of *brahma-kṣatra* status. On the other hand, in Phase II attempts were made by the ruling elites to align with the political powers who belonged to the traditional *kṣatriya varṇa* thus asserting their claims to *kṣatriya* status. In the context of Rajasthan, it has been explained that the network of marriage alliances of newly emerging ruling elites into the traditional ruling families of *kṣatriyahood* is assimilative in nature.[56] However, in the case of the Eastern Chālukyas of Vengi, the marriage alliances played the role of assertion and stabilization of their political power at times of political instability thus underpinning the significiant political implications for the family.

To conclude, in Part I of this chapter, we had focussed on the study of the nature of genealogies, and the ideological role they played in the consolidation of political power of the ruling elites, in their attempts to evolve new state structures, in two different chronological phases. In Phase I the ruling elites attempted to claim a *brahma-kṣatra* ancestry, though this has not been mentioned directly in the inscriptions. Though scholars have expressed different views with regard to the caste of the Chālukyas, based on the descriptions found in the literary and inscriptional sources from the legendary descriptions given in the *Praśastis*, however it is evident that the early Chālukyas came into power claiming a *brāhmaṇical gōtra* status during the last decades of the fifth century in the geographical area of the Deccan. Similarly, an attempt has been made by us to show the continuity of relationship between the Bādāmi Chālukyas and the Eastern Chālukyas. In Phase II the ruling elites attempted to seek legitimization in the pure *kṣatriya varṇa* through mythical genealogies. In this regard *brahma-kṣatra* status of Phase I, can be regarded as an 'Intermediary" status before the new ruling families could formulate a claim to pure *kṣatriya* origin as ultimate aim of legitimation.[57] Thus, the process of fabrication of genealogies and the innumerable claims made to attain *kṣatriya* status helped the ruling elites to claim an ideological legitimacy. At the same time they strived to establish the theory of *varnāśramadharma* as an organising principle in society. Further the ideals of *Cakravarti, Mahārājādhirāja* helped the ruling elites to seek political validation. Similarly, in this phase we have also shown the linkages that were established between the Eastern Chālukyan family and other Minor Chālukyan families. In part II of this chapter, we have discussed the significance of maintaining marriage networks between various ruling families which is seen as a process of asserting their claims to pure *kṣatriyas* status and secondly, to consolidate their power in times of political instability. Thus, the social and ideological variables in this chapter have been understood as an attempt made by the ruling elites for sustaining political descent of the elite power through self assertion and defining their own identity.

References

1. B.D. Chattopadhyaya, 'Origin of the Rajputs: The Political Economic and Social Processes in Early Medieval Rajastan', *IHR*, vol. iii, no. 2, July, 1976, pp. 60-78.
2. Romila Thapar, 'Genealogy as a Source of Social History' in *AISH*, New Delhi, 1978a, pp. 326-332.
3. *Ibid*, p. 328.
4. F.E. Pargiter, *Ancient Indian Historical Tradition*, Delhi Rpt, 1972, p. 17.
5. Romila Thapar, 'Social Mobility in Ancient India with Special Reference to Elite Groups' in *AISH*, New Delhi, 1978b, pp. 133-134.
6. Romila Thapar, Op.cit., 1978a, p. 332
7. *Ibid*, p. 332.
8. B.D. Chattopadhyaya, 'Political Processes and Structures of Polity in Early Medieval India: Problems of Perspective.' *Social Scientist*, vol. 13, 1985, p.8.
9. *Ibid*, p. 8.
10. Romila Thapar, *Op.Cit.*, 1978a, p. 327.
11. *Ibid.*, p. 354.
12. B.N.S. Yadava, 'The Accounts of the Kali Age and The Social Transition from Antiquity to the Middle Ages.' *IHR*, vol. 5, 1978, p. 46.
13. B.N.S. Yadava, *Society and Culture in Northern India (In the 12th Century)*, Allahabad, 1973, p. 6 and p. 30.
14. Suvira Jaiswal, 'Studies in Early Indian Social History: Trends and Possibilities', *IHR*, vol. VI, 1979-80, pp. 33-35.
15. B.D. Chattopadhyaya, *Op.cit.*, 1985, p. 8.

16. B.N.S. Yadava, *Op.cit.*, 1973, p. 32.
17. *Ibid*, p. 30.
18. B.D. Chattopadhyaya, *Op.cit.*, 1976, p. 61.
19. B.N.S. Yadava, *Op.Cit.*, 1973, p. 32.
20. Surajit Sinha, 'State Formation and Rajput Myth in Tribal Central India', in Hermann Kulke, ed. *The State in India, 1000-1700*, Delhi, 1995, pp. 338-339.
21. S. Sankaranarayan, *'Vishnukundis and Their Times'*, Delhi, 1977, pp. 25-26.
22. Ķesavan Veluthat, 'The Status of the Monarch: A Note on the Rituals pertaining to Kingship and their Significance in the Tamil Country (A.D. 600-1200)'. *PIHC*, Session 43, 1982, pp. 148-153.
24. N. Venkataramanayya, *The Eastern Chalukyas of Vengi*, Madras, 1950, pp. 1-10.
25. B.V. Krishna Rao, *History of the Eastern Chalukyas of Vengi (610-1210 A.D.)*, Hyderabad, 1973, pp. 1-404.
26. Suravaram Pratapa Reddy, *Andhrula Sanghika Charitra*, 1950, Hyderabad, p. 1.
27. N.R. Vijaya, 'Evolution of Prasasti in the Inscriptions of the Eastern Chalukyas', *PAPHC*, Warangal, 1990, p. 76.
28. *Ibid*, p. 76.
29. Suvira Jaiswal, *Op.cit.*, 1979-80, p. 59.
30. The term *Gōtra* means Santati (Lineage), race, *Kula* (family) or clan. It is understood as an eponymous, exogamous caste that takes its name from some mythical or religious person. *Gōtra* is regarded as a status symbol that determined the position of a clan or a family in the social hierachy. *Encydopaedia of Religion and Ethics* (ed) by James Hastings, vol. 6, Rpt. 1974, R.N. Nandi, 'Gotra and Social Mobility in the Deccan', *PIHC*, 32 session, 1970, pp. 118.
31. G. Yazdani, *Early History of Deccan*, vol. I, 1982, p. 205 and K.V. Ramesh, *Chālukyas of Vatapi*, Delhi, 1984, pp. 13-14.
32. *Vāyupuranam*, (ch; 26: 72-73) in G.P. Bhatt (ed) *Ancient Indian Tradition and Mythology*, vol. 38, 1988, p. 679.
33. B.V. Krishna Rao, *Op.cit.*, 1973, pp. 54-56.
34. *IA*, vol. VII, 1978, pp. 209-217.
35. *EI*, vol. IX, 1907-08, pp. 317-319.
36. *EA*, vol. III, 1974, pp. 1-5.
37. *EA*, *Op.cit.*, 1974, p. 2.
38. Kesavan Veluthat, *The Political Structure of Early Medieval South India*, New Delhi, 1973, p. 31.
39. Suvira Jaiswal, *Op.cit.*, 1979-90, p. 32.

40. *Ibid*, p. 32.
41. S. Sankaranarayanan, *Op.cit.*, 1977, pp. 25-26.
42. Kesavan Veluthat, *Op.cit.*, 1993, p. 31.
43. *EA*, vol. III, 1974, pp. 6-15.
44. *EI*, vol. VI, 1900-01, pp. 348-361.
45. Kesavan Veluthat, *Op.cit.*, 1993, p. 346.
46. K.S. Kameswara Rao, "Social Foremation during Eastern Chalukyan Period", *PAPHC*, Nagaram, 1987-88, pp. 61-62.
47. Romila Thapar, *Interpreting Early India*, New Delhi Rpt. 1974, p. 155.
48. Ibid, p. 155.
49. B.D. Chattopadhyaya, Op.cit., 1976, p. 75.
50. Surajit Sinha, Op.Cit., 1995, p. 316.
51. *EI*, vol. XIII, 1925-26, pp. 58-60.
52. Kesavan Veluthat, Op.Cit., 1993, p.31.
53. *EA*, vol. III, 1974, pp. 16-28.
54. K. Suryanarayana, *Feudatories under Eastern Chalukyas (History and culture of Andhras* Delhi, 1987, p. 2.
55. Kesavan Veluthat, Op.cit., 1993, p. 33.
56. B.D. Chattopadhyaya, Op.cit., 1976, p. 75.
57. Ibid, p. 69.

CHART-I

PRAŚASTIS OF THE CHĀLUKYAS OF BĀDĀMI

S. No.	*Name of the Inscription/ King/Date*	*Dynastic Praśasti*	*Personal Praśasti*	*Titles*	*Religion/Deity*	*Reference*
1.	The British Museum Plates, Pulakēśi I (543-567 A.D)	Chālukyas belonging to MG, SoH. Three generations of kings predecessors Jayasiṁha (GF) Ranarāga (F)	King a great warrior and lover of peace	The Great King The Supreme King	Nārāyaṇa, King performed/ASMY	*IA*, Vol. VII, 1878, pp. 209-217
2.	Nērūr grant Mangalēśa (592-610 A.D.)	HP of MG	Possessing states-manship modesty, tenderness, sincerity truthfulness, and valour	—	God Bhagavān Pul I Performed. Agni-shtōma, Vājapēya, Paundārika & Aśva-mēdha sacrifices	*IA*, Vol. VII, 1878, pp. 161-162.
3.	Haidarābad grant Pulakēśi II (610-642-43 A.D.)	Three Generations of rulers from Pul I to Kirtivarman	Statesman	Supreme Lord	Nārāyaṇa	*IA*, Vol. VI, 1877, pp. 72-75
4.	Aihōle inscription Pulakēśi II (S. 556)	Six generations starting from Jayasiṁha Vallabha to Pul. II and their military achievements			Jīnēndra	*EI*, Vol. VI, pp. 1-12, *IA*, Vol. VIII, 1879, pp. 237-245

S. No.	*Name of the Inscription/ King/Date*	*Dynastic Praśasti*	*Personal Praśasti*	*Titles*	*Religion/Deity*	*Reference*
5.	Kolhapuram Plates Vikramāditya I (655-681 A.D.)	The genealogy from Pul. I is given. MG, descendants of Hariti, Nourished by Sapta-Mātrikas	The defeater of hostile kings	—	Nārāyaṇa performed ASMY	*EA*, Vol. IV 1975, pp. 9-12.
6.	Lakshmēshwar inscription Vinayāditya I (681-696-97 A.D.)	Descent from Pul. I mentions Kīrti varman, Pul. II, Vikramāditya I	Kigs as heroic and Valorous	—	Viṣṇu in boar form	*IA*, Vol. VII, 1878, pp. 110-111
7.	Kottūru grant Vijayāditya Satyaśraya (696-733 A.D.)	—	—	*Śrī Prithvivallabha, Mahārājādhirāja, Paramēśvara*	—	*El*, Vol.XXX, 1953-54 pp. 69-71
8.	Nārvan Plates Vikramāditya II (S. 664) (733-744-45 A.D.)	Descent from Pul. I Mentions Predecessors except Mangalēśa	—	—	—	*El*, Vol. XXVII, 1947, pp. 125-131
9.	Kendūr Plates Kīrtivarman II (S. 672) (744-45-757 A.D.)	Genealogy begins with Pul. I	—	—	—	*El*, Vol. IX, 1907-08, pp. 200-206
10.	Vakkalēri Plates Kīrtivarman II (S. 679)	-do-	—	*Mahārājādhirāja Paramēśvara Bhaṭṭārika Śrī Prithvivallabha*	—	*El*, Vol. V, 1898-99 pp. 200-205

CHART-IIA

PRAŚASTIS OF CHĀLUKYAS OF VENGI-PHASE I (7TH C.A.D.-9TH C.A.D.)

S.No.	*Name of the Inscription/King/Date*	*Dynastic Praśasti*	*Personal Praśasti*	*Marriage alliances*	*Titles*	*Religion Deity*	*Reference*
1.	Timmāpuram plates Kubja Viṣṇuvardhana I 625-641 A.D.	Descent from SoH. Belongs to MG. Mentions 3 generations of Kings Predecessors viz., Rr, Rv, Kvl and Pul II of BCD	King as great warrior		*Mahārāja Vishamasiddhi*	*Bhagavāt Vishṇu*	*EI*, Vol. IX, 1907-08 pp. 317-319
2.	Satāra Cp grant (624-641 A.D.)	Descent from SoH. MG. Mentions KVV I as son of KvI and Grandson of Rv of BCD	King praised by taking analogies of *Mahābhārata* heroes e.g., referred to as Pārtha (Arjuna) in puissance etc.		*Vishamasiddhi*	*Swāmi Mahāsēna*	*IA*, Vol. XIX, 1890 pp. 303-311
3.	Chīpurupalle CP grant (624-641 A.D.)	Mentions KVV I as younger brother of Pul. II	King as Manu in courteous behaviour, Prithu in reputation and Possession of wisdom.		*Vishamasiddhi Mahārāja*	—	*IA*, Vol. XX, 1891, pp. 15-18.

S.No.	Name of the Inscription/King/Date	Dynastic Praśasti	Personal Praśasti	Marriage alliances	Titles	Religion Deity	Reference
4.	Puli: ımra plates Prithvı Jayasingha Vallabha (632-663 A.D.)	HP, of MG. Jayasimha Vallabha mentioned as Grandson of KvI	King praised by taking analogies from *Mahābhārata* as a diplomat like Bṛhaspati, invariable like Arjuna, righteous like Yudhiṣthira modest like Manu and a scholar of śāstras		*Sarvasiddhi Prithivallabha*	—	*EI*, Vol.XIX, 1927-28 pp. 254-258
5.	Nidupāru grant Jayasiṁha Vallabha (641-673 A.D.)	3 generations of the family given. Kv I and KVV I described as GF and F of the king	—		*Sarvasiddhi Mahārāja*	—	*EI*, Vol.XVIII, 1925-26, pp. 52.58
6.	Uchchāti grant Jayasiṁha Vallabha I (641-673 A.D.)	-do-	—		*Mahārāja*		*EA*, Vol.V, 1988, pp. 19-20.
7.	Pedda Vēgi Grant Jayasiṁha Vallabha I (641-673 A.D.)	3 generations of Kings predecessors KvI (GF) of BCD and KVV I	—		*Sarvasiddhi Mahārāja*		*EA*, Vol. V, XIX, 1927-28, pp. 258-261
8.	Piṣtapura grant Jayasiṁha Vallabha I	HP, MG, mentions 3 generations of King's predecessors	—		*Sarvasiddhi*	Performers of ASMY	*Bhārati*, Vol. 40, Dec. 1963, pp. 17-20

S.No.	*Name of the Inscription/King/Date*	*Dynastic Praśasti*	*Personal Praśasti*	*Marriage alliances*	*Titles*	*Religion Deity*	*Reference*
9.	Kondanāgaru grant Mahārāja Indravarman (673 A.D.)	King as Grandson of Mahārāja KvI and son of KVV I	—	—	*Śrī Tyāgadhēnu*	—	*EI*, Vol.XVIII, 1925-26, pp. 1-5
10.	Koneki grant Viṣṇuvardhana II (673-681 A.D.)	Names of Rr and KvI of BCD as GGGF and GGF of the king	—	—	*Mahārāja* Describes Indravarman Mahārāja with epithets : *Tyāgadhēnu, Vigrahasiddhi, Simhavikrama, Rājalōkśraya.*	—	*EI*, Vol. XXXI, 1955-56, pp. 74-80
11.	Rēyūru Grant Viṣṇuvardhana II (668-669 A.D.)	HP of MG. Genealogy commences from Śrī Viṣṇuvardhana. Mentions 3 generations of king's predecessors	King as valorous. Righteous protector of *Dharma*, Universal Emperor	—	—	*Mahēśvara Kārtikēya*	*IA*, Vol. VII, 1878, pp. 185-191
12.	Maṭṭevāda Plates Viṣṇuvardhana II (673-681 A.D.)	Genealogy begins with KvI of BCD Names of KVV I and Jayasiṁhavallabha are mentioned	Describes king as good musician and prosperous like Lord *Viṣṇu*		—	*Viṣṇu Kārtikēya*	*IA*, Vol. VII, 1878, pp. 191-192

S.No.	*Name of the Inscription/King/Date*	*Dynastic Praśasti*	*Personal Praśasti*	*Marriage alliances*	*Titles*	*Religion Deity*	*Reference*
13.	Chendalūr Plates Mahārāja Sarvalōkaśraya (681-705 A.D.)	3 generations kings mentioned viz. Mahārāja Viṣṇuvardhana (F), Mahārāja Indrabhaṭṭāraka (FG) and KVV I (GGF)	Describes king as Valourous. Obtained *Vijayasiddhi*	—	Mahārāja, *Vijaya Siddhi* Indrabhaṭṭāraka : with epithet *Simhavikrama* : Viṣṇuvardhana II as *Makaradhvaja*	—	*EI*, Vol. VIII, 1905-06, pp. 236-241
14.	Chendara Grant Jayasiṁha II (705-711 A.D.)	HP of MG. Names of Kings's (GF) and (F) are mentioned	Describes king as valiant, Charming	—	—	Lord *Nārāyaṇa*	*EA*, Vol. V, 1988, pp.20-21
15.	Kondakaripḷola grant Viṣṇuvardhana II (718-752 A.D.)	Names of King's (GF) and (F) are mentioned	—	—	*Vishamasiddhi Samasta Bhuvanāśraya Tribhuvanaṁkuśa*	—	*EA*, Vol. V, 1988, pp. 21-23.
16.	Ipūr Plates Viṣṇuvardhana II (718-752 A.D.)	-do-		Prithivipōti (W) of Viṣṇuvardhana III, (D) of Maghinduvarāja of Pallava Dynasty	-do-	—	*EI*, Vol. III, 1925-26, pp. 58-60
17.	Alluvālu grant Vijayāditya (735-770 A.D.)	Genealogy of 3 generations of Chālukyan family mentioned, viz. Mangi Yuvarāja, Viṣṇuvardhana II and Vijayāditya I	Describes kings as a vanquisher of neighbouring kings by the might of his sword		*Samastabhuvanāśraya Mahārājādhirāja, Paramēśvara, Bhaṭṭāraka*	—	*EA*, Vol. III 1974, pp. 1-5

S.No.	Name of the Inscription/King/Date	Dynastic Praśasti	Personal Praśasti	Marriage alliances	Titles	Religion Deity	Reference
18.	Two new copper plate inscriptions Vijayāditya I (753-770 A.D.)	-do-	-do-	—	*Samastabhuvanāśraya, chakravarti, Paramabrāhmaṇya, Vijayasiddhi, Bhaṭṭāraka Vikramarāma Tribhuvanaṁkuśa*	*Mahēśvara Nārāyaṇa*	*JAHRS*, Vol. V, July 1930, I, pp. 51-56
19.	Ēdēru Plates Narēndra Mrigarāja Vijayāditya II (799-843 A.D.)	HP of MG, Genealogy starts with Vikramarāma Vijayāditya I. Mentions Mahārāja Viṣṇuvardhana as (F) of Vijayāditya II	Describes king as religious and victorious like Viṣṇu	—	*Mahārājādhirāja, Paramēśvara, Bhaṭṭāraka*	*Viṣṇu*	*EI*, Vol. V, 1898-99 pp. 118-142
20.	The Varppoṁgu Plates Vijayāditya II (806-846 A.D.)	-do-	Describes king as an Emperor, Paramount sovereign over all feudatory chiefs	—	*Samastabhuvanāśraya, Mahārājādhirāja, Paramēśvara Bhaṭṭārka Chakravartin*	—	*EA*, Vol. III, 1974, pp. 5-6
21.	Korrapārru grant Vijayāditya II (806-846 A.D.)	HP of MG, Genealogy starts with Vikramarāma Vijayāditya I. Mentions Mahārāja Viṣṇuvardhana as (F) of Vijayāditya II	Describes king as an Emperor, Paramount, Soverign over all feudatory chiefs	—	*Paramamahēśvara*	*Viṣṇu*	*SII*, Vol. I, 1987 pp. 31.

CHART-IIB

PRAŚASTIS OF CHĀLUKYAS OF VENGI-PHASE II (9TH C.A.D. TO 12TH C.A.D.)

S. No.	*Name of the Inscription/ Kings/Date*	*Dynastic Praśasti*	*Personal Paraśasti*	*Marriage Alliances*	*Titles*	*Religion/ Deity*	*Reference*
22.	Chimbulūru grant Guṇakanalla Vijayāditya III (844-888 A.D.)	A new type of Praśasti emerges. Enumerates the chronological order of all the previous kings line of descent with the length of their reign	—	Chella/Challaka (D) of Vallabhēndra Amōgavarsha I of the Rāshtrakūta dynasty (W) (Q) of GV III	—	—	*EA*, Vol. III, 1974, pp. 6-15
23.	Guntur Plates Vijayāditya III (844-888 A.D.)	-do-	King had qualities like bravery generosity endurance etc.	Silāmahādēvi of Rāshtrakūta dynasty (W) of Kali Viṣṇuvardhana (M) of Vijayāditya III	*Mahārāja* Vijayāditya II as *Chālukyārjuna*	—	*EI*, Vol. V, 1898-99 pp. 122-126
24.	Satalūru Cp. grant Vijayāditya III (844-888 A.D.)	-do-	Praised as Gunaka-Mallān, i.e. most virtuous	—	*Nirpatimārtāṇda Vīramakara-dhvajaḥ*, *Manuja Prākāra*, etc.	Vijayāditya II as builder of 108 temples to god Śiva	*JAHRS*, Vol. V, 1930, pp. 101-116

S. No.	*Name of the Inscription/ Kings/Date*	*Dynastic Praśasti*	*Personal Paraśasti*	*Marriage Alliances*	*Titles*	*Religion/ Deity*	*Reference*
25.	The Mōga Grant Chālukya Bhīma I (892-922 A.D.)	HP of MG. Genealogy starts from KVV I upto CB I in a chronological order	Defeated Karṇātas and Lāṭās	Mentions (m.a.) between SC of 3 families, viz. Tailambā (D) of Sarvarāja (SC) (M) Yuddhamalla their (D) is Śrī Mahādēvi (W) of Vijayāditya of Ktr Vaṁśa	*Sarvalōkāśraya*, *Paramēśvara* *Mahārājādhirāja* *Parama* *Mahēśvara*	—	*EA*, Vol. III, 1974, pp. 28-42
26.	The Kākumrānu grant Chālukya Bhīma I (S. 814)	-do-	King Victorious over many neighbouring kings enhance his glory	Gāmakāmba (Q) (D) of Nisśannabhūpāla (FC) (W) of Vikramāditya of CB I	—	—	*EA*, Vol. III, 1974, pp. 16-28
27.	The Telugu Academy plates (or) Attili grant	—	—	—	*Sarvalōkāśraya*, *Śrī* *Viṣṇuvardhana*	Worshipper of *Brāhmaṇas*	*JBORS*, Vol, III, II, 1922, pp. 83-98
28.	Bezavāda Plates Chālukya Bhīma I (892-922 A.D.)	HP of MG, Genealogy begins with KVV I, described as (B) of Satyaśraya Vallabhēndra of BCD upto CB. I.	King, as glorious hero, respected the learned.	—	*Mahārājādhirāja*, *Paramēśvara*, *Paramabhaṭṭāraka*	*Nārāyaṇa*	*EI*, Vol. V, 1898-99, pp. 127-131

S. No.	Name of the Inscription/ Kings/Date	Dynastic Praśasti	Personal Paraśasti	Marriage Alliances	Titles	Religion/ Deity	Reference
29.	Masulipatam plates, Amma I (918-925 A.D.)	Genealogy begins with KVV I, ends with Amma I. The reigns of all kings given	Describes the king as the lord of the earth. His fame as pure as jasmine and moon	—	*Bhirudhānka Mahārāja Viṣṇuvardhana*	*Śiva*	*EI*, Vol. V, 1898-99, pp. 131-134
30.	Ēdēru plates, Amma I (918-925 A.D.)	-do-	He is called *Rājamahēndra* Described as mighty, patient and wise.	—	-do-	*Śiva*	*SII*, Vol. I, pp. 26-43
31.	The Velaṁbarṟu grant, Ammarāja Viṣṇuvardhana I (922-929 A.D.)	Genealogy begins with KVVI, ends with Amma I. KVV I (B) of Pul. II of BCD	—	Lōkamahādēvi (W) of Vijayāditya IV and (M) of Amma I.	*Sakalalōkāśraya Viṣṇuvardhana*	*Nārāyaṇa*	*EA*, Vol. III, 1974 pp. 43-46
32.	Chēvuru Plates (922-929 A.D.)	Doesnot contain usual genealogy unlike the other grants. Mentions only 2 names of Kings immediate predecessors	—	—	*Sarvalōkāśraya, Mahārājādhirāja, Paramēśvara Paramabhaṭṭāraka,* etc. Vijayāditya IV mentioned with epithet *Samasta Bhuvanāśraya*	*Mahēśvara*	*EI*, Vol. XXVII, 1947, pp. 41-47

S. No.	Name of the Inscription/ Kings/Date	Dynastic Praśasti	Personal Paraśasti	Marriage Alliances	Titles	Religion/ Deity	Reference
33.	Masulipatam plate, Chālukya Bhīma II (934-945 A.D.)	HP of MG, KVV I (B) of Pul. II of BCD. Names of Kings from KVVI to CB II mentioned in chronological order	King asylum of all mankind, devoted to religion	Mēlāmbā (W) of Vijayāditya IV (M) of Chālukya Bhīma II	*Mahārājādhirāja Paramēśvara, Viṣṇuvardhana*	—	*EI*, Vol. V, 1898-99, pp. 134-139
34.	Kolavennu plates Chālukya Bhīma II (934-945 A.D.)	HP of MG. Genealogy begins with KVV I upto CB II mentions CB I as (B) of Ammarāja I by a different (M)	*Rājamārtāṇḍa* or possessor of insurmountable greatness, proficient in all arts, supreme master, supreme lord	—	*Rājamārtāṇḍa*	*Viṣṇu*	*SII*, Vo. I, pp. 43-46
35.	Nammūru grants Ammarāja II, (945-970 A.D.)	Genealogy begins with KVVI, ends with Ammarāja II	King as the 'lord of the earth'	Lōkamahādēvi (M) of Amma II	*Samastabhuvanāśraya, Mahārājādhirāja, Paramēśvara, Paramabhaṭṭāraka*	*Mahēśvara Umā*	*EI*, Vol. XII, 1913-14 pp. 61-64
36.	Kaluchumbaṛṛu Grant Ammarāja II (934-945 A.D.)	HP of MG. Genealogy begins with Pul. II of the BDC ends with Ammarāja II	Kings as mighty like Indra, Glorious like sun etc.	Chamekāmbā of Pattavardini family courtesan and favourite mistress of Amma II Lōkamahādēvi is mentioned as (M) of Amma II	*Mahārājādhirāja, Paramēśvara, Paramabhaṭṭāraka*	Patron of Jainism	*EI*, Vol. VII, 1902-3, pp. 178-192

S. No.	Name of the Inscription/ Kings/Date	Dynastic Praśasti	Personal Praśasti	Marriage Alliances	Titles	Religion/ Deity	Reference
37.	Maliyapuṇḍi grant Ammarāja II. (945-970 A.D.)	Genealogy begins with KVV I (B) of Pul. II of BCD upto Ammarāja II.	King as Eastern Lord of mountains, very pious etc.	Lōkamahādēvi (W) of CB II and (M) of Ammarāja II.	*Samastabhuvanā-śraya, Mahārājādhirāja*	Jainism, Lord *Jinēndra*	*EI*, Vol. IX, 1907, pp.47-56
38.	Vemalūrpādu grant (945-970 A.D.)	-do-	King being mighty like Indra, glorious like sun, etc.	-do	—	*Mahēśvara*	*EI*, Vol. XVIII 1925-1926, pp. 226-235
39.	Tāṇḍikonda grant Ammarāja II (945-970 A.D.)	Genealogy begins with KVVI (B) of Pul. I, of BCD upto Ammarāja II.	—	—	—	*Kālāmukha* sect of *Pāśupata Śaivas, Śiva*, mentions Śaivate teachers of *Kālāmukha* sect.	*ARE*, 1916-17, pp. 90-91, El, Vol. XXIII, pp. 162-164.
40.	Masulipatam plates Ammarāja II (945-970 A.D.)	Genealogy begins with KVV I (B) of Pul. I, of BCD, upto Ammarāja II	King as asylum of the whole world	Lōkamahādēvi (W) of CBII and (M) of Ammarāja II	*Mahārāja, Rājādhirāja, Paramēśvara Paramabhaṭṭāraka*		*EI*, Vol. V, 1898-99, pp. 139-142
41.	Kandyan plates Dānarnava/ Dānapa (S. 892)/ (970 A.D.)	Gives the line of succession from KVVI upto Ammarāja II	King as Just, Proficient in all sciences and arts, an able administrator. Also called Bhīma	Ankidēvī/ Ankimahādēvī Urjapāya (D) of Kalinga King, first (W) of CBII, (M) of Dānarnava	*Viṣṇuvardhana Mahārājādhirāja Paramēśvara*	*Śiva*	*JAHRS*, Vol. XI, ii 1938, pp. 80-88

S. No.	Name of the Inscription/ Kings/Date	Dynastic Praśasti	Personal Praśasti	Marriage Alliances	Titles	Religion/ Deity	Reference
42.	Māṅgallu grant (970-973 A.D.)	-do-	-do-	-do-	*Samastabhuvanaśr-aya Śrī Vijayāditya Mahārājādhirāja Paramēśvara, Paramabhaṭṭāraka Paramabrāhmaṇyaḥ*	*Viṣṇu* in the form of *Vāmana*	*EA*, Vol. I, 1969, pp. 57-70, *EI*, Vol, XXXI, 1955-56, pp. 37-44.
43.	Raṇastipūṇḍi grant, Vimalāditya (1011-1018 A.D.)	A detailed Pg. Genealogy of CF traced to *Brahma*. Belongs to CV family. Mentions 59' generations of kings in this line. Mentions Chālukyas as HP, MG, Mentions historical genealogy of the Chālukyas, starting from Viṣṇuvardhana	A lengthy personal eulogy given, drawing analogies from MB heroes. King compared to Sahadēva well-versed in arts poetry and royal sciences. Destroyer of enemies at war etc.	Āryamahādēvī (W) of Dānarnava (M) or Vimalāditya	*Birudāṅka Bhīma Tribuvanaṁkuśa, Mummadi Bhīma, Bhūpa Mahēndra*	*Sambhu/Śiva Mahēśvara*	*EI*, Vol. VI, 1900-01, pp. 348-361
44.	Kōrumelli plates Rājarāja II (1022-1061 A.D.)	-do-	—	Kundavamahādēvī (D) of Rājarāja of Chōla family (W) of Vimalāditya and (M) of Rājarāja II	*Sarvalōkāśrya, Śrī Viṣṇuvardhana Mahārājādhirāja, Paramēśvara, Paramabhaṭṭāraka, Paramabrāhmaṇyaḥ*	*Nārāyaṇa Viṣṇu*	*IA*, Vol. XIV, 1885, pp. 48-55

S. No.	Name of the Inscription/ Kings/Date	Dynastic Praśasti	Personal Praśasti	Marriage Alliances	Titles	Religion/ Deity	Reference
45.	Telugu Academy plates, Śaktivarman II (1061 A.D.)	A detailed Pg. Genealogy of CF traced to *Brahma*. Belongs to CV family. Mentions 59 generations of king's in this line. Mentions Chālukyas as HP, MG, Mentions historical genealogy of the Chālukyas, starting from Viṣṇuvardhana	King described as the supreme master kings; valorous truthful, energetic	(1) Medavamahādēvī, Chōla princess (W) of Vimalāditya (M) of Vijayāditya VII. (2) Madavamahādēvī Haihaya princess. (W) of Vijayāditya VII (M) of Śaktivarman II.	*Samaraika Bhairava*, *Sarvalōkāśraya*, *Śrī Viṣṇuvardhana*, *Mahārājādhirāja*, *Paramēśvara*, *Paramabhaṭṭāraka* *Paramabrāhmaṇya*, *Parama Mahēśvara*, *Satyaśradēva*	*Mahēśvara*	*JAHRS*, Vol. V, 1930, pp. 33-49
46.	Two New CP inscriptions Vijayāditya vII (1061-1075 A.D.)	A detailed P, Belongs to CV family. List of 59 kings enumerated. Chālukyan belong to MG, HP. Genealogy of the whole dynasty given starting from Viṣṇuvardhana to Rājarāja II.		Mēdava Chōla Princess (W) of Vimalāditya (M) of Vijayāditya VII	*Sarvalōkāśraya*, *Mahārāja*	—	*JAHRS*, Vol. IX, i, 1934, pp. 24-35

S. No.	Name of the Inscription/ Kings/Date	Dynastic Praśasti	Personal Praśasti	Marriage Alliances	Titles	Religion/ Deity	Reference
47.	Tēki plates Kulōttunga I Rājarāja Chōda Gaṅga (1075-1118 A.D.)	A detail Pg. Belongs to CV family. List of 59 kings enumerated. Chālukyas belongs to MG, HP, Genealogy of the whole dynasty given, starting from Viṣṇuvardhana to Rājarāja II.	—	Madhurāntakī (W) of Kulōttunga	*Sarvalōkāśraya, Mahārājādhirāja, Paramēśvara, Paramabhaṭṭāraka*	*Śiva Mahēśvara*	*EI*, Vol. VI, 1900-01, pp. 334-347
48.	Bhīmavaram inscriptions (1075-1118 A.D.)	-do-	—	—	*Parāntaka, Sarvalōkāśraya, Viṣṇuvardhana, Mahārāja,*	*Viṣṇu Lakṣmī*	*EI*, Vol. VI, pp. 219-223
49.	Chellūr grant Vīrachōda (1078-1084 A.D.) (1084-1094 A.D.)	-do-	King as valorous Supreme master of kings etc.	(1) Ammaṅga of Chōla dynasty (W) of Rājarāja Narēndra. (2) Madhurāntakī as Chōla Princess (W) of Kulōttunga I.	*Viṣṇuvardhana*	*Śiva, Viṣṇu Lakṣmī, Umā, Mahēśvara*	*SII*, Vol. I, pp. 51-62
50.	Pithāpuram plates Vīrachōda (1078-1084 A.D.) (1089-1094 A.D.)	-do-	-do-	-do-	-do-	-do-	*EI*, Vol. V, 1898-99, pp. 70-100

CHART-III

PRAŚASTIS OF THE MINOR CHĀLUKYAN FAMILIES (9TH C.A.D. - 12TH C.A.D.)

S. No.	*Name of the Family/Locality*	*Name of the Inscription/King/Date*	*Dynastic Praśasti linkage with ECV*	*Titles*	*Political status*	*Religion/Deity*	*Reference*
1.	Chālukyas of Mudigonda	Mogalucheṛuvula grant, Kusumāyudha IV (1050-1075 A.D.)	Belongs to MG, HP, Genealogy of 3 generations of rulers starting from Kokkirāja to Kusamāyudha IV	*Parama Mahēśvara, Parama, Brāhmaṇya,*	semi-independent owed allegiance to Chālukyas of Vengi	*Nārāyaṇa*.	*IMCDAP*, K, Suryanārāyaṇa 1993, pp. 34-35
2.	-do-	Krivvaka grant (or) Kūkunūru grant Kusumāditya (1150-1175 A.D.)	Descent from *Viṣṇu* through *Brahma* Chālukyas belonged to *Candravaṁśa*. Genealogy starts with Kariya Goṇaga 8th ruler of the dynasty and ends with the Kusumāditya	Mārbbala Kēśari	-do-	*Nārāyaṇa Paramēśvara*	*EA*, Vol. I, 1974, pp. 39-49 Bharati, Nov. 1979, pp. 32-39

S. No.	Name of the Family/Locality	Name of the Inscription/King/Date	Dynastic Praśasti linkage with ECV	Titles	Political status	Religion/Deity	Reference
3.	Chālukyas of Jananāthapuram	Edaṛupalli re-issued grant Viṣṇuvardhana (1124-1151 A.D.)	Paurāṇic and mythical genealogies of the family. Mentions names of Pul. I, KVI, Pul II, HP, MG. Gives names of rulers of ECV, starting from KVV. I to Vikrama Chōda. Then mentions rulers of C.J., starting from Bēta Vijayāditya to Viṣṇuvardhana	*Sarvalōkāśraya, Mahārājādhirāja, Rājarāja, Paramēśvaraḥ, Paramabhaṭṭārakaḥ, Paramabrāhmaṇyaḥ, Parama Mahēśvaraḥ*	—	*Nārāyaṇa Paramēśvara*	*IMCDAP, K* Suryanārāyaṇa 1993, pp. 60-67
4.	-do-	Pithāpuram Pillar Incription Mallapa Dēva II (A.D. 1202)	-do- CJ names extended upto Mallapa II	Paramēśvarāja/ Purandaraḥ Paramabhāgavataḥ Paramabrāhmaṇyaḥ	—	—	*IMCDAP, K* Suryanārāyaṇa 1993, pp. 75-80
5.	Chālukyas of Nidadavōlu	Ganapavaram Inscription, Gōkarāja (A.D. 1174)	Describes kings as belonging to Lunar race, MG.	—	*Manmahā-Mandalēśvara*	—	*IMCDAP, K* Suryanārāyaṇa 1993, p. 122

CONSOLIDATED KEY FOR CHARTS I, IIA, IIB AND III.

ASMY	=	Asvamēdha Yajña	Ktr	=	Kātakarāya
B	=	Brother	KvI	=	Kīrtivarman I
BCD	=	Bādāmi Chālukyan Dynasty	KVVI	=	Kubja Viṣṇuvardhana I
CBI	=	Chālukya Bhīma I	M	=	Mother
CBII	=	Chālukyas Bhīma II.	m.a.	=	Marriage alliance
CJ	=	Chālukyas of Jananāthapuram	MB	=	Mahābhārata
Cp	=	Copper plate	MG	=	Mānavya Gōtra
CV	=	Chaṇḍravaṃśa	(mar)	=	Married
D	=	Daughter	PG	=	Paurāṇic Genealogy
ECV	=	Eastern Chālukyas of Vengi	Pul	=	Pulakeśin I
F	=	Father	Pul. I	=	Pulakeśin II
FC	=	Feudatory Chiefs	Q	=	Queen
GF	=	Grand Father	Rr	=	Ranarāga
GGF	=	Great Grand Father	Rv	=	Ranavikraman
GGGF	=	Great Great Grand Father	SC	=	Sāmanta Chief
GV III	=	Guṇaga Vijayāditya III	W	=	Wife
HP	=	Hariti putrās			

Chapter-IV

ECONOMIC LINKAGES

In recent years it has been realized that the underlining importance of the early medieval economy was largely based on the system of land grants. Land grants can be defined as `gifting of land (*bhūdāna*) made by the king or the state initially to the religious beneficiaries viz., the *brāhmaṇas* and the Buddhist monks and later, to the secular donees. The former were given ostensibly for the purpose of extending vedic learning where as the latter for governance and with the motive of expanding agricultural land, resource mobilization and redistribution.[1] The system of land grants was rooted in the concepts of *Dāna* and *Dakṣhina*, which were given primarily to the priests and *brāhmaṇas. Dāna* etymological means giving or gifting materials such as gold, cattle etc.[2] However, a change has been perceived in the concept of *Dāna* during the early medieval period onwards, when land predominantly replaced the earlier practice of gifting cattle, gold etc., as a major commodity of gift exchange.[3]

This chapter entitled, focuses mainly on the economic process as an important factor in determining the nature of the state. They were important mechanisms adopted by the newly emerging ruling elites for the consolidation of their economic power. To highlight the nature of these changes as perceived in the donations of land and other grants to various social groups the study of economic transformation during the early medieval period becomes imperative as an interdependent factor to understand the larger processes of the nature of political power and the economic power of the newly emerging ruling elites, namely, the Eastern Chālukyas of Vegni. Intially, the Eastern Chālukyas who were the offshoot of the Bādāmi Chālukyan dynasty had migrated from the Western Deccan to the region of Vengi as conquerors and had established themselves in an alien land. The region of Vengi at the time of the Eastern Chālukyan rule encompassed a broader area of the Andhra country, extending from the river Manneru in the south to the Mahēndra mountains in the north.[4] It was a most fertile region and can be defined in Subba Rao's terminology as a "nuclear zone" or an "area of attraction".[5] As discussed earlier in Chapter II, it has been understood that the geographical importance of this region had attracted many ruling elites in the past, from other parts of the country. In fact, the conquest of Vengi by Pulakēśin II has been understood as a means to enhance resource mobilization from this region. Thus, the establishment of the Eastern Chālukyan kingdom in the region of Vengi should be understood from this perspective. In order to sustain the kingdom in an alien land, the new ruling elites had to evolve certain economic mechanisms such as granting of land initially, to the religious beneficiaries and later, to other beneficiaries to consolidate their political and economic powers in an alien land.

So far in understanding the region, the period under study has not attracted enough attention from historians inorder to elaborate on the economic processes of state formation. Eminent scholars such as N. Venkataramanayya, B.V Krishna Rao, and others have simply described the role of ruling elites in terms of the donations of lands they made to religious and non-religious beneficiaries. In fact, a study of the nature of grants and their analysis as economic mechanisms and as a means for the stabilization of power and for resource mobilization has been given marginal importance in hitherto writings on dynastic histories. Therefore, in this regard, we have made a small attempt to analyse the economic processes along with the nature of changes it led to in the period of our study.

To initiate our understanding of the nature of the economy in the early medieval Andhra country, under the rule of the Eastern Chālukyas, we have taken up an analysis of the nature of land grants in two different phases. Phase I of our study covers the period between the 7th century A.D. to the 9th century A.D. and Phase II commences from the 9th century A.D. and extends upto the 12th Century A.D. The inscriptions belonging to the Minor Chālukyan families of Mudigonda, Nidadavōlu and Jananāthapuram also come under the second phase.

This division into two phases is significant as they reflect changes in the economic structure of land grants which can be considered as a direct result of the political and social transformations that had necessiated the ruling elites to make alterations as demanded by the time and circumstances. To understand the nature of these changes initiated by the ruling elites for the period and the region under study, we have relied largely on the inscriptional sources which were like legal documents that were specifically meant for recording land grants and other economic transactions and this information formed their central theme.[6] From these inscriptions we get to know about the name and status of the donor and the donee, the specifications of the grant or gift, the occcasion and the purpose of the gift, the various social groups involved in economic transaction and also the economic and administrative immunities attached to such grants. These various aspects helped us in comprehending the importance of land grants as a mechanism of appropriation of land revenues by different levels of state power, transfer of ownership rights, the nature of peasant labour, mode of exchange between various segments of society and the religious institutions, the spread of new kinds of settlements and most importantly, the role of state in all these activities, which explain the economic variable adopted by ruling elites in the consolidation of the power. (Chart IVA, IVB, & Vx y, z).

Economic structure in the early medieval period has been characterised by some scholars by the prevalence of dominant features discerned in the decline of trade, commerce and urban life, and the consequent growth of self-sufficient economy which was largely agrarian in character. Further, in this view the relative scarcity of metallic coins during this period had necessiated that the rulers hence forward make all the payments in the form of land grants and revenues to priests and other officials in return for the services they have rendered to the state. Hence, these scholars emphasized on the external factors for the internal transformation of society and economy.[7] As an alternative to this view some of the recent writings have emphasised on the breakdown of the early historical civilization which was envisaged in the internal social contradictions. An attempt has been made in these writings to show that a deep social crisis was pressaging the process of feudalism of Indian society. This was manifested in the descriptions of the Kaliyuga texts and in various epic and purāṇic passages datable to the third and early fourth centuries A.D. One way to redress this class antgonism was to find new mechanism of surplus extraction. Subsequently, the state began to assign land revenues directly to priests, military chiefs, administrators for their support.[8]

Such a mechanism of transfer of land of various sizes to variety of donees helped the king to appropriate the surplus in the form of rent.[9] Further, this process also brought under purview the question of land ownership rights. It can be said that the donation of land necessarily led to a significant change in the land ownership patterns.

Prior to this historiographical position, traditional scholarship held that in the legal texts of the period, it was indicated that the entire land belonged to the ruling authority. This theory of royal ownership was justified through the practice of donating large-scale land grants to priests and temples, vassals and officials, in return for their services.[10] Pertinently, due to this development there arose the question of multiplicity of rights held over land by different sections of people such as the *Rāja, the Svāmin*, and the *Karṣaka.*[11] Thus, as was conceived by the medieval Indian jurists, ownership rights in landed property was duly sub-divided into the *Svatva* of property rights of the king, the *Svatva* those of the land owners, the *Svatva* of the tenant farmer etc., within their respective boundaries.[12]

As new rulers in an alien land, the Eastern Chālukyan rulers had to encounter with the already existing owners of land at different levels, such as the cultivators of the land (*Kutumbins*), the controllers of the cultivators namely the *Grāmabhōgikas* who acted as intermediaries and the different levels of the state officials such as the *Vishayapatis* and *Rāshtrakūtas.* Since land during this period was shared between these three levels of competitors, naturally the revenues would also be shared by them, though the share of the produce was not equal and considerably differed from landed peasantry to that of the cultivators, who got the meagre share.[13] The existence of such ceaseless competition between these three categories would obviously bring into question the rights of the conqueror as the owner of the entire land. The *Smṛti* and the *Dharmaśāstra* texts have approved the ownership of land by the conqueror. This would certainly entail the Eastern Chālukyan rulers as the owners of the conquered kingdom of Vengi. Further, this also entrusted them with the right to dispose the land at their own will.[14]

In phase I, Eastern Chālukyan rulers as new comers in an alien land, after establishing themselves politically through military conquests, which had already been discussed in Chapter II, had adopted certain new economic mechanisms to stabilize their political and economic powers. Politically, it has been discussed in Chapter II, how the ruling elites pacified local chiefs through economic mechanism of donating land grants. Therefore, our main concern in this chapter is to understand the economic mechanism of integration of economy and various social groups into the state structure as this would necessarily involve the study of nature of land grants and other resources made by the ruling elites, to various social groups.

As conquerors of an alien land, the first and foremost task before the ruling elites was to consolidate their power and accumulate resources through which they attempted to strengthen the economic base of the newly formed state structure. Initially, this was made possible through the mechanism of reinstating some of the conquered local chiefs on stipulated conditions of payment of regular tributes to the State. This not only made these local chiefs to remain subordinate and loyal but also helped the new rulers to appropriate revenues to the State. Secondly, stabilization of power was sought through granting of land in the form of *agrahāras* and villages to various *brāhmaṇas* and other powerful local chiefs such as the Dūrjayas of Giripaschimasima and the Mastyas of Oddadi. Further, the new ruling elites imported large number of *brāhmaṇas* from their native place into the conquered region of Vengi. Most of these *brāhmaṇas* were conferred with land grants.[15]

In phase I as the powerful ruling elites of the Vengi region we find that most of the land grants were being donated by the kings of the main ruling family (Chart IVA, ii, 1-8, 9-19,21-27). The only instance where the donor is mentioned to be queen was the lpur plates (Chart IVA, ii, 20). Almost all the grants that were made by the ruling elites were given to the members of the *brāhmaṇa varṇa*. This is indicated by the use of the appellation *Śarman, Śvamin, Bhaṭṭāraka* which are suffixed to their names (Chart IVA, iii,1-27). It has been noted in the inscriptions during this phase that most of these grants were given only to those *brāhmaṇas* who have mastered in all the sciences, *vēdas, śāstras and smṛtis.* According to R.S. Sharma, donations to such highly scholared *brāhmaṇas* is significant as these grantees brought new knowledge which improved cultivation and at the same time inculcated in the aborigines a sense of loyalty to the established order which was upheld by the rulers, who could therefore dispense with the service of extra staff for maintaining law and order.[16] However, it has been postulated that the most important function of the immigrated *brāhmaṇa* was to provide religio-political legitimation to the new ruling elites. This has been regarded by Kulke as "an urgent necessity inorder to claim a regular system of imposts and later, revenues. This happened in different ways. One way for the *brāhmaṇas* was to create genealogies connecting to the mythical past. Further, *brāhmaṇas* vested the new ruler with the paraphernalia of Hindu royalty".[17]

It is interesting to note that during this phase apart from *brāhmaṇas* we also find some of the bōya priests being conferred with land grants which are chiefly in the form of *agrahāra* villages. Bōyas were actually the aboriginal tribes inhabiting the border regions of the present day Nellore District. Their primary pursuits were in hunting and gathering.

The ethnographic accounts of the British officials described them as an 'old fighting caste'.[18] Because of their militant character and their prowess in fighting, the services of the bōyas was deemed necessary by the new ruling elites to consolidate their power in an alien land. Subsequently, a considerable number of bōya priests were given land grants in the form of *agrahāra* villages. This process of donating land to bōyas through acculturation, necessarily led to their elevation to higher *varṇa* status in the brāhmaṇical ideology.[19]

The earliest reference to bōyas is found in the Kondanāguru grant of Indravarman (Chart IVA, iii, 12). It mentions the bōyas as witnesses of the grant and also contains their signatures. This reveals the recognition of the high socio-economic status of the bōyas in the village of Kondanāguru.[20] However, it is in the Rēyūru grant[21] of Vishnuvardhana II (673-681 A.D.) and the Chendalūru grant[22] of Sarvalōkāśraya Mangi Yuvarāja that we come to know about the bōyas being conferred with land grants. This is attested from the names of the *brāhmaṇa* donees that are suffixed with the term *bōya.* This process indicates the first attempt of the Eastern Chālukyas to breakup the solidarity of the bōyas as a separate group, and reconcile some of them to their newly established rule through conferring land grants to their priests. The bōyas also had to be placated on the political front as they acted as the buffers between their own kingdom and the troublesome *kottams* of the Pallava kingdom.[23]

Therefore, the *brāhmaṇa* immigration, on the one hand, and the bōya settlement on the other, reveal that the main concern of the state was not only the migration of upper castes, but it also recognised the services of the tribals and other lower castes as essential for society. The services of the former were used chiefly for creating a congenial atmosphere for pacification and integration, and the latter for the expansion and stabilization of the state.[24]

Most of the land donations that were made by ruling elites in phase I consisted of a plot of land or a field or a village or several plots. Inscriptions during this phase describe the founding of new *brāhmaṇa* villages by converting some portions of land or villages into *agrahāras. Agrahāras* were actually described as tax free grants. The other forms in which land was donated in phase I are noted to be in the form of villages (Chart IVA, iv, 2,4,12,14,18,21,26,27) fields, house-sites (Chart IVA, iv, 20,25). In some cases land was donated by certain measurements mentioned as *nivartanas* (Chart IVA, iv, 1,8) *Puttis* (Chart IVA, iv, 5) and *Khāndis* or *Khāndikas* (Chart IVA, iv, 19,23,25). But these occur only in few grants. From these various types of land endowments, we came to know that most of the land grants during this phase are bigger in size. This will further explains the State's attempts to bring more virgin land under cultivation. It has been noticed that the inscriptions of this Phase showed that most of the land endowments that were made by the ruling elites appear to be already settled villages. This was presumed based on the information furnished in the inscriptions on the witnesses and executors who were present during land transactions. During this phase inscriptions mention about the existence of dominant social groups such as the *vishayapatis, sāmantas, grāma-bhōgikas, mahattaras, rāshtrakūtas* and *niyōgikas*. Also the ***kutumbins*** or the cultivators were mentioned as those who constituted the majority of the village population. (Chart IIA, vi, 2-27). *Vishayapatis* are the governors of a district called Vishaya. *Sāmantas* were the military chiefs. *Grāma-bhōgikas* are described as one who enjoyed the village as a free-holding, which implies that he is exempted from all taxes and at the same time probably held rights on the land. *Mahattaras*, are the village headman. *Kutumbis* were the actual cultivators or ryots who cultivated the land and were required to pay taxes. *Rāshtrakūtas* are the village headman who are also interpreted as a land holders. *Naiyogikas* are officers incharge of administrative unit. It has been noted that the officials present during land transactions are noticed to be relatively lesser in number in this phase. In most of the land grants, Executors were specifically mentioned signifying the important role they played in enacting land grants to various donees. This clearly indicates that there existed a hierarchy of officials administering the villages they inhabited. Thus, they necessarily acted as important levels between the State and the villages.

It is observed that the ruling elites converted some of these already settled villages as *agrahāras* which are exempted from the payment of all kinds of taxes (Chart IIA, v, 3,6,7,10,11). Generally, in most of the *agrahāras*, the *brāhmaṇās* did not plough the land for themselves. They frequently leased out the land to the Kutumbis who cultivated these lands and at the same time paid the revenues to the State. However ,sometimes when *brāhmaṇa* villages were founded in the virgin lands, some scholars postulated that the rulers may have assigned groups of agricultural labourers to them to clear and develop these lands.[25]

On the other hand some of the lands that were donated to *brāhmaṇas* appeared to be unsettled villages. This has been inferred from the absence of witnesses who generally present themselves while the land was being transacted. (Chart IVA, 5,1,5,13,18,26). Unsettled villages were usually given by the ruler, in far off places from the regions where they had strong base. This can be exemplified from inscriptions wherein we find that far off places from the core area of Vengi were used to be donated. For example Timmapuram, Chipurupalli, Nidupāru, Rēyūru, (MAP IV) and other places are located far off from the core region of Vengi appears to be an unsettled land. The main concern of ruling elites in giving land grants in far off unsettled aeas was related to their political and economic concerns of statilization of power.[26]

Interestingly, some of the inscriptions during this phase mention that villages were apportioned into shares among *brāhmaṇas* or groups of *brāhmaṇas.* The shares of land was not necessarily divided into equal parts as sometimes some *brāhmaṇas* are mentioned to have got more shares than the others (Chart IVA, iii, 1,13,15,27). According to Honore this method of apportioning land among several beneficiaries corresponded to "split ownership", in which large number of people held their rights in land.[27]

Further, it has been noticed that some of the grants made to *brāhmaṇas* need not necessarily be *agrahāra* villages which were tax free grants, but in some cases villages were given which were probably tax paying. This supposition can be buttressed from the fact that most of these village grants were not stipulated with the economic immunities mentioned in inscriptions such as *Sarvakara Parihāra* (Chart IVA, vii, 2,3,6,7,11,13,21-25,27) and *Sarva Siddhidatti* (Chart IVA, vii, 10) which means a tax free *agrahāra.* Similarly, some grants did not carry along with them administrative immunities such as *anavamarśyam* meaning not to cause obstruction to the grants, (Chart IVA, vii, 3, 11, 23) which are usually specified while the *agrahāra* villages were granted. It can be presumed that probably it was from these villages that the State accumulated resources that provided economic base to the State in phase I, as the *agrahāra* villages were tax free and the revenue would go in this regard to the landed intermediaries and officials of the State, rather than to the State.

The land that was donated during this phase reveal the emerging agrarian character of the Eastern Chālukyan economy. This is inferred from the inscriptions of this phase which show that certain amount of land was given for sowing 12 Khandis of grain or paddy and some times 8 Khandis of land are mentioned as being donated (Chart IVA, iv, 18,23,25). This implies that paddy constituted the main crop during the Chālukyan period. This further, reveal that considerable extent of fertile tracts or nuclear zones were acculturated through land donations. Further, there was also mention of flower gardens being donated (Chart IVA, iv, 19). This shows that there was a considerable amount of `cultivable waste land' which was used for developing flower gardens.[28] To understand the nature of economy that had emerged during phase I of our study, we have examined the nature of settlement patterns during this phase.

The settlement patterns in Phase I reveal that the majority of the settlements were suffixed with `*ūru* (Chart IVA, iv, 1, 4, 7, 11, 12, 13, 16, 19, 23, 27), *vāti* or vāda (Chart IVA, iv, 4, 5, 10, 17, 20, 25), and *Palli* (Chart IVA, iv, 3). These suffixes indicate tribal or small village hamlets and connotes the existence of largely rural settlements. Interestingly, during this phase *Pura* occurs thrice in the form of Chērupura (Chart IVA, iv, 3), Āsanapura (Chart IVA, iv, 4) and Pistapura (Chart IVA, iv, 26). These indicate the existence of a settlement larger than a village settlement.These are an indicative of being a military camp rather than an urban centre or town, as no numismatic evidence is found here, suggesting the existence of trade and commerce. Further, inscriptions also mention them as military camps from where the ruling elites issued grants. Most of the settlements in phase I are noticed to have located in the Krishna-Godavari basin (MAP IV) which has been discussed by us in Chapter II as constituting a fertile region that has been called by Subba Rao as "a nuclear area of attraction". This also probably indicates that the ruling elites during this phase consciously granted villages in new cultivable lands thereby enabling them to control the economic surplus of these lands. It is interesting to note that one of the grants of Jayasimha Vallabha I mentions an *ādivāsa* village (Chart IVA, iv, 7). It has been mentioned in this grant that the western portion of the *Ādivāsa* village and some of the fields in Gudivāda were adjoined together and were constituted as an *agrahāra*. The term *ādivāsa* is understood as a tribal settlement. This, then clearly indicates the acculturation of tribal settlements by converting them into villages. This process of acculturation of pastoral villages suggests to a substantially pastoral and agrarian economy co-existed during phase I.

From this analysis in Phase I, it is understood that transfer of ownership rights to *brāhmaṇas* and other powerful pastoral communities like *bōyas* did not necessarily lead to the loss of these privileges by the king, as was postulated by the Marxist scholars. On the other hand it can be argue that though the creation of *agrahāras* did not lead to appropriation of revenue by the State as most of these were tax free and the revenue would go to the local landed intermediaries. However the main concern of the ruling elites in phase I was to devolve upon the *brāhmaṇas* the difficult task of creating validity for the `royal' rights in their settlements and also other neighbouring villages.[29] Also *brāhmaṇas* constructed elaborated genealogies for ruling elites and provided legitimation to their rule. Further, contestation by existing agricultural groups was numbed by the role of the *brāhmaṇas* as leaders of the new ideology of the State. Simultaneously, *agrahāras* also helped in developing a village-level administration necessary for the implementation of royal demands.[30]

On the other hand, the study of nature of grants in Phase II, reflect a significant change with regard to the status of the donor, donee and nature of grants which necessarily effected the nature of economy that prevailed during this phase. Having acculturated most of the fertile tracts of the Krishna, Godavari basin which considerably helped in the extension of the kingdom, and also stabilized their power in the newly created settlements the main concern of the ruling elites in this phase was to appropriate more revenues to the State. This was essential for the State to meet its growing military expenditure, as this phase witnessed constant wars between the Eastern Chālukyan rulers and other contending neighbouring rulers. Therefore, the very purpose of making land donations during this phase appeared to be distinct from Phase I where the ruling elites made land grants to seek ideological support and simultaneously attempted to augment the rural agrarian economy.

A glance at the inscriptions during this phase show that though the majority of donations were made by the members of the main ruling family comprising chiefly kings (Chart IVB, ii, 28, 30, 34-35, 37, 43, 46-51, 53-58, 60, 61) however, some of the inscrptions shows that grants were also made by ministers (Chart IVB, iii, 33) and queens (Chart IVB, iii, 31). Some of the grants were made by the rulers at the request of feudatory chiefs and other favourities of the king (Chart IVB, ii, 33,45,52). This indicates that the prerogative of making land grants during this phase was confined not only to the members of the main ruling dynasty, namely the kings but was also enjoyed by other dominant social groups of the society who made donations of land. Similarly, in this phase the nature of donees is also found to be distinct from Phase I. In this phase it has been noticed that most of the land grants that were made was not exclusively confined to the *brāhmaṇa varṇa* which was the case in the earlier phase. Apart from the *brāhmaṇas* as major recipients (Chart IVB, iii, 28,30-33,42,44,46), we have instances in the inscriptions showing merchant guilds (Chart IVB, iii, 35,58), warriors (Chart IVB, iii, 39-41), ministers (Chart IVB, iii, 44, 54, 56), women musicians (Chart IBV, iii, 34,51) and Jain and brāhmaṇical temples (Chart IVB, iii, 29,47,49,60) as receiving grants. Endowments to bōyas continued even in this phase (Chart IVB, iii, 59). The increasing political constraints during this period had necessiated the ruling elites to confer grants to warriors, generals and other parties as well as to temples as they provided political and ideological support to the State. Most of the grants were created as service tenements. This resulted in emergence of a class of warriors as land holders which is seen in the rise of the *Sāmanta* system which according to B.N.S. Yadava became the key word of Indian Feudalism.[31] These *sāmantas* apart from paying yearly tributes also rendered military services to the State. The system did emerge out of a decentralization of the Chālukyan State but rather can be looked upon as a means of integrating different localities conquered into an economically viable system of political governance. Further, there was a proliferation of these grants in the second phase, since we note that the donee after receiving his due portion of land, in turn, in his capacity as a donor made a grant of some portion of the acquired land to other persons. This process is strongly indicative of the proposition that there existed private property in land. Thus, for instance, inscriptions (Chart IVA, ii, 9, 16), (Chart IVB, ii,32,36) that show the transfer of landed property of both the donor and the donee explains the complicated nature of rights held in private property of land.

The nature of grants that were donated to these various donees differed considerably in their size. While in Phase I most of the grants appear to be big in size, in Phase II it has been noticed that villages were frequently apportioned or only land of small size was donated. The mention of the terms such as *Khandi* occurs more frequently (Chart IVB, iv, 28,29,37,46). Apart from *agrahāras* as major land grants we also find a variety of grants being donated such as fields, tax on *ēruvāka khara, dhavana* etc. (Chart IVB, iv, 33), *vrittis* (Chart IVB, iv, 33), *mānya* (Chart IVB, iv, 44), hamlets or small villages (Chart IVB, iv, 41), alms-houses (*sattra*) (Chart IVB, iv, 47), donation of betel (Chart IVB, iv, 58) and gift of lamp, cattle, ghee to the deity in the temple (Chart IVB, iv, 56) were also being donated by the ruling elites and other social groups of the society, in the second Phase. This substantially explains in explicit terms the changes perceived in the nature of grants made from "*villages*" and "*agrahāras*" to ultimately commodities. This has to be closely linked to who the donor was. In the first phase, it has been noted that the donors largely constituted from the main ruling family whose primary concern was to expand and consolidate their political and economic power. Therefore, they made large donations in the form of land. However, in the second phase there was the gradual decline in the donations of large lands which only indicates that the numerous villages that were donated in the earlier phase had by now created a powerful class of landed aristocracy. Secondly, it also reflects the declining power of the king as the owner of the land grants. Grants were continued to be made by ruling elites but during this period only small portions of land was granted. Apart from this a variety of commodities were also donated depending on the economic capacity of the donor. Most of the grants that were donated to *brāhmaṇas* were mostly villages and *agrahāras* which are apportioned even in this phase. Further, even in this phase we find some of the land grants were not being mentioned with economic and administrative immunities (Chart IVB, 28,29,31,32,36,46,49,55-59). Interestingly, it has been noted in Phase II that some of the land grants made to the warriors, merchants, mucisians, also carried along with them certain economic and administrative immunities. (Chart IVB, 34,35,37,39-41,45,47,49,51,60). At the time when the State's power was becoming fragile due to external threats and the rise of fissiparious tendencies within, the kingdom, such tax-free grants to these various social groups indicates the necessity of the ruling elites to make these grants as they rendered military support, wealth and political stability to the State.

The period between 10th and 11th centuries A.D. is regarded as crucial for the State. During this period, the State made constant attempts to assert its authority and for that reason evolved a new mechanism to increase its rental income. Since most of the grants in earlier phase were created into numerous free holdings this appeared to be a fiscal constraint on the growth of political authority in the second phase. This might explain the growing patronage of temple institution and corresponding decline in the patronage of *brahmadēyas* and *agrahāras*. Unlike the free holdings the temples replenished the revenues of the State besides providing a stronger basis of legitimization.[32] Therefore, in this phase land grants to temples and religious priests become more apparent (Chart IVB, iii, 29,45,47,49,60) than in Phase I.

In contrast to the study of the grants made by the main ruling family, in Phase II we have also attempted to look at the nature of grants under the Minor Chālukyan families of Mudigonda, Jananāthapuram and

Nidadavōlu, and this enabled us to understand the economic integration of local economies into the larger economic structure of the state through mobilization of resources. In the earlier chapters it has been discussed that politically and ideologically these minor Chālukyan families owed their allegiance to the Eastern Chālukyas. Though these minor ruling families enjoyed semi-independent status, they did recognize the suzerainity of the Eastern Chālukyan rulers. This can also be seen in the way the minor Chālukyan economy was integrated into the larger economic structures of the Eastern Chālukyan economy.

Interestingly, it has been noted that the grants that were made by the Mudigonda Chālukyan family were in the form of land donations. The limited number of inscriptions that were available for this family show that the donors included not only the rulers of the family (Chart Vx ii, 3,4) but also subordinate chief (Chart Vx, iii,1) and a *pergere* or *Preggaḍa* (Chart Vx, ii, 7). The donations that these minor chiefs made were in the form of *agrahāras* granted chiefly to the *brāhmaṇas.* This indicates that the minor Chālukyan family of Mudigonda was a powerful local family that exercised considerable influence in its locality. On the other hand, the grants made by the other minor Chālukyan families of Jananāthapuram and Nidadavōlu differed both in terms of the donors, donees and nature of donations, from those of Chālukyas of Mudigonda and the Eastern Chālukyan grants. The study of grants of these two families show that apart from the members of the rulers of these minor families (Chart Vy, ii, 13-15), we come to know about the donations being made by other social groups of the society such as queens (Chart Vy, 2,ii, 5-8, 10-b), man-Mahamandalēśwaras (Chart Vz, ii, 17,19,22), *Preggaḍa* (Chart Vz, ii, 20), merchant (Chart Vy, iuii, 11), prince (Chart Vy, ii, 12). This indicates that by this time a considerable majority of other social groups were becoming prominent. This also reveals their rising socio-economic status in the society.

Most of the grants that were donated to the deity in temples by these social groups were in the form of commodities. The items of donations were in the form of perpetual lamp (akhandadīpam) gifted along with cows, in order to supply ghee. The usual custom was to donate 50 cows for an *akhandadīpam* (full lamp) (Chart Vy, iv, 5-10), (Chart Vz, iv, 16,17,20,21) and 30 or 25 for an *aradīpam* (half lamp) (Chart Vz, iv, 19). This clearly shows pastoral nature of the minor Chālukyan economy.

Further, the crop patterns in this phase reveal that most of the crops that were grown constituted chiefly paddy, as the grants mention of land donations being made to grow paddy. (Chart IVB, iv, 28,29,37,46). This indicates that a substantial portion of rich rice producing zones were brought under cultivation.[33] With the emergence of temple, betel leaves and areca-nuts started gaining importance as they essentially served the ritual purpose in the temple. (Chart IVB, iv, 37)

In order to understand the nature of economy in Phase II which has been regarded as distinct from Phase I, the study of the nature of settlements that existed in Phase II is important as this will necessarily help us to distinguish the nature of economy in both the phases. The differential characters and typologies of settlements such as *'Ūru' 'Grāma', 'Vāda'* which are observed in phase I are also found in majority of the inscriptions in Phase II (Chart IBV, iv, 28-61). By this time a large number of nuclear agrarian areas were integrated. The interesting phenomenon observed during this phase was the emergence of new temple settlemnts such as Drakshārāmam, (Chart Vz, i, 17,22), Bhīmavaram (Chart Vy, i, 12, 13), Ganapavaram (Chart Vz, i, 10), (MAP IV) which came to prominent picture under the grants made by the minor Chālukyan families.

Most of these temple settlements seem to have been situated away from the areas where these minor Chālukyan families controlled. Further most of these temples were constructed and patronized by the Eastern Chālukyan rulers in the fertile tracts of the Godavari basin (MAP IV). This indicates that the minor Chālukyan rulers accepted the legitimation of the Vengi Chālukyas. At the same time this also led to acculturate their economy, which is substantially pastoral in nature, as the grants they made were mostly from the surplus of the pastoral economy, with that of the economy of the Vengi rulers which was emerging as a full-fledged agrarian economy. In this context temple emerged as an integrating force of various pastoral and tribal communities into the State and acted as a legitimizer of political power and thereby helped in extending the horizon of the State's authority.[34]

Further, land grants to temples and *brāhmaṇas* in certain key *agrahāras* is also seen as an important mechanism as it led to the growth of temple centred commodity production.[35] Most of the temple settlements are noted to have located along sea coast such as Drākshārāmam, Pithāpuram. This facilitated revival of tendencies that indicated growth of trade and markets. Some grants that were made to merchant groups such as traders, oil mongers (Telikis) (Chart IVB, iii, 35,58), supports our arguement that the agrarian economy was developing to be able to sustain trade and commerce during this period. This view is further buttressed by the discovery of hoards of gold coins belonging to the Eastern Chālukyan rulers especially from the reign of Śaktivarman I.[36] From the study of these temple settlements and nature of grants, we concluded that the Eastern Chālukyan economy during this phase was not a full fledged urban economy as the process of urbanization had been just started. This happened in a few select areas. However, in some sub-regions its character was different as it was not a fully developed agrarian economy, since it was still dominated by pastoral and agrarian social groups.

Based on this information available in the inscriptions it can concluded that grants were continued to be made to pastoral and tribal groups like the *bōyas* and secondly, most of the grants made to temples especially by the minor Chālukyan rulers was surplus from the pastoral economy. All these helped the State to economically integrate diverse regions and people.

Our next focus, in this phase was on the role of social groups involved in land transactions. The inscriptions during this phase show that there was a considerable increase in the number of officials present during the land transactions to various beneficiaries. Apart from those mentioned in Phase I, we have in addition officials such as *mantri, purōhita, yuvarāja, dauvārika* and *pradhāna* (Chart IVB, vi, 51,56,58), Chart Vy, v, 13,14). *Mantri* has been interpreted as a Minister, *Purōhita* as priest, and *dauvārika* as a door-keeper. Further *Kutumbins* are again mentioned as witnesses of the grants as they were the actual cultivating peasantry in the villages. These officials and village headmen controlled administration at the local village levels. They were the executors and village kutumbins were the witnesses of the grant. They acted as channel between the main rulers and the village through economic linkages of tax collection and were indeed an important lever of state control.

It has been noticed by R.S. Sharma and other scholars that most of the land grants made to the *brāhmaṇas* during the early medieval period carried along with them certain economic immunities.[37] The study of fiscal and administrative immunities in both the phases such as exemption from the payment of taxes and the transfer of all dues to the *brāhmaṇa* intermediaries, meant that they wielded considerable economic and political powers in their localities. In both the phases, the ruling elites made land grants which were exempted from the payment of all taxes. This is indicated by the use of such terms as *Sarva-*

Karaparihāra (Chart IVA) and *Sarvasiddhidatti* (Chart IVA, vii, II) which means a tax free *agrahāra.* Similarly, in the Phase II, apart from some of the land being exempted from tax payment, we have the mention of certain terms which indicates the forms of taxes from which the donee was exempted. They are *Siddhaya* which is a regular or agricultural income, *abhinava* which was a kind of cess or a tax. *Krīdara-śulka* and *avēndayas* were further mentioned as names of taxes. The mention of these tax names indicates that these were the popular taxes from which the state received its revenues. The inscriptions, however, are not clear on the issue of how these taxes were distributed. While most of the grants that were donated to *brāhmaṇas* were made tax-free, on the other hand, the non-mention of such specificities of economic immunities in a larger majority of inscriptions suggests that the State received its income from the villages. R.S. Sharma has postulated that such transfer of fiscal immunities to *brāhmaṇa* donees had its far reaching implications on the social structure of the early medieval period. It has been noticed that the growth of land owners in the *agrahāra* villages led to the subjection of peasantry through the forceful collection of multiplicity of taxes which are often not clearly mentioned when the grant was made. In other words, it was left to the discretion of the donees to exact taxes as they wished. This clearly alludes to uncertainities being faced by the peasant cultivators. It is interesting to notice that we do not find the direct mention of *viṣti* in the Eastern Chālukyan inscriptions. However, this does not necessarily mean that there was a total absence of *viṣti* in the early medieval Andhra country. Since, as B.N.S. Yadava puts it, the non-mention of *viṣti* in the inscriptions does not imply that there was no forced labour.[38] This conclusion was derived by Yadava as some grants refer significantly to the transfer of peasants without any land or village along with them, to a god. They revealed the continuous process of coercive labour, the dependence of peasants and the increasing restrictions on their mobility. The multiple taxes that were forcefully collected from the peasants, who were in fact the actual cultivators of land clearly indicates the existence of a tax payer. It was often the taxes that were collected from the peasants in the largely non-beneficial tenure areas that constituted the income of the State.

The extensive economic privileges, thus granted to donees were further reinforced by various administrative immunities attached to the grant. This is indicated by the mention of terms such as not to cause obstruction to the grant *anavamarśyam,* (Chart IVA, 3,11,23) (Chart IVB, 30,31,44,51,54) *apravēśyam* not to be entered by soldiers (Chart IVB, vii, 53) are indicators to this tendency. However, it has been noticed that not many grants were clearly specified with administrative immunities. These administrative immunities helped the donees to exercise effective political and economic control over the stratified peasantry. Further, the mention of such ideological imprecations at the end of the grants such as the violation of the grant would be punished by a sixty thousand years in hell, and preserving the grant would be rewarded by the same number of years in heaven were all effective means by which the donee kept control over the people in the donated areas. Such threats were deemed necessary to subdue the peasantry against their exploitation. This would suggest the State's objective may have been not to transfer complete rights over land and still maintain some control over the donated lands. An important question that has to be posed in this connection is whether the non-transfer of administrative immunities suggests the check on the exploitation of subject peasantry from the landed intermediaries? This may not have been the case because in terms of economic immunities the donees have considerable power. This would suggest one of the mechanisms of the ruling elites to maintain peace and tranquility in the country, by preventing any sort of contestation to their power both from the landed intermediaries and the peasant classes.

The ostensible purpose for which most of the grants made in the early medieval period, were not for rendering civil and military services but for economic and spiritual purpose. In the inscriptions, it has been noticed that there was an interesting change in the purpose for which the grants were made by the ruling elites. The ostensible purpose for which the land grants were made during the first phase, was mainly for the increase of king's own religious merit, for the acquisition of reputation, good health and longevity of life. (Chart IVA, v, 2,3,6,14,15,18). Occasionally, land was granted for religious purpose also. The Satāra copper plate grant of Kubja Vishnuvardhana I states that the grant was made for the purpose of maintaining the five great sacrifices of the *bali, chāru, vaiśvadēva, agnihōtra and havane.* The purpose for which grants were made in the first phase were mainly for the acquisition of personal and material benefits. On the other hand in Phase II, the inscriptions clearly state the purpose for which these grants were made is quite different from what has been noticed in the earlier phase. During this phase most of the grants were made irrespective of caste and class considerations. The grants that were made to secular persons such as warriors was mainly in recognition of the services rendered by them and as mark of loyalty and obedience. (Chart IVB, v, 34,40). The temples were given grants, during this phase, for maintaining dining halls and to undertake the necessary repairs (Chart IVB, v, 45,47,48), and for offering *bali, naivēdya* and music to the God (Chart IVB, v, 49).

However, this information blurs the real motive for making grants which were understood to be far more complex and related to many issues of ownership rights in the country side, methods and mode of agricultural expansion and finally interest of the State in getting revenue which underlines the economic processes that the ruling elites had to address as a means for resource mobilization and stabilization of power. Thus, we conclude that the economy during this period in both phases was in transition wherein a full fledged agrarian economy was in the process of establishing its hold over major nuclear areas. In some areas the pastoral groups continued to dominate whereas in others, like major *agrahāras* settlements, the temple grew to become the nuclei of a market indulging in non-agrarian activity.

Reference

1. R.S. Sharma, *Indian Feudalism*, New Delhi, 1980 (1ed 1965) pp. 2ff.
2. Romila Thapar, "*Dāna and Dakṣina* as forms of Exchange" an *AISH*, New Delhi, 1978, p. 106.
3. *Ibid*, p. 118.
4. B.V. Krishna Rao, *Eastern Chalukyas of Vengi*, Hyderabad, 1978, p. 47.
5. B.V. Suba Rao, *The Personality of India, Pre and Proto-Historic foundation of India and Pakistan*, Baroda, 1958, p. 85.
6. D.C. Sircar, *Indian Epigraphy*, Delhi, 1965, p. 134.
7. D.N. Jha, "Early Indian Feudalism - A Historiographical Critique", Presidential Address, *PIHC*, 40 ss, Waltair, 1979, p. 20.
8. B.D. Chattopadhyaya, *The Making of Early Medieval India*, New Delhi, 1994, pp. 3-4.
9. D.N. Jha, *Op.Cit.*, 1979, p. 20.
10. R.S. Sharma, *Op.Cit.*, 1965, p. 124.
11. *Ibid*, p. 124.

12. B.N.S. Yadava, *Society and Culture in Northern India, in the 12th century A.D.,* Allahabad, 1973, p. 257.
13. Dharma Kumar, 'Private Property in Asia?", The Case of Medieval South India,' *CSSH,* vol. 27, No.2, April, 1985, pp. 341-42.
14. Y. Kumaraswamy, 'Traces of Feudalism during the Eastern Chalukyan period' *PAPHC,* Warangal, 1983, p. 30.
15. B.S.L. Hanumantha Rao, *Social Mobility in Medieval Andhra,* Hyderabad, 1995, p. 37.
16. R.S. Sharma, *Op. cit.,* 1865, p. 281.
17. Hermann Kulke, 'The Early and the Imperial Kingdom: A Processural Model of Integrative State Formation in Early Medieval India', In Hermann Kulke (ed) *The State in India, 1000-1700,* New Delhi, 1995, pp. 239-240.
18. P.S. Kanaka Durga and Y.A. Sudhakar Reddy, 'Kings Temples and Legitimation of Autochthonous Communities, *JESHO,* vol. XXV, 1992, p. 159.
19. Suvira Jaiswal 'Studies in Early Indian Social History: Trends and possibilities', *IHR,* vol. VI, 1979-80, p. 27.
20. B.S.L. Hanumantha Rao, *Op.cit.,* 1995, p. 40.
21. *IA,* vol. VII, 1878, pp. 185-191.
22. *EI,* Vol. VIII, 1905-06, pp. 236-241.
23. B.S.L. Hanumantha Rao, *Op.cit.,* 1995, p. 40.
24. P.S. Kanaka Durga and Y.A. Sudhakar Reddy, *Op.cit.,* 1992, p. 161.
25. Dharma Kumar, *Op.cit.,* 1985, p. 348.
26. *Ibid,* p. 344.
27. *Ibid,* p. 351.
28. P.S. Kanaka Durga and Y.A. Sudhakar Reddy, *Op.cit.,* 1992, p. 149.
29. Hermann Kulke, *Op.cit.,* 1995, p. 243.
30. *Ibid,* p. 243.
31. B.N.S. Yadava, *Op.cit.,* 1973, p. 136.
32. R.N. Nandi, 'Growth of Rural Economy in Early Feudal India' Presidential Address, PIHC 45th session, 1984, p. 17.
33. P.S. Kanaka Durga and Y.A. Sudhakar Reddy, *Op.cit.,* pp. 163-164.

34. *Ibid*, p. 147.
35. R. Champalakshmi, 'Urbanization in Medieval Tamil Nadu', in S. Bhattacharya and Romila Thapar (ed), *Situating Indian History*, Delhi, 1986, p. 37-38.
36. B.D. Chattopadhyaya, *Coins and currency system in south India (C.A.D. 225-1300)* 1977, p. 31.
37. R.S. Sharma, *Op.cit.*, 1965, pp. 2-4.
38. B.N.S. Yadava, *Op.cit.*, 1973, p. 172.

CHART - IVA

NATURE OF GRANTS - PHASE I (7TH C.A.D. - 9TH C.A.D.)

S. No.	*Name of the Incription/Date*	*Donor/Status*	*Donee/Status*	*Nature of Grant/Location*	*Purpose of Grant*	*Witnesses/ Executors*	*Economic/ Adminstrative immunities*	*Reference*
1.	Timmāpuram plates (624-641 A.D.)	Kubja Viṣṇuvar-dhana I. (MR)	40 (BR) of Chhandōga school	4000 (Niv) of (L) Kumūlūra (V) Paḷaki (Vis)	—	—	—	*EI*, Vol. IX, 1907-08, pp. 317-319.
2.	Satāra Copper Plate Grant 632 A.D.)	Kubja Viṣṇuvar-dhana I (MR)	Achalaśvāmin Vēdaśvāmin Dēvaśvāmin Adityaśvamin Nāgakumāra of Ghritakauśika Gōtra	Alandatīrtha (V) Śrīnilaya Bhōga	For self merit and maintenance of 5 sacrifices	*Vishayapatis, Samanatas, Grāmabhōgi-kas, Mahatt-aras & Kutum-bins*	*SKPH, Apravēśyam*	*IA*, Vol. XIX, 1891, pp. 310-311
3	Chipurupalle Copper plate grant (624-661 A.D.)	Kubja Viṣṇuvar-dhana I (MR)	Viṣṇu Śarman, Mādhava Śarman of Taittirīya Charaṇa, Gautama Gōtra (BR)	Kālvakoṇḍa (V) converted into (A) Dimili (Vis) Cheṛpura (Taluk)	For self merit	*Kutumbis* of Kālvakoṇḍa Aṭavidūrjaya as (AP)	*SKPH, Anavamarśyam*	*IA*, Vol. XX, 1891, pp.17-18
4	Niḍūparu grant (641-673 A.D.)	Jayasiṁha I (MR)	Kāṭiśarman of Taittirīya (Charaṇa) Hārīti Gōtra	Niduparu (V) Gaṇḍēruvāti (Vis) Grant issued from Āsanapura	—	(BR) Minister of the king (AP)	—	*EI*, Vol. VIII, 1925-26. pp.55-59

S. No.	*Name of the Incription/Date*	*Donor/Status*	*Donee/Status*	*Nature of Grant/Location*	*Purpose of Grant*	*Witnesses/ Executors*	*Economic/ Adminstrative immunities*	*Reference*
5	Uchchāti garant (641-673 A.D.)	Jayasiṁha I (MR)	Mātriśarma (Dvivedi)	24 (Pu) of (L) Uchchāti (V) Nathavāda (Vis)	—	—	—	*EA*, Vol. V, 1988, pp.19-20
6	Three grants 'A', 'B', 'C', (18th regnal year of the king) Grant 'A'	Ptithivi-Jaya-siṁha I (MR)	Vinayā Śarman (BR), Viṣṇu Śarman (BR) of Kauthema Chhandōga	(A) Ādivāsa (V) Pḷakki (vis)	—	Paramēśvara Varman (AP)	SKPH	*EI*, Vol.XXXI, 1955-56, pp.129-132
7	Grant 'B'	Prithivi-Jaya-siṁha I (MR)	Svāmiyaśas Viṣṇuyaśas of Chhandōga school. Vatsa Gōtra	32 (Niv) of (L) converting it into (A) Kundūru (V) Pḷakki (Vis)	—	Rāshtrakūtas, Naiyōgikas, & Kutumbins of Pḷakki (Vis) Bhīmaśarman (AP)	SKPH	*EI*, Vol. XXXI, 1955-56 pp.133-136
8	Grant 'B'	Svāmiyaśas Viṣṇuyaśas (BR)	Viṣṇuśarman (BR) Students of the Bahuṛicha and Gavishmi Gōtra	9th portion of the above grant.	—	Bhīmaśarman (AP)	—	*Ibid.*, pp. 136-138
9	Grant 'C'	Jayasiṁha Vallabha (MR)	Svāmiyaśas Viṣṇuyaśas (BR)	(A) Kuḍivāda (V)	—	Rāshtrakūtas, Naiyōgikas, & Kutumbins of Pḷakki (Vis) Bhīmaśarman (AP)	SKPH	*Ibid.*, pp. 129-138

S. No.	*Name of the Incription/Date*	*Donor/Status*	*Donee/Status*	*Nature of Grant/Location*	*Purpose of Grant*	*Witnesses/ Executors*	*Economic/ adminstrative immunities*	*Reference*
10	Pulibūrma plates (632-663 A.D.)	Prithivi-Jayasiṁha (MR)	Rudraśarman (B) Gautama Gōtra (Dvivēdi) Taittīrūya School	Sarvasiddhi (V) made it into an (A), Guddavādi (Vis)	—	*Nivāśins & Adhyakśas, Hastikōśa, Vīrakōśa* (AP)	*Sarvasiddhi-Datti Anavamarśyam*	*EI*, Vol. XIX, 1927-28, pp.254-255
11	Pedda-Vēgi grants	Jayasiṁha Vallabha (MR)	Sōmaśarman (BR) Taittirīya School, Gārg-gasya Gōtra	Kambaṛu (V) converted into (A)	For increas-ing the *Dhar-ma* of donor & his parents	Nivaśins of Kambaṛu (V) Narasiṁha Śarman (AP)	*SKPH*	*Ibid.*, pp. 256-261
12	Koṇḍanāguru grant (673 A.D.)	Indravarman (MR)	Cheṇḍaśarman (BR) Bharadvāja Gōtra, Vājasanēya Charaṇa	Koṇḍanāguru (V)	—	Indravarman (AP) elder son of the king. Contains signatures of 4 Bōyas who acted as witnesses	—	*EI*, Vol. XVIII, 1925-26, pp.1-5
13	Rēyūru grant (673-681 A.D.)	Viṣṇu-vardhana II (MR)	59 BR, 36 belong to different occupational groups of the Bōya Community	Rēyūru (V) apportioned into shares	self merit	—	*SKPH*	*IA*, Vol. VII, 1878, pp.185-191

S. No.	Name of the Incription/Date	Donor/Status	Donee/Status	Nature of Grant/Location	Purpose of Grant	Witnesses/ Executors	Economic/ Adminstrative immunities	Reference
14	Koṇeki Grant (673-681 A.D.)	Vishun-vardhana II (MR)	Viduśarman (BR) of Taittirīya Charaṇa	Koṇeki (V) Palli rāshtra with exclusion of DL	Self merit	*Rājapurusha, Talavāra, Dandanāyaka Rāshtrika, Grāmēyaka Chētaka*	—	*EI*, Vol. XXXI, 1955-56 pp.74-80.
15	—do—	Viduśarman (BR)	15 (BR)	120 shares in Koṇeki (V) with 6 DL	—	—do—	—	*Ibid.*, pp. 74-80
16	Chendulūr Plates (681-705 A.D.)	Sarvalōkāśraya (Mangi Yuva-rāja (MR)	6 (BR) of Chhandōga school. 5 of them mentioned with suffix Bōya.	Chendarūra (V) divided into 2 shares each, Kamma Rāshtra (Vis)	—	Villagers of the district *Naiyōgikas* Narabhāskara (AP)	—	*EI*, Vol. VIII, 1905-06, pp. 236-241
17	Chendara grant (705-717 A.D.)	Jayasiṁha II (MR)	Dugamaḍi-śarma (BR) of Āpsthamba sūtra, Kanva Gōtra	Chendara (V) Pennātavādi (vis)	Self merit	Vissaranu (AP)	—	*EA*, Vol.V, 1988, p. 20-21

S. No.	*Name of the Incription/Date*	*Donor/Status*	*Donee/Status*	*Nature of Grant/Location*	*Purpose of Grant*	*Witnesses/ Executors*	*Economic/ Adminstrative immunities*	*Reference*
18	Koṇḍakaripḷola grant (5th regnal year of the king) (718-75 A.D.)	Viṣṇu-vardhana II (MR)	Nandiśarman (BR) of Taittirīya Sūtra	(L) Sufficient for sowing 12 (Kh) of grain Koṇḍakaripḷola (V) Pennātavādi (Vis)	Self merit	—	—	*EA*, Vol. V, 1988 pp. 21-23
19	Ipūr Plates (23rd year of the king)	Pṛithivipōthī (W) of Viṣṇu-vardhana III	Kēśavaśarman (BR) Atrēya-Gōtra, Hiraṇyakēśi Sūtra	A (F), (HS) with (FG) Jalayūru (V) Pḷōlnāṇḍu (vis)	—	Vātaṭṭa (AP)	—	*EI*, Vol. XIII, 1925-26, pp. 58-60
20	Mūsinikoṇḍa grant (718-725 A.D.)	Viṣṇu-vardhana III (MR)	Kālibhadra-chārya (a Jaina teacher) of Kavurūri gaṇa Ānvaya-Sangha	Mūsinikoṇḍa (V) Tōṅka-Nātavādi (Vis)	For the benefit of the Jaina temple, Nadumbi-Vāsadi	Avyana/ Ayyana Mahādēvi (AP)	—	*ARE*, 1916-17, p. 42.
21	Alluvālu grant (753-770 A.D.)	Vijayāditya I (MR)	Gōlaśarman (BR) Bharadvāja Gōtra, Āpastambha Sūtra	Alluvālu (V) Palli-Nādu (Vis)	—	—	*SKPH*	*EA*, Vol. III, 1974, pp.1-5

S. No.	*Name of the Incription/Date*	*Donor/Status*	*Donee/Status*	*Nature of Grant/Location*	*Purpose of Grant*	*Witnesses/ Executors*	*Economic/ Adminstrative immunities*	*Reference*
22	Two new copper plate inscriptions 'A'	Vijayāditya I (MR)	Mādhavaśarma II (BR) (Dvivēdi) (BR)	8 kh of (L) together with crops, Gommalūru (V) Gudrahāra (Vis)	—	*Kutumbins, Rāshtrakūtas* (Bhaurama) (AP)	*SKPH, Anavamarśyam*	*JAHRS*, Vol. I, July, i, 1930 pp.51-56
23	'B' II set	—do—	—do— (Chaturvēdi)	12 Kh of (L) together with crops Dinakādu (V) Prakunōra (Vis)	—	—do—	—do—	*JAHRS*, Vol. V, July, 1930, pp. 51-56
24	Ēdēru Plates (799-849 A.D.)	Vijayāditya II (MR)	Paḷḷa-bhaṭṭāraka (BR) St. of Taittirīyavēda	A (F) Sown with 12 kh of kodrava grain & a dwelling place in Va(nḍ)rupiṭēyu Kaṇḍeṛuvādi (Vis)	—	Boḷama (E) *Kutumbins, Kūṭakas*	—do—	*EI*, Vol. 5, 1898-99, pp.118-142
25	Varppoṁgu plates	—do—	Chandaśarman (BR) (Chaturvēdi)	Varppoṁgu (V) Pishṭapura (vis)	—	—	—	*EA*, Vol. III, 1974, pp. 5-6

S. No.	*Name of the Incription/Date*	*Donor/Status*	*Donee/Status*	*Nature of Grant/Location*	*Purpose of Grant*	*Witnesses/ Executors*	*Economic/ Adminstrative immunities*	*Reference*
26	Koṟṟapaṟṟu grant	Vijayāditya II (MR)	24 (BR) 6 belonging to Hiranyakēśsi-sūtra, 18 Āpastamba sūtra	Koṟṟapaṟṟu (V)	—	Nṛipa Rudra (E) *Kutumbis* & *Rāshtrakūtas*	*SKPH*	*SII*, Vol. I, 1987, pp. 31-36

CHART - IVB

NATURE OF GRANTS—PHASE II (9TH C.A.D. - 12TH C.A.D.)

S. No.	*Name of the Inscription/Date*	*Donor/status*	*Donee/status*	*Nature of Grant/Location*	*Purpose of Grant*	*Witness/ Executors*	*Economic/ Administrative immunities*	*Reference*
27	Permajīli grant	Viṣṇuvardhana (V) (MR)	Agniśarman (BR)	(L) Sowable with 12 (kh) of paddy Permajīli (V) Pagunavāra(vis)	—	Jayarūpa (AP)	—	*ARE*, 1911-14, pp. 5-86.
28	Addanki stone Inscription (844-845 A.D.)	Paṇḍaraṅga (Official of Guṇaga Vijayāditya III	Āditya-Bhaṭāra (G)	(L) Sowable with 80 (kh) of Paddy at Dammavuram	—	—	—	*EI*, Vol, XIX, 1927-28, pp.271-277
29	Masulipatam Plates (844-888 A.D.)	Gunaga Vijayāditya (III) (MR)	Vinayādiśarma (BR) of Taittirīya - School	Traṇḍa(par)ṛu (V)	—	*Kutumbis*, headed by *Rāshtrakūtas* Paṇḍaraṅga(AP)	*SKPH*, *Anavamarśyam*	*EI*, Vol. 1898-99, pp.122-126
30	Chimbulūru grant (844-888 A.D.)	Chella/Challaka of Vallabhēndra (W) of Vijayāditya III	Vēdayya Śarman (BR)	Chimbulūru (V) Gūdrahāra (vis)	—	*Paṇḍaraṅga Rāshtrakūta Pramukhas*	—	*EA*, Vol. III, 1974,pp.6-15

S. No.	*Name of the Inscription/Date*	*Donor/status*	*Donee/status*	*Nature of Grant/Location*	*Purpose of Grant*	*Witness/ Executors*	*Economic/ Administrative immunities*	*Reference*
31	Chimbulūru grant	Vēdayya Śarman (BR)	(BRs) (Chaturvēdis)	Chimbulūru (A)	—	Paṇḍaraṅga (AP) *Rāshtrakūta Pramukhas*		*EA*, Vol. III, 1974 pp. 6-15
32	Satalūru Copper plate grant (844-888 A.D.)	Guṇaga Vijayāditya (MR) at the instance of his brother Nṛipakāma	100 (BR)	Śāntagrāma (V) Gudrahāra (vis)	—	Paṇḍaraṅga (AP)	*SKPH*	*JAHRS* Vol. V, Oct., 1930, pp.101-116
33	Mōga Grant (892-922 A.D.)	Chālukya Bhīma I (Mr)	Śrī Mahādēvi (W) of Vijayāditya of the Kātakarāja Vaṁśa	Mōga (V)	In memory of the Services rendered by Vijayāditya	Kaḍeyarāja (AP)	*SKPH*	*EA*, Vol. III, 1974, pp.28-42
34	Kākumrānu grant (892-922 A.D.)	—do—	Pōlayana (M) (Paṭṭapusetti) (Leader of a Caravan)	Kākumrānu(V) (Omgēru-mārga (vis)	— —	*Rāshtrakūta Pramukhas*	*SKPH*	*EA*. Vol. III, 1974, pp.16-28
35	Kākumrānu grant	Pōlayana (M)	86 (BR) (FO) & Chāmanabhaṭṭa & Suvarnakāra Bhīmanāyaka	(A) 10 shares tax on Eruvāka, hara, dhāvana, Vrittis, etc.	—	*Rāshtrakūta Pramukhas*	—	*EA*, Vol. III, 1974, pp.16-28

S. No	*Name of the Inscription/Date*	*Donor/status*	*Donee/status*	*Nature of Grant/Location*	*Purpose of Grant*	*Witness/ Executors*	*Economic/ Administrative immunities*	*Reference*
36	Telugu Acadamy plates or Attili grant (892-922 A.D.)	Chālukya Bhīma I (MR)	Challava (Musician)	A (F) Sowable with 50 (kh) of paddy, (HS), a ground occupied by 1000 betel-nuts	—	*Kutumbis, Rāshtrakūtas Kadēyarāja* (AP)	*Anavamarśyam*	*JBORS*, VIII, pt. ii, June 1922, pp. 83-98
37	Bezvāda plates (892-922 A.D.)	—do—	Pōtamayya (S) of Kramapāṭha	Kūkiparṟu (V) Uttara-kandeṟuvādi (vis)	On the occasion of King's Coronation ceremony	*Kutumbis Rāshtrakūtas Kādēyarāja* (AP)	*SKPH, Anavamarśyam*	*EI*, Vol. V, 1898-99, pp.127-137
38	Masulipatam Plates (918-925 A.D.)	Amma I (MR)	Mahākāla (gen)	Drujjūru (V) Pennātavādi (vis)	—	*Kutumbis Rāshtrakūtas Kādēyarāja* (AP)	—do—	*EI*, Vol.V, 1898-99, pp.131-134
39	Chevūru plate	—do—	Vēmarāja (war) of Kōna family	Umukilī (V) Gudravāra (vis)	Loyalty & obedience rendered by Vēmarāja to Amma I	Nivāśins of the (dist) Katakēśvara (AP) *Rāshtrakūtas*	*SKPH*, except the traditional fixation of 80 *gadyānakas*	*EI*, Vol. XXVII, 1947, pp.41-47
40	Ēdēru Plates (918-925 A.D.)	—do—	Kuṇtāditya (War)	Goṇṭūru (V) with 12 hamlets	—	*Kutumbis*	*SKPH*	*SII*, Vol I, pp.36-47

S. No.	Name of the Inscription/Date	Donor/status	Donee/status	Nature of Grant/Location	Purpose of Grant	Witness/ Executors	Economic/ Administrative immunities	Reference
41	Velaṁbaṟṟu grant (915-925 A.D.)	Amma I (MR)	Kodāli Śarman (BR) Taittirīya Brahmachārin (Karpatiṇ (Bikshu)	Velaṁbaṟṟu (A) Velanāntipalli (vis)	—	Kādēyarāja	*SKPH*	*EA*, Vol. III, 1974, pp. 43-46
42	Masulipatam Plates (934-945 A.D.)	Chālukya Bhīma II (MR)	Viddamayya(s) of Kramapatha	(F) Akulamanaṇḍu (vis)	—	*Rāshtrakūtas Kutumbis*	*SKPH*	*EI*, Vol. V, 1898-99, pp.134-139
43	Vēmalūrpādu plates (934-945 A.D.)	Ammarāja II (MR) at the request of Durgarāja (Feudatory chief)	Musiya or Musiya śarman (BR) (Min) under Durgarāja	(A) or Manya	—	Durgarāja (AP)	*SKPH* *Anavamarśyam* the grant regarded as a sin	*EI*, Vol.XVIII, 925-26, p.226-235
44	Kaluchumbaṟṟu grant (934-945 A.D.)	Ammarāja at the request of Chamekāmba (W) (Q)	Arhanandin (a Jaina teacher)	Kaluchumbaṟṟu (V)	For the maintenance of the dining hall repairs of the Jaina temple	*Rāshtrakūtas*	*SKPH*	*EI* ,Vol.VII 1905-06, pp.179-192
45	Nammūru grant (934-945 A.D.)	Ammarāja II (MR)	Viṣṇuśarman (BR)	A (F) Sowable with 12 (KH) of grain Nammūru (V)	—	*Nivāśin's* of Gudla-Kandērvād (vis)	—	*EI*, Vol. XII, 1913-14, pp.61-64

S. No	Name of the Inscription/Date	Donor/status	Donee/status	Nature of Grant/Location	Purpose of Grant	Witness/ Executors	Economic/ Administrative immunities	Reference
46	Maliyapūṇḍi grant (934-945 A.D.)	Ammarāja II (MR)	Śrīmandirādēva (Sptd) Katakābharaṇa Jinala (A Jaina temple	Maliyapūṇḍi (V) Kamma-nāṇḍu (vis) & and alms house (Sattra)	Repairs, Offerings worship etc.	*Kutumbis, Rāshtrakūtas,* and *Nivāśins* of the dist.	*SKPH*	*EI,* Vol. IX 1907-08, pp.47-56
47	Vandram plate (945-970 A.D.)	—do—	Turkkiya-Yajvan, surnamed VipraNārāyaṇa (BR)	Tāndēṛu (V) Beṭipuṇdi (V) together with the share of gold	For the donee's devotion to the king	*Kutumbis, Rāstrakūtas* inhabiting-12 (V) chief one Prāndoṛu Kātakarāja (AP)	*SKPH*	*EI,* Vol. IX, pp.131-135
48	Tāṇḍikoṇḍa grant (958-959 A.D.)	—do—	Prabhūtarāśi III of Śiva Temple called Samasta-bhuvanāśraya Vijayavāṭi (Bezwada)	4 (V) Tāṇḍikoṇḍa Amalapūṇḍi, Gollapūṇḍi, Āsurulapaṛṛu	for increase of property, longivity, free from disease of his people, for repairs of the temple, offering *bali*, *naivēdya*, music to god and *sattra*	Kaṭakanāyaka (AP)	*SKPH*	*EI,* Vol. XXIII, 1945-46 pp.162-164

S. No	Name of the Inscription/Date	Donor/status	Donee/status	Nature of Grant/Location	Purpose of Grant	Witness/ Executors	Economic/ Administrative immunities	Reference
49	Masulipatam plates	Ammarāja II (MR)	Yuvarāja Ballāladēva Vēlabhaṭa (named) Boḍḍiya	2(F) Nōmi & Pūtośa (Pa)ri(ya) Pambaṟṟu (V) Gudrāvāra (Vis)	—	*Kutumbis Rāshtrakūtas*	—	*EI*, Vol. V 1898-99 pp.139-142
50	Kāndyam plate (970 A.D.)	Dānarnava	Maliya & Gōṇḍiya (2, Princes of Minor Chālukyan family	300 (V) Pottapi-nāḍu (vis)	—	*Mantrin, Purōhita, Sēnapati Rāshtrakūtas* Kātakarāja (AP)	*SKPH* Molestation of the gift considered as a great sin. The *Yuvarāja* was to protect & enforce this gift with the aid of 2032 soldiers	*JAHRS*, Vol. XI, Part i & ii, 1930 pp. 80-88
51	Māṇgallu grant	Dānarnava at the request of Kākartya Guṇḍyana	Dommana of Kutsa-gōtra	(A) Māṇgallu village Natavādīvishaya	For religious ceremony named Karpaṭi-vrata	*Kutumbin' Rāshtrakūtas Pramukhas*	*SKPH*	*EA*, Vol, I, 1969, pp.57-70
52	Rāgōlu Plates (1000-1011 A.D.)	Śaktivarman I (MR)	Kumāraśarman Vājasanēyi (Sakha) (BR)	(V) Converted into (A) Rākalu or Rāgōlu (V) Kalinga (Vis)	For self Merit	*Nivāśins* Kalinga (vis) Śaktivarman (AP)	*SKPH, Apravēśam*	*EI*, Vol XII 1913-14, pp.1-3

S. No	*Name of the Inscription/Date*	*Donor/status*	*Donee/status*	*Nature of Grant/Location*	*Purpose of Grant*	*Witness/ Executors*	*Economic/ Administrative immunities*	*Reference*
53	Ranastipūṇḍi grant	Vimalāditya (MR)	Vijjiya Peggaḍa Vajra (Minister)	(A) Ranastapūṇḍi (V), Guddavāḍi (vis), Pṛuvaḷa (V)	Self Merit	*Rāshtrakūtas & Kutumbis* of the (Vis)	*SKPH Anavamarśyam*	*EI*, Vol, VI, 1901-02, pp.348-361
54	Korumelli Plates (S.944)	Rājarāja II (MR)	Chīdamārya (BR) of Āpastamba Sūtra	Korumelli (V) Guddavāḍi (vis)	—	—	—	*IA*, Vol. XIV, 1885, pp.8-55
55	Telugu Academy plates (1061 A.D.)	Śaktivarman II (MR)	Adapa Appanna (sūdra or kṣatriya (officer of the king)	(V) Converted into (A) Numiyavāda Prōlunāṇḍu (vis)	—	*Rāshtrakūta, Pramukhas, Kutumbins, Mantri, Purōhita, Sēnāpati Yuvarāja, Pradhāna,* Kaṭakādi-pathi (AP)	—	*JAHRS*, Vol. V, July 1930, pp.39-49
56	Two New copper plate Inscriptions, (Ryāli)	Vijayāditya (VII) (MR)	Pampanabhaṭṭa (BR)	Krumdiya (V) (Drākshārāma) Mavindēru (Y) (Korumelli)	—	—	—	*JAHRS*, Vol. I, July 1930, pp.24-35

S. No.	Name of the Inscription/Date	Donor/status	Donee/status	Nature of Grant/Location	Purpose of Grant	Witness/ Executors	Economic/ Administrative immunities	Reference
57	Tēki plates (1084 A.D.)	Kulottunga I or Rājarājachōda-gaṇga (MR)	1000 Teliki Families of which 10 are mentioned, viz. Velumanūllu Pattipālu etc.	Donation of betel in the golden vessel by the ruling family to the married couple of the Teliki family.	Donees loya-lty and devo-tion to the king's family	*Rāshtrakūtas, Kutumbins, Mantri, Purōhita, Sēnapati Pradhāna, Yuvarāja, Dauvārika*		*EI*, Vol. VI, pp.334-347
58	Bhīmavarmam Pillar inscriptions (S, 1037)	Mādhava or Rājavallabha (Officer of Kulottunga I)	Pāpana-Bōya	Gift of (LM) to (G) Nārāyaṇa of Mandayar temple, (20-Bu) Chālukya-Bhīmavaram	—	—	—	*EI*, Vol. VI, pp.219-223
59	Chellūru Grant (21st year of the king)	Vīrachōda (MR)	Temple of Viṣṇu founded by Medamārya, (Sēnapati) of the king	Kolaṛu (V) Chellūru (A) Guddavāṭi (vis)	Daily Performance of *Chāru, Bali* & *Pūja*, Repairs of gaps and cracks.	*Rāshtrakūtas, Kutumbins, Mantri, Purōhita, Sēnapati Pradhāna, Yuvarāja, Dauvārika* Pennāchāri (AP)	*SKPH*	*SII*, Vol. I, pp. 51-62

S. No.	*Name of the Inscription/Date*	*Donor/status*	*Donee/status*	*Nature of Grant/Location*	*Purpose of Grant*	*Witness/ Executors*	*Economic/ Administrative immunities*	*Reference*
60	Pithāpuram Plates 23rd year of the king	Vīrachōda (MR)	536 (BR)	Vīrachōda CVM (V) converted into (A) formed by uniting Mālaveli (V) with 12 (hamlets and Ponnatoṛṛa (V) Prōlunāṇḍu (Vis) & Ālami (V), Uttaravarusa (Vis)	—	Pancha Pradhāna (AP)	Remitted *Siddhaya Avendaya, Abinanava* & *Krīdara-sulka* and other revenues	*EI,* Vol. V, 1898-99, pp.70-100

CHART - Vx
NATURE OF GRANTS MINOR - CHĀLUKYAN FAMILIES CHĀLUKYAS OF MUDIGONDA

S. No.	*Name of the Inscription/ Date*	*Donor/Status*	*Donee/Status*	*Nature of Grant/Location*	*Purpose of Grant*	*Witnesse/ Executors*	*Economic/ Administrative Immunities*	*Reference*
1	Koravi Epigraph	Goṇangayya (SR of MC family)	Peddana	Koravi (V)			Mentions punishments and tributes to be paid by the people	*EA*, Vol. I, pp.119-145
2	Nārāyaṇagiri inscriptions	Gaṇgappayya (perggere or pregaḍe)	God Mallikārjuna	not clear	—	—	—	*IMCDAP*, K. Suryanara-yana pp.33-34
3	Mogalucheṛu-vula grant (1175-1200 A.D.	Kusumāyudha	Donamayya (BR) & 30 other (BR)	Mogalucheṛu-vulu (V) Mardikoṇḍa (Vis)	—	Nivāśins of Manchikonda (vis) Rashtrakuta Pramukhas, Kutumbis	Sarvakara Parihārikritya	*IMCDP*, 199 pp.34-37
4	Krivvaka grant of Kukkunūru grant (12th C.A.D.)	Kusumāditya	Ministers (BR)	Kirvvaka (A) Kūkkunūru (V) Visurunāḍu (vis)	For Loyalty and services rendered by his ministers	Kusumāditya (A)	ministers raised to the position of Mahāmaṇḍaleś-vars confering on them the office of Makara Tōrana	*EA*, Vol. II, 1974 pp.39-40 *Bharati*, Nov. 1979, pp.32-39

CHART - Vy

NATURE OF GRANTS - CHĀLUKYAS OF JANANĀTHAPURAM

S. No.	*Name of the Inscription/ Date*	*Donor/Status*	*Donee/Status*	*Nature of Grant/Location*	*Purpose of Grant*	*Witnesse/ Executors*	*Economic/ Administrative Immunities*	*Reference*
5	Drākshārāma Inscription (1128 A.D.)	Rājalādēvi (Q) of Gaṇga Ananthavarman Chōda Gaṇga Dēva	Bhīmēśvara (G)	50 (BU) & gift of (LM)	PL	Peddanācharya (Writer)	—	*IMCDAP*, 1993, pp. 43-44
6	Drākshārāma inscription (1128 A.D.)	Kalyānadēvī (Q) of Gaṇga Ananthavarman Chōda Gaṇga Dēva	—do—	—do—	—do—	—	—	*IMCDAP*, 1993, p. 46; SII, Vol. IV, No. 1198, p. 413
7	Drākshārāma inscription (1128 A.D.)	Śrīyadēvī (Q) of Gaṇga Ananthavarman Chōda Gaṇga Dēva	—do—	—do—	—do—	Peddanācharya (Writer)	—	*IMCDAP*, 1993, pp. 46-47
8	Drākshārāma inscription (1128 A.D.)	Līlāvatidēvī (Q) of Gaṇga Ananthavarman Chōda Gaṇga Dēva	—do—	—do—	—do—	—do—	—	*IMCDAP*, 1993, pp. 47-48
9	Drākshārāma inscription (1129 A.D.)	Bhīmināyaka (Chief of Visnuvardhana)	—do—	—do—	—do—	—	—	*IMCDAP*, p. 50

S. No.	*Name of the Inscription/ Date*	*Donor/Status*	*Donee/Status*	*Nature of Grant/Location*	*Purpose of Grant*	*witnesse/ Executors*	*Economic/ Administrative Immunities*	*Reference*
10	Juttiga inscription (1141 A.D.)	Prōlipāva (D) of Chengama	Vāsukīravi Somēśvara Mahādēva (G)	—do—	—do—	—	—	*SII*, Vol. X, No. 110, p. 50
11	Rājahmundry inscription (1145 A.D.)	Prōliseṭṭi (M) of Penugonda	Vīrabhadrē-śvara Paṭṭisam (G)	Ghee for lightening of LM	—	—	—	*SII*, Vol. X, No. 116, p. 53
12	Bhīmavaram inscription (1176 A.D.)	Vīranarēndra (Prince)	Rājanārāyaṇa (G) Chālukya Bhīmapuram	Gift of LM	—	—	—	*SII*, Vol. V, No. 61, p. 22
13	Bhīmavaram inscription (1176 A.D.)	Sarvalōkāśraya Viṣṇuvardhana Mallapa (II)	—do—	12 Puttis of (L)	For *Naivēdya*	—	*SKPH*	*SII*, Vol. V, No. 91 pp. 34-35
14	Eḍaṛupalli re-issued grant	Śrī Viṣṇuvardhana	78 (BR)	Eḍaṛupalli (V)	—	*Nivāśins* of Guddavādi (vis) *Rāshtrakūta Pramukhas, Kutumbins, Mantri, Yuvarāja, Sēnāpati Purōhita*	*SKPH*	*Bharati*, Jan. 1968, p. 3
15	Pithāpuram grant. (1202 A.D.)	Mallapadēva (II)	Kunti-Mādhava (G)	Gudivāda (V) Prōlananti (Vis)	—	Rāshtrakūta Pramukhas, Kutumbins & Nivāśins of (Vis)	*SKPH*	*EI*, Vol. IV, p. 226

CHART - Vz

NATURE OF GRANTS OF THE CHĀLUKYAS OF NIDADAVŌLU

S No.	*Name of the Inscription/ Date*	*Donor/status*	*Donee/status*	*Nature of Grant/Location*	*Purpose of Grant*	*Witnesses/ Executors*	*Economic/ Administrative intiel immunities*	*Reference*
16	Drākshārāma Inscriptions	(Q) of Vēngi Malla	God Bhīmēśvara	Gift to (LM) & 50 excellent (BU)	—	—	—	*IMCDAP,* 1992 pp. 119-120, SII, Vol. IV, N. 1076, p. 258
17	Tadikalapūḍi Inscription (1141 A.D.)	Vēngi Ayyapadēva (man Mahā-maṇḍalēśvara)	Mahādēva (G)	Gift of (LM) with 50 (BU)	For the merit of his parents	Nāgāchārya (writer)	—	*IMCDAP,* 1993, p. 120
18	Drākshārāma Inscription (1149 A.D.)	Mallarāja	Bhīmēśvara (G)	Gift of 2 (LM)	For the merit of his father Vēngīśvara	—	—	*IMCDAP,* 1993, p. 121
19.	Ganapavaram Inscription	Gōkarāja (Man-Mahā-Maṇḍalēśvara)	Śrī Śvarṇīśvara, Mahādēva (G)	Gift of 30 Cows	For the upkeep of (LM)	—	—	*IMCDAP,* 1993, pp. 122-123

S No.	*Name of the Inscription/ Date*	*Donor/status*	*Donee/status*	*Nature of Grant/Location*	*Purpose of Grant*	*Witnesses/ Executors*	*Economic/ Administrative intiel immunities*	*Reference*
20	Drākshārāma Inscription (1177 A.D.)	Tripurāntaka (Preggada)	Śrī Bhīmēśvara Mahādēva (G)	50 Cows	For the upkeep of lamp	—	—	*SII*, Vol. IV, No. 1169, p. 399
21	Drākshārāma Inscription (1196 A.D.)	Valyama	-do-	50 He-(Bu)	-do-	—	—	*IMCDAP*, 1993, p. 124
22.	Tadikalapūdi Inscription (1208 A.D.)	Vēngī Mahādēva rāja (Man-mahā-maṇḍalēśvara)	Haruṇīśvara (G)	Gift of (LM)	For (PL)	—	—	*SII*, Vol. V, No. 203, p. 75

CONSOLIDATED KEY FOR CHART IVA, IVB AND V

A	=	*Agrahāra*	L	=	Land
AP	=	*Ajñapti*	LM	=	Lamp
BR	=	*Brāhmaṇa*	M	=	Merchant
BU	=	Buffaloes	MR	=	Main Ruler
CVM	=	Chatur Vēdi Maṇgala	Niv	=	*Nivarthans*
D	=	Daughter	PL	=	Perpetual Lamp
DL	=	*Dēvabhōga* land	PU	=	*Puttis*
F	=	Field	Q	=	Queen
FG	=	Flower Garden	S	=	Student
FO	=	Former Owners	SKPH	=	*Sarva kara Parihāra*
G	=	God	Sptd	=	Superintendent
GEN	=	General	V	=	Village
HS	=	House site	Vis	=	*Viṣhaya*
KH	=	*Khuṇdis*	W	=	Wife
			War	=	Warrior

Chapter - V

SOCIO-INDEOLOGICAL PARAMETERS

An understanding of the various processes involved in the formation and consolidation of power by the rulng elites, namely the Eastern Chālukyas of Vengi, will not be complete without comprehending the crucial role played by the socio-ideological parameters that helped them in legitimizing their political authority through controlling society at various levels.

In the context of the emergence of new regional kingdoms in almost all the major regions of the Indian sub-continent as a result of the socio-economic transformation during the early medieval period, it becomes imperative for these States to seek new ways of social and ideological mechanisms in controlling society as part of process of the consolidation of their power. Hence, it would be pertinent to state here that the inter-relationship between the ideology of these new States and the socio-ideological variables should be seen as intinsically linked to provide integrative mechanisms for the assertion of political authority. At one level, as seen in Chapter III, the process of legitimation was sought through fabrication of genealogies connecting to the mythical families of *Suryavaṃśi* and *Chandravaṃśi* lineages so as to strengthen the image of the ruling elites themselves. This was accomplished by the temporal power with the help of *brāhmaṇas* who constituted the sacred domain.[1] The process also involved the improving and asserting *varṇa* status by the ruling elites and this has been already discussed by us elsewhere. It has been argued by us of how the Eastern Chālukyan rulers made constant attempts to assert their kṣatriyahood first, by seeking *brahma-kṣatra* origin and later, through linking up their ancestry to mythical genealogies of *Candravaṃśi* lineage and thereby claim a pure *kṣatriya* status.

The essence of the social processes are pertinently related to how the ruling elite used the *varṇa* ideology to control society. It is well known that for ancient India stratification was made possible theoretically through *varṇa* ideology. According to the *Dharmaśāstra* norms, the main duty of the king was to protect the *Varnāśramadharma.* Traditionally, *varṇa* ideology appeared to be very conservative restricting any sort of transgression from the comprehensive framework of theoretically articulated *varṇa* ideology of the texts. Not withstanding these rigid norms, it has been argued by many scholars that caste always retained the requisite amount of flexibility and an attitude of accommodation.[2] This was explicit in the concept of *varnasaṃkāra* itself which the legal texts explained in their earliest writings. The important characteristic of the theory of *varnasaṃkāra* was the proliferation of castes and *jātis*, both horizontally and vertically.[3] The new States during the early period, although they theoretically adhered to the Dharmaśāstric norms, nevertheless encouraged the proliferation of castes and *jātis*, through opening the channels of social mobility at different levels of the *varṇa* system. This process of allowing certain caste groups to raise their ritual as well as actual status helped the State in drawing many loyal subjects. The process of proliferation of castes and *jātis* was further accelerated by the system of donating land grants to the *brāhmaṇa* ideologies in the peripheral areas. These *brāhmaṇas* acted as chief agents in the process of the acculturation and assimilation of various aboriginal and tribal groups into the caste system.[4]

At the ideological level, it was the religious process that played a crucial role in providing religious legitimation for the newly emerging ruling authorities. The early medieval period saw a great spurt in strengthening the Purāṇic religion based on theistic worship which led to the simultaneous growth of multifarious sectarian strands like Śaivism and Vaiṣṇavism. These new religious sects were entrenched themselves in the concept of *Bhakti.* The ascendancy of *bhakti* ideology acted as a governing principle in establishing the spirit of loyalty and devotion towards the king, suggesting clearly a hierarchy of domination and subordination.[5]

The main locus of the *bhakti* ideology was rooted in the institution of the temple. This led to the patronage extended by ruling elites to large scale construction and repairs of temples. Through these temples, ruling elites attempted to create a new and centralised ritual structure by seeking identification with the divinity enshrined in the temple.[6] Also associated with the legitimation and consolidation process was the acculturation and integration of cults and deities into Pan-Hinduism.[7]

The earliest attempts to study the complex nature of socio-religious aspects of Indian society was made under the auspices of the imperialists and orientalists. In their observations they provided an unchanging image of Indian caste system and religious ideology. Hence, they projected these factors as overladen with spiritual ethos impeding any progress in Indian society.[8]

The image that has been provided in the writings of the imperialists and Orientalists remained to a large extent in the descriptions of nationalist historians, the regional historians and those who wrote on the social history of the period. Scholars belonging to these schools understood society and religious conditions of the period within the normative frame work of the fourfold division of society based on *varṇa* ideology. Other descriptions on society include dress, ornaments, food, sports etc. While dealing with the religious history, most of these writings emphasized on the existence of dominant religions such as Hinduism, Buddhism, Jainism, Śaivism, Vaiṣṇavism, and their associated rituals, fairs, festivals, temples and monasteries. According to Vaidehi Krishna Murthy, "the hierarchical structure with the *brāhmin* at the top and the *Caṇḍāla* at the bottom became much more strengthened than in the past. This was to a great extent due to the decline of Jainism and Buddhism and the revival of Hinduism. Eventhough, Śaivism and Vaiṣṇavism of the period stood for a certain kind of equality among the devotees of Śiva and Viṣṇu, they did little to modify the rigours of caste". However, she admits the flexible nature of caste system, which is seen in terms of proliferation of sub-castes through the process of social mobility. Thus, an attempt has been made by the scholar to co-relate the social structure of caste with that of religion.[9] In contrast to the hypothesis postulated by conventional historians, the Marxist scholars viewed the socio-ideological variations of Indian society in terms of the breakdown of *varṇa* structure. This break down has been explained in terms of the emergence of new mode of production dominated by land grant economy which they have characterized as `Feudal' in nature. According to R.S. Sharma, "the rise of quasi-feudal mode of production modified the *varṇa* divided society which is seen in terms of the proliferation of castes at different levels of the *varṇa* hierarchy.

Similarly at the religious level, feudal development was seen in terms of the evolution of *Bhakti* ideology that permeated through various religious sects such as Śaivism, Vaiṣṇavism. The core of the *bhakti* ideology according to these scholars is reflected through the complete dependence of the tenants or semi-serfs on the land owners in the medieval times. Thus, the Marxist writings emphasized on the crucial importance of economic change in the socio-ideological spheres.[10]

As an alternative, the recent writings tried to integrate the various processes of state formation of which the socio-ideological variables formed the major mechanism of consolidation of power. This trend of integrative processes is observed in the writings of eminent scholars like B.D. Chattopadhyaya, Hermann Kulke and others. According to B.D. Chattopadhyaya, the major processes operating at the socio-ideological level are the transformation of tribes into peasantry which was done through the process of acculturation and secondly, through cult appropriation and integration.[11] Thus, in his opinion "common modes of royal legitimation and inter-related phenomenon such as the practice of land grants, the creation of *agrahāras,* the emergence of major cult centres and temple complexes, social stratification subscribing to the *varṇa* order, all these were manifestations of the manner in which local states mediated in the absorption of ideas and practices which had been taking shape as a wider temporal and ideological processes."[12] Similarly, Hermann Kulke, postulates that the royal legitimation to power could be stabilized through ritual means such as integration of autochthonous deities as tutelary deities, construction of imperial temples and a systematic and large-scale settlement of *brāhmaṇas* in the peripheral areas.[13] Hence, these scholars regarded socio-ideological variables as integrated elements through which State sought legitimation and controlled society. These various socio-ideological processes operated in most of the new States that had emerged in the early medieval period.

Therefore, our main concern here would be to delineate the study on the *varṇa* ideology and the religious affiliation of the ruling elites towards different social groups and religious sects. This enabled us to understand not only the social and religious conditions prevailing under the Eastern Chālukyan period but at the same time it also helped to comprehend the ruling elites attempts to control society through these variables. This study has been undertaken by two different phases. The division has been made due to the changes perceptible in the nature of patronage extended by the ruling elites to different social groups and to various religious sects that dominated the period under study. This also explains the encouragement given to the construction of temples in honour of various deities and development of religious centres.

In phase I, the Eastern Chālukyas of Vengi, as new ruling elites who were still in the process of forming an independent State in an alien land had to follow a two fold policy to consolidate their authority. This was done by them, firstly through the mechanism of conciliation and pacification of the local military chiefs and intellectual leaders, namely the *brāhmaṇas.*[14] In this process, they imported some of the above sections of people from their native place. This was done by the ruling elites with the intention that these *brāhmaṇas* would render legitimation to their power in an alien land.

One dimension of acquiring support from *brāhmaṇas* was by donating land grants to them. In phase I, the new ruling elites made large scale donations of land to *brāhmaṇas* in the form of *agrahāra* villages (Chart IVA, iii, 1-20, 22-27). Most of the grants were made to individual *brāhmaṇas* and some times to group of *brāhmaṇas* (Chart IVA, iii, 1, 2, 14, 17, 27).

As religious specialists these *brāhmaṇas* played a decisive role in colonising the peripheral areas. Further, the high scholarship of *brāhmaṇas,* as well versed in vēdas and their affiliated schools shows their intellectual calibre as highly educated. This is evident from Phase I where *brāhmaṇas* were being mentioned with suffixes such as *Dvivēdi,* (Chart IVA iii, 5, 11, 23) and *Chaturvēdi* (Chart IVA, iii, 24, 26). This shows that these scholars are well versed in either two or four vēdas. Further, most of the *brāhmaṇas* are mentioned as belonging to Taittirīya Charaṇa (Chart IVA, iii, 3, 4, 6, 11, 13, 15, 19, 25) and others as belonging to Chhandōga school (Chart IVA, iii, 1, 7, 8, 17) and Vajasanēya Charaṇa (Chart IVA, iii, 12). This reveals that ruling elites conferred land grants mostly to *brāhmaṇas* of high scholarship, as they generated a sense of loyalty among tribal people towards the established order. These *brāhmaṇas* on the other hand with their superior material culture not only taught new scripts, language and rituals to the preliterate people but also acquainted them with plough cultivation, new crops, seasons calendar, preservation of cattle wealth etc.[15] All these necessarily helped the tribal people to improve their status. By spreading vēdic learning and brāhmaṇical order in the aboriginal tracts, these *brāhmaṇas* tried to bring the tribal people into the vortex of caste system. Further, land grants to *brāhmaṇas* encouraged the phenomenon of social mobility. This was made possible through the processes of assimilation and acculturation of various aborginal tribal groups and persons belonging to other lower *varṇas* into the higher *varṇa* structure. Such a phenomenon is observed due to the rise in actual status of some sections of the lower *varṇa* groups to economic and political power. Thus, the bōyas who were initially tribal people got acculturated into the *varṇa* ideology at different levels.[16]

In Phase I, the process of acculturation of bōyas assumed a new dimension. It has been noticed that new ruling elites could not subdue the powerful bōya tribes and annex their region into the newly established Eastern Chālukyan kingdom. Therefore, alternatively they had to pacify them through donation of land grants to bōya priests. The records in Phase I, shows that bōya priests with brāhmaṇical suffix *śarma* which means a vēdic scholar reveals the process of acculturation. This helped the bōya priests to grow higher up in social hierarchy and gain equality of ritual purity with the *brāhmaṇas* of the traditional "Hindu" order. From the standpoint of State, this process of acculturation of formidable tribal groups into the brāhmaṇical order helped in strengthening their power in the border regions.

Scholars have expressed divergent views regarding the social mobility of the bōya *brāhmaṇas.* At one level, scholars like P.V. Parabrahma Sastry identifies the existence of two types of bōyas in the Andhra region. One group has been recognised by him as the aboriginal tribes who, in his opinion did not give up their caste status and therefore social mobility among these tribes was refuted by the scholar. The other group constituted the Bōya officers who were connected with the Pallava administration. They are identified as *bhōjakas.* In his view ruling elites made endowments to these bōyas or *bhōjakas* who were chosen from different classes of the society. In this regard, he attempts to explain how the term *bhōjaka* was replaced by its prakrit variant Bōya or Bōi, which is seen as frequently occuring in the Eastern Chālukyan inscriptions. Therefore, he envisages social mobility among the bōya officers rather than among bōya tribes.[17] On the other hand scholars like B.S.L. Hanumantha Rao, regards that land grants to bōya tribes, who inhabited the region between the Pallava kottams and the Chālukyan kingdoms, by the early rulers of the Eastern Chālukyan dynasty helped these tribal groups to acquire proficiency in vēdic learning. Subsequently, the bōya *brāhmaṇas* came to be treated on par with the traditional *brāhmaṇas.*[18]

Another mechanism through which some of the other forest tribes were allowed to raise their status was mainly through the process of recruiting them into the higher administrative structure. As it has been already stated, the new ruling elites in order to stabilize their power needed the support of local chiefs. Therefore, in an alien land one way of seeking support from these local chiefs was by raising their status in the administrative apparatus. The Chipurupalli plates[19] of Kubja Vishnuvardhana mentions about one Atavi Dūrjaya. He was mentioned as the leader of a forest tribe in the Kalinga region. Further, it has been mentioned that he was raised to the status of a general under Kubja

Vishnuvardhana. Similarly, Buddhavarman of the Pattavardhan family who claimed himself to be the proud member of the *Chaturtha kulajas* was also raised to the status of a general.[20]

Thus, during the first phase, most of the grants were made in the form of *agrahāra* villages, which were conferred predominantly to the *brāhmaṇa* groups and sometimes even acculturating aboriginals into the *brāhmaṇa varṇa.* This explains the phenomenon of acquiring support and loyalty from dominant sections of the society in an alien land. This, further helped the ruling elites to gradually consolidate their power and initiate the process of formation of a new state structure.

The early medieval period saw a great spurt in the revival of brāhmaṇical religion so as to counter the dominance of heretical religions, namely Buddhism and Jainism. The dominance of Vēdic religion during this period was attested by the patronisation extended to *brāhmaṇas* through land grants. In Phase I, we notice the tendency among the ruling elites to patronise predominantly the members of the *brāhmaṇa varṇa.* This clearly reflects the Eastern Chālukyan rulers religious leanings were more towards Brāhmaṇism in Phase I. This is evident from the large scale donations of *agrahāra,* villages to *brāhmaṇas* (Chart IVA, ii, iii, 1-27). Further, repeated references to brahches of Vēdic and its affiliated learning namely Chhandōga school (Chart IVA, iii, 1,7,8,17). Taittiriya school (Chart IVA, iii, 3-6,11,13) in the first phase point to the general dominance of Brāhmaṇism. The brāhmaṇic religion was mainly based on vēdic and purāṇic ideologies of the brāhmaṇical order. The dominance of this religion is also attested by, the use of appellations such as "*Parama brāhmaṇyas*" (Chart IIA, v, 18) by the Eastern Chalukyan rulers. Brāhmaṇism is also associated with the performance of Vēdic sacrifices such as *Vajapēya, Aśvamēdha, Agnishtōma, Paundārika* etc. Reference to these sacrifices was made in the first phase (Chart I, v, 1-2,5) of the Bādāmi Chālukyan rulers. Eastern Chālukyan rulers seems to have given up the practice of performing vēdic sacrifices. However, we find constant references to these sacrifices in their inscriptions. This was made with reference to their parent branch. Other important features of Brāhmaṇism are performance of *Vratas,* taking pilgrimage to sacred places and making gifts to *brāhmaṇas* and religious institutions, such as temples. All these were done by the ruling elites in phase I.

During early medieval period Brāhmaṇism got crystallised into Śaivism, Vaiṣṇavism, and Śaktism. Hence, in phase I we find that along with Brāhmaṇism there existed side by side Purāṇic theism in the form of Śaivism and Vaiṣṇavism.[21] In Vaiṣṇavism, *viṣṇu* is manifested as the supreme God. An important feature of Vaiṣṇavism is that it is based on the theory of *Avatāras*. This helped the religion to absorb the local deities and grow as a syncretic religion. The evolution of Viṣṇavism in the early medieval period revolved around the cult of *Vāsudēva-Kṛṣṇa*, the leader of the famous epic namely, the *Mahābhārata*. *Vāsudēva-Kṛṣṇa*, is defined as Bhagavat and is identified with Nārāyana and Viṣṇu, who were held supreme among Brāhmaṇists.[22] The existence of Vaiṣṇavism in this phase is attested from the *praśasti* sections of their inscriptions. In these sections, Eastern Chālukyas attributed their origin to Lord Nārāyana (Chart IIA, vi, 14,18). Further, inscriptions during this phase also make a mention about Viṣṇu (Chart IIA, vi, 1,12,19,21). The Praśastis of the ruling elites under consideration proclaim themselves as *Bhagavannārāyaṇa Prasāda Samsadite Vara Varāha Lañchana*. Further, in phase I Lord Viṣṇu occurs quite frequently (Chart IIA, vi, 1,12,19,21). There are also instances to show how the ruling elites tried to draw references with Lord Viṣṇu and other *Mahābhārata* heroes (Chart IIA, ii, 1-4, 12,19). All these, clearly reflect the ruling elites affiliation towards Vaiṣṇavism during phase I.

This imilarly, Śaivism also existed during this phase. This can be attested from the *praśasti* sections where the Chālukyas had described themselves as protected by Swāmi Mahāsēna and *Karttikeya* (Chart IIA, vi, 2, 11, 12, 18). From the later half of phase I, we notice that the ruling elites under consideration assuming titles such as *Paramēśwara*, *Paramamahēśvara* (Chart IIA, v, 19-20). This further suggests that by this time Śaivism gradually started gaining influence among the ruiing elites. An interesting feature associated with the worship of Śiva was the installation of Bānalingas. Bānalingas were installed in honour of the deceased. Inscriptions in Phase I (Chart IIB, 24) mention Vijayāditya II as the builder of 108 temples to God Śiva under his surname Narendrēśvara. The idea of Bānalingas might have induced this ruler to construct so many temples at every place where he fought with his enemies.[23] Thus, by the later half of this phase, Śaivism emerged as an important and dominant religion which got its social base both from the ruling elites and the large majority of local population.

An interesting feature of all these religious sects in the early medieval context, was that they were greatly influenced by tantric dogmas. The tantric system is characterised by the worship of Śakti or the female energy of Śiva. The presence of female principle in the name of Śakti gradually developed into an independent cult called Śaktism.

The important aspect of this new cult was the appropriation of autochthonous cults. This cult emerged as a prominent cult among the ruling dynasties in the early medieval period.

An important feature of Śaktism is that it was associated with the cult of *Saptamātrikas.* The *Saptamātrikas* included the seven mothers namely, Brahmi, Mahēśvari, Kaumāri, Vaiṣṇavi, Varāhi, Indrāni and Camuṇdi.[24] In the inscriptions of the ruling elites under consideration, they described themselves as *Mātrigaṇaparipālitānaṃ* that is those who were protected by the seven mothers of mankind. The cult of *Saptamātrikas* involved the worship of mother goddess in seven forms. The other deities that are worshipped during this period were Śiva with his variant names such as Narendrēśwara, Bhimēśwara, Mallikārjuna, Svarnēśvara, Harunēśvara, Vāsukīravi Somēśvara Mahādēva, etc.

Though, Brāhmaṇism was the dominant religious ideology of the ruling elites and Śaivaism and Vaiṣṇavism simultaneously gaining prominence during phase I, yet we still find Jainism receiving patronage from the ruling elites but this was only to a limited extent. Its support was mainly drawn from some loyal officials, queens and chieftains. In phase I, the inscriptions of early Chālukyan rulers of Bādāmi show their rulers as being sympathetic towards Jainism. The Aihōle inscription[25] of Pulakēśin II (Chart I, v, 4) mentions Jinēndra as an important deity worshipped. This clearly shows that he was an ardent follower of Jainism.

Even the Eastern Chālukyan rulers in this phase are said to have made sufficient grants to Jain temples. The Kaluchumbaṟru grant of Vishnuvardhana II was made to Jain teachers for the maintenance of Jaina basadis (Chart IVA, ii, 21). This shows their sympathetic attitude towards Jainism.

At the social level, incorporation of several tribes and castes and formation of new sub-castes based on regional and occupational identities were taking place. This resulted in caste proliferation leading to the complexity in social formation. Another noteworthy aspect that had emerged as a dominant feature during this phase, is the construction of temples by the ruling elites as this is often associated with the royalization of the local cult centres.[26] Associated with the growth of the sectarian religion and temple construction was the ideology of *bhakti.* The purāṇic ideology of *bhakti* appears to have percolated to the south through the temple centred *brāhmaṇa* settlements.[27] These changes in the ideological and social strands were also prominently figured in phase II. Brāhmaṇism though continued to exist even in this phase, however got crystalized and gave place to the dominance of new religious sects such as Śaivism, Vaiṣṇavism, and Śaktism.

Śaivism, during this phase emerged as a dominant religious ideology of the ruling elites. This can assumed from the large number of inscriptions in which the ruling elites used such titles as *Parama-mahēśvara, Paramēśvara, and Mahēśvara* (Chart IIB, v, 25, 28, 32, 33, 35, 42, 44, 45) in describing themselves. This clearly revealed not only the ruling elites leanings towards Śaivism but it also explains their attempts to equate themselves with the dominant religious ideology associated with lord Śiva.

The Bānalingas which were described as associated with Śaivism in phase I are also found in phase II. During this phase Rājarājanarēndra is also said to have installed Bānaliṇgas in the honour of his general Brahma Mahārāja and two other generals. These generals have sacrificed their life in a fierce battle. It was under these circumstances that Rājarāja I is said to have set up in memory of Rājarāja Brahma Mahārāja a temple dedicated to God Śiva called Rājarājēśwara at the village of Kalidindi.[28]

The important aspect of Śaivism during this phase is the emergence of radical Śaivite sects like the Pāsupatas and Kālāmukhas. These two sects also received patronage from the ruling elites. From phase II that is from about the 9th century A.D. onwards the Kālāmukhas occupied a prominent place among the Śaivite sects in Andhra country. They received patronage from ruling elites (Chart IVB, iii, 49). From the Taṇḍikoṇḍa grant[29] of Ammarāja II (A.D. 958-59), it appears that Simhaparishad branch of Kālāmukhas who belonged to the family of Śri Lākulisa are mentioned as being donated with the grant of four villages along with three milch cows by Ammarāja II. It also mentions the succession of nine pontiffs, who were incharge of the Jaina institutions at Bezwada. The first pontiff was mentioned as Lākṣipu paśupati and the last pontiff of the Jaina institution was Prabhutarāsi III. They were a Śaivite sect of social and religious reformers and drew within their vortex large sections of populations.

Apart from Śaivism, Vaiṣṇnvism in some form or the other also gained support from the ruling elites during this period. The fabrication of mythical genealogies connecting the Eastern Chālukyan descent to the *Mahābhārata* heroes, namely, the Kauravas and the Pāndavas from the later half of this phase (Chart IIB, ii, 43-50) indicates their affiliation towards Vaiṣṇavism. Further, it has been noticed that during this phase Rājarāja Narēndra had encouraged the translation of *Mahābhārata* intō the vernacular language in accordance with the brāhmaṇical ideology so as to claim greatness along with the Kauravas and the Pāndavas. C.R. Reddy opines that "the real motive underlying the translation of the *Mahā*bhārata into Telugu with its pro-brāhmaṇic interpretations was a propaganda through the vernacular, as a counter blast to the Jaina and Buddhist propaganda".[30]

In course of time Vaiṣṇavism gave place to the development to three important sects namely Vīkhanāsa, Pañcaratras, and Śrīvaiṣṇavism. Under the missionary zeal of Ramanujacharya, brāhmaṇism was made reconciled with Bhāgavatism. Ramanuja seems to have tried to build up the Śrivaiṣṇava system as a bridge between Vikhanāsa and Pañcharatra.[31] However, it should be mentioned here that during the period under study Śrīvaiṣṇavism was not very popular.

An important aspect of these new sectarian religions is that they exercised tremendous influence not only on ruling elites and large sections of people but also on heretical sects like Jainism. Further, the influence of Jainism was still seen to a limited extent in the Andhra counrty inspite of its relative decline all over the country. In the wake of constant threats encountered from the Rāshtrakūtas, who were ardent patrons of Jainism and the Eastern Chālukyan rulers who were often shrunk to subordinate position by the former in their constant wars were compelled to patronize Jainism, despite of them been staunch supporters of brāhmaṇism and its purāṇic elements of Śaivism and Viṣṇavism.[32] During this phase, Jainism seems to have incorporated within its fold the features of the sectarian religions.[32] Hence, during this phase, we still find Jainism being continued to receive royal patronage. This was reflected in the inscriptions of this phase where the ruling elites have made endowments to Jaina temples (Chart IVB, 1, 45, 47). Ammarāja II patronized Jainism, inspite of him being a devote Śaivite. One interesting point about his Jain grants was that they were made at the request of others (Chart IVB, i, 15, 47). This was done mainly with the intention of pleasing his officers and keep them loyal to him. In doing this, he was prompted by his anxiety to consolidate his own position on the throne in the face of troubles from his cousins.

The emergence of theistic worship of sectarian gods found its institutional base in temples. This led to the proliferation of temple construction in different parts of the Indian sub-continent.

In Phase I the temple construction activity was first undertaken by Vijayāditya II. He is said to have constructed 108 temples dedicated to

God Śiva (Chart IVB, vi, 24). The process, thus initiated in the later half of Phase I was accelarated in Phase II, where we have instances of ruling elites as having shown great interest in the erection of huge temples dedicated to both Śiva and Viṣṇu. The popularity of these sectarian religions can be assigned by the proliferation of temples at different centres. Some of them were even developed as important tīrthas or holy places. Among these important religious centres in this period include the Pañcarāmas, Pithāpuram, Vijayawāda, Bāpatla, Simhāchalam and Srīkūrmam. The origin of the Pañcarāmas is attributed to a legendary story. According to this myth, it has been stated that the temples for God Śiva were founded when the skull of the demon named Tārakāsura burst into five pieces and fell in five different places. These five places henceforward came to be popularly known as the Pañcarāmas. The Pañcarāmas or the five great Śaivite centres includes Pedda-Dakarēmi or Drākshārāma, Skandārāma, or Kumārārāma, Bhīmārāma or Chālukya Bhīmavaram, Kshīrārāma and Amarārāma or Amarāvati.[34] Interestingly, the inscriptions of this phase reveal that while the ruling elites have erected temples dedicated to Lord Śiva, we have instances of merchants and sēnapatis having encouraged the construction of temples dedicated to Viṣṇu (Chart IVB, ii, 59, 60, Vz, iii, 23). This clearly reflects the popularity of Śaivism among the ruling elites and that of Vaiṣṇavism among other dominant sections of the society.

These temple institutions emerged as crucial centres for linking up local systems into larger organisational units as every person or group who controlled political or economic power joined in the pattern of religious patronage. Thus, the long term support of religious institutions such as temples or monasteries constituted the most important forms of legitimation and control of the society.[35]

An important aspect that is associated with the legitimation process of local state structures in the early medieval context was through the process of seeking affiliation with a deity or a sacred centre. This practice that was initiated under the Pallavas and augmented by the Cōlas in Tamilnadu and the Gaṇgas in Orissa in the 11th-12th centuries A.D. appears much earlier in our case study. In phase II, in the reign of Chālukya Bhīma I, Lord Śiva came to be identified under the name of Bhīmēśvara. From then onwards Lord Bhīmēśvara became the tutelary deity not only of the Chālukyan rulers of Vengi, but also to the other minor Chālukyan dynasties. The various donations made by these minor ruling chiefs to God Bhīmēśvara in the form of cattle, shows the prominence of this deity under the minor Chālukyan families. Further, in one of the inscriptions Polamayya a merchant (Pattapu-setti) is said to have erected the temple of Chālukya Bhīmēśvara at Prayaga. This is a clear indication of raising the status of the central cult to the pan-Indian importance. Similarly, Chālukya Bhīma also came to be identified with Chālukya Bhīmēśvaram or Bhīmēśvaram which emerged as an important sacred Śaivite centre during this phase (MAP IV). This dual process of identifying with the deity or a sacred centre provided legitimation to the royal authority[36] and simultaneously this also helped them in consolidating their power.

Synchronous to these processes of legitimation is the new ideology of *bhakti. Bhakti* emerged as a dominant ideology of the new religious sects such as Śaivism and Vaiṣṇavism in the early medieval period. The cult of devotion and loyalty towards the deity became the rallying points of *Bhakti* ideology. *Bhakti* received its support through the institutionalization and construction of temples. The temple complex included within its organizational layers, vast sections of population who controlled political or economic power. All these groups directly came under the influence of *bhakti* ideology. The concept of *bhakti* with its emphasis on devotion, loyalty and complete surrender towards the deity, provided legitimation for the ruling elites.[37] The ideology of *bhakti* opened up new avenues for social mobility. Consequently, many social groups irrespective of their caste status got incorporated into the domain of *bhakti* ideology. This also had its effect on the ruling elites approach towards various social groups. This change can be clearly evidenced in phase II where the ruling elites extended their patronage to various social groups apart from *brāhmaṇas.*

In phase II, there was a perceptible change in the attitude of ruling elites towards different *varṇa* categories. While in phase I we find them encouraging predominantly the members belonging to the *brāhmaṇa varṇa* through the process of conferring land grants, in phase II the ruling elites extended their patronage not only to *brāhmaṇas* but also to persons belonging to other *varṇa* categories such as the *vaiśyas,* and the *sūdras* by conferring land grants. It is observed that from this period onwards the Chālukyas preferred to create more military fiefs than *agrāharas* (Chart IVB, iii, 34, 35, 39-41, 51). In situations of the disturbed political conditions that shook the stability of the State from both within and outside the kingdom the ruling elites were compelled to adopt a new approach in their socio-economic policy during this phase. Further, many social groups belonging to the lower *varṇas* were seem to have raised their status and therefore also received patronage from the ruling elites.

Though, the ruling elites claimed themselves to be *kṣatriyas* and whose inscriptions mention them as the protectors of *varnāśramadharma*, however, they had encouraged the upward mobility of other *varṇas* especially those belonging to the *sūdra varṇa* who claimed themselves to be *Chaturthakulajas*. This was done by offering material incentives in the shape of a military fief or a position in the army (Chart IVB, 39-41).

In this regard it would be pertinent to quote Romila Thapar. According to her view, "Mobility within the ranks of bureaucratic office was related to mobility within the wider context of society itself. Bureaucratic status becomes a means of obtaining social status for the kin group. Therefore upward mobility even when possible was slow. Acceleration of the process would occur during periods of political crisis and instability".[38] Thus, in Phase II during the period of political crisis, the ruling elites confered military fiefs to the *sūdras* who formed the bulk of the population, thus contributing for the social mobility of the *sūdras* to the occupational status of the *kṣatriyas* (Chart IVB, 39-41). An interesting reference to the *sūdra* being raised to the status of a *brāhmaṇa* is evident in this phase. The Telugu Academy plates[39] of Śaktivarman II refers to one Adapa Appanna whose *varṇa* status is identified as a *sūdra.* He was mentioned as having been granted the village of Numiyavāda which has been converted as an *agrahāra.* Since *agrahāras* were grants given only to the *brāhmaṇas,* therefore this is a clear indication of a *sūdra* being raised to the ritual status of a *brāhmaṇa.*

The ruling elites during this phase extended their patronage even to the vaiśya community. The mention of the merchant receiving grant (Chart IVB, 35) attests this fact. Patronization of rich vaiśyas by donating land grants was deemed necessary by the ruling elites as they constituted the wealthy sections of the society.

The proliferation of Jātis or sub-caste is an essential feature of the early medieval society. During this period the existing *varṇas* multiplied into many castes and sub-castes based on their occupations and regional idententies. This phenomenon has been described by M.G.S. Narayanan as *jāti* formation or *jātikarana.*[40] Thus, in our case study the bōyas who were raised to the status of *brāhmaṇas* were mentioned with their occupations such as Dūdibōya (cotton bōya), Kōil bōya (Priest bōya), Mandu bōya (medicine bōya) etc. Similarly, the *brāhmaṇas* and the vaiśyas during this period were identified on the basis of their regional identities such as Velanāti *brāhmaṇas,* Venginäti *brāhmaṇas,* Kammanāti *brāhmaṇas* and Pākanāti *brāhmaṇas* and Kammakōmatis.[41]

Further, an important sub-caste among the *sūdras* that has been mentioned in the inscriptions of this phase are the Teliki Community (Chart IVB, iii, 58). The Telikis belonged to the community of oil-mongers. They organised themselves into a guild known as Telikivevuru or teliki-1000 with their head quarters at Bezwada. This community aspired for a high status, which was acquired by them by rendering meritorious services to the ruling elites namely, the Eastern Chālukyas of Vengi.

The Teki plates[42] of Kulōttunga I mentions that the Telikis were rewarded with privileges which were designed to assure for them a certain favoured position in the society at the times.

By the early medieval period, untouchability appears in its fullest form in terms of rigid caste rules imposed on them. The Caṇḍālas formed an important section of the population. They were placed outside the *varṇa* hicrarchy. This was mainly because of the menial occupations they performed that were tabooed in the *varṇa* ordered aryan society.[43] During this period, Caṇḍālas are employed as talaries or watchmen of the villages and some of them even held positions in administration.[44] This is a clear indication of the untouchables being allowed mobility in terms of occupational status.

Further, the new ideology of *bhakti* which provided space to all these social groups tried to control these social groups through establishing parallelism between the deity and the king. For instance, the deity in the temple, which is the central concept, is equated with the king. This helped in establishing a parallel world of authority that is reconstructed on the spiritual plane. This phenomenon is also observed in phase II. The sculptural representation of the Chālukya Bhimēśvara temple depicts the king Chālukya Bhīma I as being accompanied by his consort queen (Pattapu rāni). They were further depicted as attended by lady attendants and others just as the chief deity of the temple who was accompanied by his consort and served by a whole army of musicians, dancing girls, story tellers, actors, garland makers and priests-in-attendance. All this created a parallelism between the deity and the king that provided legitimacy to the new monarchy. Further, *bhakti* also acted as a governing force among various caste groups by cementing the spirit of loyalty and devotion in service to the king and thereby acted as an important agent in controlling the society.

Thus, from the socio-ideological variables in this Chapter, it is evident that the ruling elites namely, the Eastern Chālukyan rulers made constant attempts to seek socio-ideological legitimation to their political power through controlling society. Similarly, in phase II, the new sectarian religions such as Śaivism and Vaiṣṇavism opened channels to various social groups through *bhakti* ideology and thus controlled the society by establishing parallelism between the deity and the king.

References

1. B.D. Chattopadhyaya, 'Political Processes and Structure of Polity in Early Medieval India: Problems of Perspective', *Social Scientist*, vol. 13, 1985, p. 8.
2. Vivekanand Jha, 'Social Stratification in Ancient India', *Social Scientist*, vol. 19, 1991, p.30.
3. B.D. Chattopadhyaya, *The Making of Early Medieval India*, New Delhi, 1993, p. 19.
4. R.S. Sharma, *Social Changes in Early Medieval India (Circa A.D. 500-1200)*, Delhi, 1969, pp. 19-20.
5. M.G.S. Narayanan and Kesavan Veluthat, 'Bhakti Movement in South India', in D.N. Jha, (ed) *Feudal Social Formations in Early India*, Delhi, 1987, p. 367.
6. A Eschmann, Hermann Kulke et.al, (ed), *The Cult of Jagannath and the Regional Tradition of Orissa*, Delhi, 1986, (Ist ed. 1978) p. 137.
7. B.D. Chattopadhya, *Op.cit.*, 1985, p. 11.
8. Ronald Inden, 'Orientalist Construction of India', *MAS* 1986, 20, 3, pp. 427-428.
9. Alladi Vaidehi Krishna Murthy, *Social and Economic Conditions in Eastern Deccan (A.D. 1000-1250)*. Madras, 1970, p. xi.
10. R.S. Sharma, 'Problem of Transition from Ancient To Medieval Indian History', *IHR* no. 1, 1974, p. 5.
11. B.D. Chattopadhya, *Op.cit.*, 1993, p. 16.
12. *Ibid*, p. 35.
13. Hermann Kulke, "Fragmentation and Segmentation versus Integration? Reflections on the Concepts of Indian Feudalism and the Segmentary State in Indian History," *Studies in History*, vol. IV, no. 2, 1982, p. 37.
14. B.S.L. Hanumantha Rao, *Social Mobility In Medieval Andhra*, Hyderabad, 1995, p. 37.
15. R.S. Sharma, *Op.cit.*, 1969, pp. 23-24.
16. Suvira Jaiswal, 'Studies in Early Indian Social History : Trends and Possibilities', *IHR*, vol.VI, 1979-80, p. 29.
17. P.V. Parabrahma Sastry, 'The Bōyas in Andhra History' *PAPHC*, Guntur, 1986, pp. 72-73.
18. B.S.L. Hanumantha Rao, *Op.cit.*, 1995, pp. 76-84.

19. *IA*, Vol. XX, 1891, pp. 15-18.
20. K.S. Kameswara Rao, 'Social Structure of Medieval Andhra - Emergence of New Political Elites' *PAPHC*, Nellore, 1991, pp. 80-82.
21. B.D. Chattopadhyaya, *Op.cit.*, 1993, pp. 30-31.
22. B.S.L. Hanumantha Rao, *Op.cit.*, 1973, p. 245.
23. B.S.L. Hanumantha Rao, *Religion in Andhra*, Guntur, 1973, pp. 268-69.
24. K. Suryanarayana, *History of the Minor Chalukyan Families in Medieval Andhra Desa*, Delhi, 1986, pp. 244 & 254.
25. *EI*, Vol. VI, 1900-1901, pp. 1-12.
26. M.L.K. Murthy, 'Environment, Royal Policy and Social Formation in the Eastern Ghats South India, A.D. 1000-1500', Presidential Address, *PIHC*, Warangal, 1992, pp. 8-9.
27. M.G.S. Narayanan and Kesavan Veluthat, *Op.cit.*, 1987, pp. 358-359.
28. Alladi Vaidehi Krishnamurthy, *Op.cit.*, 1970, pp. 194-195.
29. *EI*, Vol. XXIII, 1935-36, pp. 162-164.
30. K.S. Kameswara Rao, 'Social Formation During Eastern Chalukyan Period', *PAPHC*, Nagaram, 1987-88, p. 62.
31. B.S.L. Hanumantha Rao, *Op.cit.*, 1973, pp. 254-256.
32. *Ibid*, pp. 168-169.
33. *Ibid*, pp. 167-168.
34. B.V. Krishna Rao, *History of the Eastern Chalukyas of Vengi* (610-1210 A.D.), Hyderabad, 1973, p. 221.
35. James Heitzman, 'Ritual Polity and Economy: The Transactional Network of an Imperial Temple in Medieval South India', *JESHO*, Vol. XXXIV, 1991, p. 26.
36. Anncharlott Eschmann, *Op.cit.*, 1986, pp. 132-137.
37. M.G.S. Narayanan and Kesavan Veluthat, *Op.cit.*, 1990, pp. 366-67.
38. Romila Thapar, *Op.cit.*, 1978, p. 142.
39. *JAHRS*, Vol. V, 1930, pp. 33-49.
40. M.G.S. Narayanan, 'Trends and Prospects of Historiography' *PIHC*, 39th ss, Hyderabad, 1978, p. 29.
41. B.S.L. Hanumantha Rao, *Op.cit.*, 1995, pp. 57-58.
42. *EI*, Vol. VI, 1900-1901, pp. 334-347.
43. Vivekanand Jha, 'Caṇḍāla and The Origin of Untouchability', *IHR*, Vol. XIII, Nos. 1-2, July, 1986, pp. 1-36.
44. M.G.S. Narayanan and Kesavan Veluthat, *Op.cit.*, 1987, p. 366.
45. S. Dasarathi, 'A Sculptural Representation of Chalukya Bhima I', *PAPHC*, Kurnool, 1985, pp. 54-55.

MAP IV
MAJOR TEMPLE SITES AND IMPORTANT SETTLEMENTS PHASE I & II
(7th CENTURY A.D.-12th CENTURY A.D.)

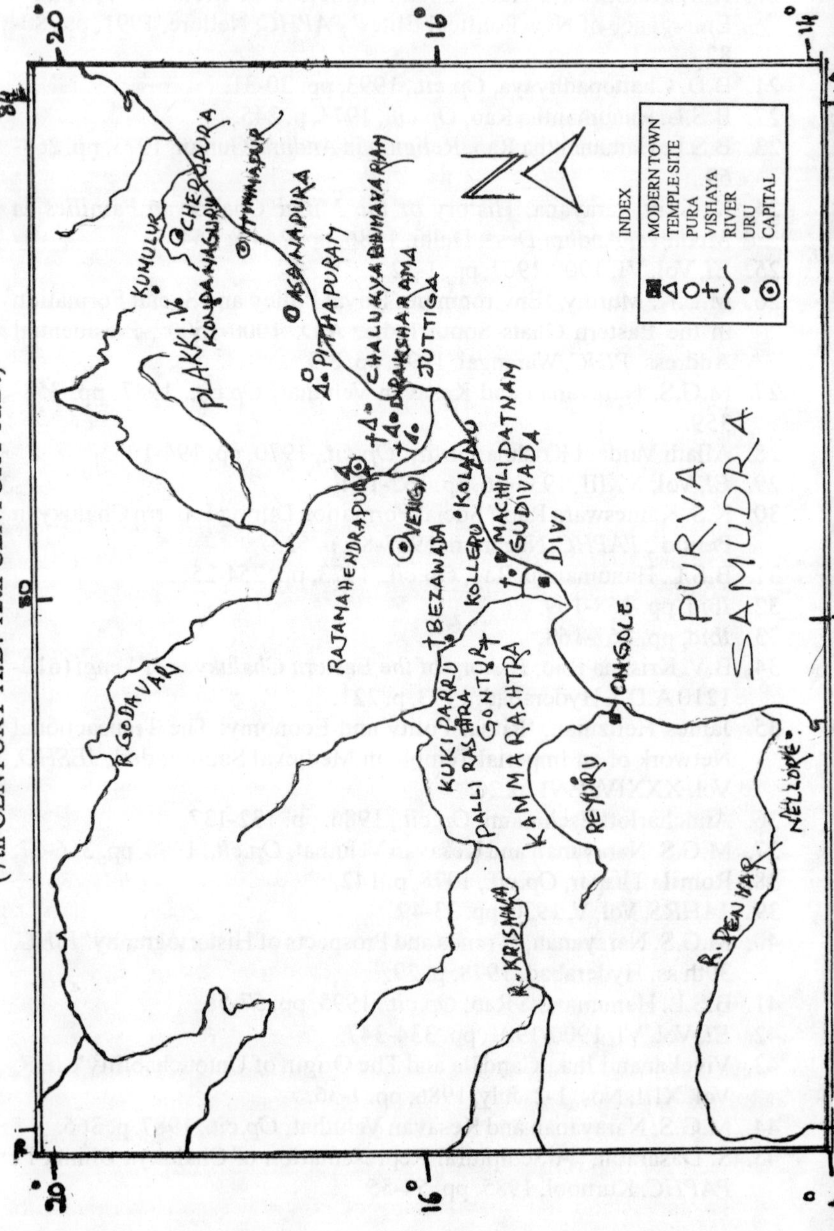

CONCLUSION

In conclusion we reiterate that the main aim of this book is to understand the nature of ruling elites in the context of the notions of social mobility and state formation in the early medieval period. For this purpose the study at the micro-level taking the Eastern Chālukyan dynasty as the case study enabled to understand various mechanisms adopted by ruiling elites to integrate local polities into larger state structure through the elements of continuity and change. The element of continuity was seen in terms of the relationship maintained by the main dynasty under consideration, namely, of the Eastern Chālukyas with their parent branch, namely, the Bādāmi Chālukyas on the one hand, and the minor Chālukyan dynasties on the other. This was mainly through ideological and social linkages. Secondly, the change in terms of the various processes adopted by the ruling elites is understood to consolidate their power that subsequently led to the formation of a new regional state structure. These various process of political, economic, social and ideological changes enabled in the greater penetration of state society into local agrarian pastoral and other peripheral levels thereby integrating them to the State system. This also enhanced the endeavours of ruling elites to consolidate their powr. Most of the earlier writings that have discussed the nature of ruling elites and the State have viewed them form a normative perspective with literary texts serving as their major sources. Therefore, in most of their writings Indian State and society were perceived as being despotic, centralized and barbaric that hindered change, thus portraying the Indian State as static. In our study we have pertinently moved away from such interpretations of conventional historiography. In doing so we had to rely on inscriptional sources which furnished us with direct information on ruling elites and State. They provided us with most of the information on political, economic, social and ideological aspects. The Structural changes that took place among the early medieval period, were undertaken by us in the broad phases of study. This chronological division has been maintained in different chapters as this enabled us to analyse element of continuity and change reflected in the relationship between various ruling elites of the period under study.

To understand the phenomenon of continuity and change in the process of formation and consolidation of ruling elites and the transformation of State polity, first and foremost, we had taken up the study on how the earlier scholars had viewed this phenomenon. The views of various scholars belonging to both conventional and recent historigraphical schools have been elaborated by us in Chapter I. In this chapter, an account of the views of four major schools existing as major historigraphical trends in comprehending the nature of Indian State and society was detailed. The first major trend in history writing was initiated under the auspicious of the Imperialist Orientalists. By using various ancient Indian literary texts as their major source material, these scholars adopted the scientific positivist method in understaning Indian State and society. Their study ended up in the formulation of two concepts, namely the Oriental Despotism and Asiatic mode of production. These two concepts were based on the misconceived notion that Indian Society was dominated by autocratic despotic rulers who owned the entire land. Further, they conceived caste and religion as major obstacles for further progress. In order to justify their racial hegemony over the colonized people, they tried to degrade Inidan culture and bluntly rejected change in Indian society.

The second major trend which emerged as a reaction against much of Imperialists and Orientalist writings was the Nationalist school. The Nationalist historians regarded Indian State as rather unitary, centrally organized with strong bureaucracy thus emphasizing on the concepts of "Golden Ages" and "Age of Empires" intercepted by "Darkages" in Indian history. This further buttressed the notion of a static society. Most of their writings were concentrated on particular geographical area with more focus on the Indo-Gangetic plains. Therefore, in most of their works Deccan was given a marginal importance. Most of these Nationalist writings gave spurt to the emergence of regional histories. In this chapter, therefore we have focussed on the books that emerged within this genre of regional historic. Most of the regional writings identified the region of historical analysis with present day boundaries of linguistic States. In this regard, in majority of the writings on early regional historics the history of Andhra Pradesh received only a peripheral attention. Therefore, we finally focussed in our study on those scholars who wrote on early Andhradēsa especially those on the Eastern Chālukyas of Vengi. Though these scholars endeavoured to elaborate the variations in the Praśasti portions of the Eastern Chālukyan dynasty yet, they have failed to study how these changes in the evolution of praśastis helped in comprehending the overall characterization of the socio-economic and idelogical spheres of activity of the ruling elites in consolidating their power.

In this chapter on historiography we have also consciouly dealt with the recent writings which are seen as making a healthy departure from earlier tendency to dynasticize history. In this regard, the Indian Marxist historians namely R.S. Sharma, B.N.S. Yadava and others have initiated a new trend with a "socio-economic orientation" to history. The Marxist scholars with their emphasis on socio-economic transformations understood the nature of Indian State and society in the early medieval period under the new paradigm of "Feudalism". In their understanding of these changes they emphasized on the breakdown of centralized State structures that led to the emergence of new ruling elities. However, with their main focus on land grants they identified change in class relationships which had an impact on defining the proliferation of castes and changing the theoretical varna structure. However, they understood the whole process as that depicting a decentralized polity where the State was seen as parting away with all its powers. Though the majority of the Marxist writings were pertained to Northern India, they tried to generalize the concept of Feudalism at the regional level also.

As against much of the earlier understandings we have, in recent years, the new approach emphasizing on social history framework. Scholars who fall in this category, namely, Hermann Kulke, B.D. Chattopadhyaya and others emphasized on the study of the dynamics of interdependent variables of socio-economic, political and ideological processes in understanding the processes of State formation. Thus, according to Hermann Kulke, the operation of various processes such as donating land to brāhmaṇas in the peripheral areas, kṣatriyization of tribal chiefs, acculturation of tribal cults and deities by the ruling elites were all seen as major ideological processes in consolidating the power of the ruling elities and the formation of states, in the early medieval Orissa. Similarly, B.D. Chattopadhyaya's studies on the process of State formation with reference to the emergence of various Rajput clans to political prominence, highlights the various political, economic, socio-ideological processes of the ruling elites. These processes are explained in terms of the fortification of rural settlements, assignment of land grants, maintaining horizontal marriage networks and finally, legitimization of their rule by establishing genealogical linkages with the kṣatriya line of the mythical past have helped the ruling elites in Rajasthan to consolidate their power in the early medieval period.

Thus, in their writings, these scholars tried to evolve the concept of integrative policy which was seen as positive way in which ruling elites consolidated their power rather then decntralizing it. By adopting the last approach of visualizing an integrative polity, we have attempted to understand the overall changes at the micro-level to comprehend the nature of ruling elites and their attempts to consolidate power in the regional state structures.

In Chapter II, the physical space of micro-region of Vengi in terms of its geography and history was highlighted. In this regard we argued that the history of a broader region can be better understood by placing the history of a micro-region within the context of studying its history against its general geographical setting. For understanding geographical significance first the physical space of micro-region of Vengi was described as part of a larger geographical entity of the Krishna, Godavari sub-region. The rich alluvial soils and strategical location of vengi as a meeting point and a natural highway converging five great routes of Kalinga, Drāvida, Karnataka, Maharashtra and Dakshina Kosala made us agree with Subba Rao's characterization of it as an "area of attraction" on nuclear region.

A major part of our discussion of the region also specially focussed on how the micro-region of Vengi came to be identified. We began this with how in the present day, Vengi is identified with a village called Pedavegi situated near Elluru in the present day West Godavari district. But over time beginning with earliest reference to Vengi in the 2nd Century A.D., its characterization has been changing. We described these changing boundaries upto the 12th century A.D. Our conclusion in this regard was that initially it formed a politically peripheral zone under the Mauryans, the Sātavāhanas and the Ikṣvakas, but subsequently it emerged as an important centre of political power during the transition to the early medieval period.

The second major aspect for description in this chapter was the military conquests undertaken by the Eastern Chālukyan rulers to expand and consolidate their power in two different phases. In this study, we emphasized on nature of their polity that was seen in two distinct phase of growth. The data from inscriptions revealed that in Phase I, the main concern of the ruling elites as new comes in an alien land was to expand their empire through military conquests and at the same time stabilize their political power with the help of local chiefs. This was made possible firstly through the process of conferring land grants and secondly by recruiting local chiefs to high positions in the bureaucratic structure.

In Phase II, the data revealed that the nature of policy underwent a change. With the riseof the hostile powers such as the Rāshtrakūtas of Malkhed, the Gangas of Kalinga and the Western Chālukyas of Kalyani, who posed threat to the stability of the Eastern Chālukyan kingdom, the ruling elites evolved a new political mechanism to consolidate their power. This was made possible with the help of Minor Chālukyan families and secondly through the mechanism of getting into matrimonial alliance with powerful neighbouring rulers and local chieftains. This clearly indicates that the nature of polity evolved under the Eastern Chālukyas was neither a centralized bureaucratic structure as envisaged by traditional historians nor, was it a feudal policy where the State was seen as parting away with its administrative power, as was postulated by Marxist scholars. We have concluded that the nature of polity under the Eastern Chālukyas was an integrative policy, where the State attempted to mediate its political authority and stabilization of power through creating semi-independent localities held by the local chieftains and the minor Chālukyan dynasty. This argument is further buttressed by the fact that most of these semi-independent localities which were integrated into the larger processes of state structure, and that provided stabilization, started emerging as defacto principalities after the collapse of the Eastern Chālukyan kingdom, by the end of 12th century A.D.

To understand the larger processes of political structure, in the context of the changing ideology of the ruling elite, we attempted to first study the pattern of changes perceived in the Genealogies and Marriage Networks in Chapter III. This study has also been undertaken by us in two different parts. In part I, the main thrust of the study was on genealogies and in part II, we discussed on marriage networks. To understand these two variables, namely, the ideological and social, we have categorized the data from inscriptions in the chart (I, IIA, IIB and III). which helped us to define the dynastic *praśastis*, the personal *praśastis*, and marriage alliances.

In phase I the Praśastis of both the Bādāmi Chālukyan rulers and the Eastern Chālukyan rulers (Chart I and IIA) it has been mentioned that the Chālukyas were decedants of *Hariti*, that they belonged to *Mānavya gōtra*, nourished by *Sapta Mātrikas* and so on. From these descriptions we argued that the early Chālukyas, whose real origins were blurred, assumed a brāhmaṇic *gōtra*, namely *Mānavya gōtra*, following the pan-Indian phenomenon. This has been understood by us as an attempt by the ruling elites to claim a *brahma-kṣatra* identity. This argument is further reinforced by the early Chālukyas describing themselves as *Hariti putras* or decendants of *Hariti*. Tradition describes *Haritiputras* as *brāhmanas* endowed with *kṣatriya* like qualities and came to be recognized by a double *varṇa* status, namely *brāhma-kṣatriyas*. From this observation, we concluded that during this phase, the early Chālukyas like other rulers such as the Kādambas before them and the early Pallavas who are contemporaneous with them attempted to seek legitimation to their power by linking up their descent to an old *kṣatriya* family, namely, that of *Harita* and secondly their claim to be the members of the *brāhmana varṇa* was established by adopting a *brāhmaṇa gōtra* namely *Mānavya*, thus imbibing in their dynastic tradition both the brāhmaṇ and kṣatra lineages. From this we concluded that the early Chālukyas were *brahma-kṣatras*, though this has not directly or explicitly referred in their inscriptions.

Similarly, during this phase, we have noted that the records of the two families bears only names of three generations of rulers, i.e., the name of the donor of the grant, his father and his grand father. In the inscriptions of the Eastern Chālukyas from Kubja Vishnuvardhana I to Vishnuvardhana II, we find reference to the Bādāmi Chālukyan rulers in terms of the paternal relations existing between them. This we concluded as manifesting traits of continuity of relationship that had existed between these two branches, inspite of the fact that the Eastern Chālukyan kingdom was established as an independent kingdom by Pulakēśin II. This is further buttressed from the assumption of similar titles by the Eastern Chalukyan rulers. Until the reign of Vijayaditya I, almost all the rulers assumed such ordinary titles like *Mahārāja*, *Vishamasiddhi*, and *Vijayasiddhi* which only indicated their military achievements as conquerors. Further, this also shows the subordinate position of the Eastern Chālukyan rulers viś a viś their affiliation to the Bādāmi Chālukyan dynasty.

In phase II, the data revealed a different picture. The genealogies belonging to the later half of the Eastern Chālukyan dynasty and its collateral branches namely, the minor Chālukyan families of Mudigonda, Jananāthapuram and Nidadavōlu, revealed a change in the descriptions of the genealogies. In the first half of this phase, the data revealed that the dynastic *Praśasti* of these rulers was not very different from phase I. However, it appears distinct in terms of the introduction of long pedigrees of the Eastern Chālukyan rulers with only a brief reference to the Bādāmi Chālukyas. The record from now onwards gave the chronological list of kings starting from the founder of that of the donor of the grant. Further, the personal *praśastis* became more elaborate with the assumption of high sounding titles like *Samastabhuvanāśraya, Mahārājādhirāja, Chakravarti* and so on.

In the later half of phase II, i.e. from the 11th century A.D. onwards, a new trend is perceptible in the Eastern Chālukyan and the Minor Chālukyan records. The data in this phase revealed that the ruling elites attempted to connect their lineage with the *Candravaṃśa* lineage of the mythical past in accordance with the *itihāsa-purāṇa* tradition of North India. Such an attempt of fabricating genealogies by the ruling elites has been concluded by us as an attempt on the part of the ruling elites to seek legitimation in the pure *kṣatriya varṇa*. In this regard the *brahma-kṣatra* status of phase I has been regarded by us as an "intermediary" status before the new ruling elites attempted to claim a pure *kṣatriya* origin to legitimize their power especially when their links with their original family had become bleak and nebulous. Further, we understood this whole phenomenon of fabricating mythical genealogies by the later rulers as a political ideology to consolidate their power in the kingdom at a time when fissiparious tendencies were emerging. By seeking an authoritative genealogical superiority they sought to naturally distance themselves from the local chiefs whom they had conquered.

In part II of this chapter, we attempted to look at the various marriage alliances maintained by Eastern Chālukyan rulers with their contemporary rulers and other local chiefs as an important mechanism for consolidation of power. The data in Phase I was sparse and revealed only one example of Eastern Chālukyan rulers entering into marriage alliance with the Pallavas, who were also *brahma-kṣatriyas*. Thus, alliance between two powerful *brahma-kṣatra* lineages implied their assertion of caste and kinship relationship through marriage alliance.

On the other hand, in Phase II, the data revealed frequent references to marriage alliances between the Eastern Chālukyan family and other contemporary dynasties such as the Rāshtrakūtas, the Chōlas, the Gaṇgas and other powerful local chiefs such as the Pattavardhanis. From the data, we concluded that while, on the one hand, the ruling elites during this phase attempted to align with rulerswho also claimed to belong to the *kṣatriya varṇa* only to assert their *kṣatriya* status, on the other hand, they aligned with local chiefs. It must be emphasized here that some of these local chiefs claimed to be proud members of the *Chaturthakulajas*. This has been regarded by us as an expediency on the part of the ruling elites because of political circumstances and therefore created new networks of social relations, as this provided yet another way of achieving sustenance and stability to their power at time of political instability. This marriage networks, according to us acted as a significant social variable in consolidation of political power by the Eastern Chālukyan rulers especially in phase II. Thus, the social and ideological variables in this chapter have been understood as an attempt by the new ruling elites for sustaining political descent of the elite power through self assertion.

In Chapter IV entitled "Economic Linkages" we have moved on to understand the economic processes of consolidation of power. In this chapter, we highlighted on the nature of grants issued by the Eastern Chālukyan family and contrasted these with those of the three Minor Chālukyan families of Mudigonda, Jananāthapuram and Nidadavōlu. This has been categorized in the form of (Charts IVA, IVB, Vx, Vy, Vz). The classfication of information from these charts helped us in understanding the important changes perceived in the nature of donations of land and other economic resources in the form of grants to various religious and non-religious authorities such as military chiefs and merchants and to temple centred organizations, in two phases of our study. In this context of understanding the economic processes, we have analyzed the various means of resource mobilization of the State. This primarily focussed on the study of the nature of settlement patterns, as a means of acculturating new lands which also included pasturages and gave us an idea of the nature of ownership patterns. Through temple centred settlements in phase II particularly evidence for the encouragement to trade and commerce was noted in some areas.

From the data charted down in Phase I, it was seen that as new ruling elites in an alien land, the Eastern Chālukyan rulers made large scale donations of land primarily to *brāhmaṇas* and also to powerful trible groups such as the *bōyas*. It is interesting to note that during this period some of the *bōyas* got acculturated into the brāhmanical order. This was done through creating *agrahāras* in already settled villages or by creating new settlements in virgin land. This can be exemplified through data where in far off places from the core area of Vengi were used to make these grants.

In phase I, we have concluded that the transfer of ownership rights to *brāhmaṇas* and other powerful pastoral communities like *bōyas* did not necessarily lead to the loss of these privileges by the king, as was postulated by the Marxist scholars. We argued, that though the creation of *agrahāras* did not lead to the a propriation of revenue by the State as these were tax free and the revenue would go to the local authorities, however, the main motive of the ruling elites in creating *agrahāras* was to devolve upon the *brāhmaṇas* the difficult task of creating validity for the "royal" rights in their settlements. Further, contestation by existing agricultural groups was numbed by the role of the *brāhmaṇas* as leaders of the new ideology of the State. Simultaneously, *agrahāras* also helped in developing a village-level administration necessary for the implementation of royal demands.

An analysis of the nature of settlement patterns in Phase I, reveals that the majority of settlements during this phase were "Ūru", "grāma" ending names. Further, the acculturation of pastoral and tribal settlements such as *Ādivāsa* village was noted in this phase. This suggests that the substantially pastoral and agrarian economy co-existed during Phase I.

However in Phase II, on one hand there is a continuity of the agrarian and pastoral economy in some tracts, in other areas especially temple centred agrarian areas emerged. During this phase, it has been noticed that most of the land grants were made to a hierarchy of officials and merchants and also to temples apart from those to *brāhmaṇas* which continued. In this Phase village grants were apportioned and were not necessarily tax free *agrahāras* as had been the case in phase I. The grants that were made by Mudigonda Chālukyas were largely in the form of land donations in contrast to the grants that were made by other Chālukyan families of Jananāthapuram and Nidadavōlu which were in the form of cattle and cattle products such as butter, ghee donated for lighting of lamps in temples. Most of these temples seems to have situated away from the areas they controlled. This indicates that the Minor Chālukyan rulers accepted the legitimation of the Vengi Chālukyas. At the same time this also led to acculturation of their economy, which is substantially pastoral in nature with that of the economy of the Vengi rulers which is emerging as a full fledged agrarian economy. Further, the grants were made to warriors, generals and other parties who paid yearly tributes to the State. During this phase temple as an institution emerged as receipent of land grants and also other resources. It became a means for integrating different economic resources. Land grants to temples in certain key agrahāras is also seen as an important mechanism as it led to the growth of temple centred commodity production. Most of the temple settlement (e.g. Drākshārāma, Pithāpuram) were located along sea-coast and this facilitated revival of tendencies that indicated growth of trade and markets. Data also revealed that land donations were made to merchant class which further supports our argument that the agrarian economy was developing to be able to sustain trade and commerce during this period. The discovery of hoards of gold coins belonging to the Eastern Chālukyan dynasty from the later half of phase II, further buttresses our argument. From the study of these temple settlements and nature of grants, we concluded that the Eastern Chālukyan economy during this phase was neither a full fledged urban economy as the process of urbanization had just been started. This happened only in a few select areas. However, in some sub-regions its character was different as it was not a fully developed agrarian economy, since it was still dominated by both pastoral and agrarian social groups. We had to arrive at this conclusion based on the data revealed in the grants that were continued to be made to pastoral and trible groups like the *bōyas* and secondly, most of the grants made to temples especially by the minor Chālukyan rulers was surplus from the pastrol economy. All these helped the State to economically integrate diverse regions and people.

Further, in this chapter the data revealed that the purpose for making grants to *brāhmaṇas*, temples and other groups was obstensibly for spiritual purpose of gaining self-glory, for repairs of temples or for loyalty and obedience rendered by the military chiefs. This information we have argued, blurs the real motive for making grants which were understood as more complex and related to many issues of ownership rights in country side, methods and mode of agricultural expansion and finally interest of the State in getting revenue which underlines the economic processes that the ruling elites had to address as a means for resource mobilization and stabilization of power. Ultimately, we concluded that the economy during this period (both phases) is in transition where in a fullfledged agrarian economy was in the processes of establishing its hold over major nuclear areas. In some areas the pastrol groups continued to dominate where as in others, like major *agrahāra* settlements, the temple grew to become the nuclei of a market indulging in non-agrarian economic activity.

Another dimension of ruling elites to consolidate their power was through socio-ideological processes. For the purpose of study in this Chapter V, we undertook a detailed examination of the socio-ideological parameters. In contrast to the discussion of social and ideological variables in Chapter III, where the ruling elites used these variables to strengthen themselves, this chapter focussed on how ruling elites tried to control society through ideological means.

The data from the inscriptions revealed that in Phase I, the ruling elites deliberately patronized the *brāhmaṇas* belonging to various *gōtras* by donating *agrahāras*. Most of the *brāhmaṇas* appeared to be specialists in the *vēdas* and their affiliated schools. The patronization of *brāhmaṇas* in Phase I, also revealed the early Chālukyan rulers religious leaning towards brāhmaṇism. The dominance of brāhmaṇism is further attested by reference to various vēdic sacrifices that were performed by the early Chālukyan rulers of Bādāmi, such as *Vājapēya, Aśvamēdha, Agnishtōma, Paundārika* etc., mentioned in the Eastern Chālukyan records. Also the assumption of titles such as *Parama-brāhmaṇya* supports this fact. From this information, it was evident that in phase I, grants to the *brāhmaṇas* as religious specialists played a dual role of colonizing the peripheral areas and generated a sense of loyalty among the tribal people towards the king. As highly scholared religious professionals they acted as important levers in disseminating *varṇa* ideology in their *agrahāras* and neighbouring settlements. Simultaneously, land grants to *brāhmaṇas* also encouraged the process of social mobility through assimilation and acculturation of various aboriginal tribal groups such as the *bōyas* and persons who were placed at lower levels of the *varṇa* system. In this way, the new ruling elites in Phase I, attempted to control the society through *brāhmaṇas* and brāhmaṇical religion. However, along with Brāhmaṇism, there co-existed elements of Paurānic religion, through mention of names of gods like Śiva, and Viṣṇu. Jainism also received patronage from ruling elites during this phase but to a limited extent.

On the other hand, in Phase II the data revealed a perceptible change in the attitude of the ruling elites towards different religious sects and social groups. During this phase, we find the dominance of such religious sects like Śaivism and Vaiṣṇavism. These two religious sects emerged in a big way so as to overshadow the earlier importance given to vēdic religion. They also emerged as a challenge to heretical sects like Jainism and Buddhism. In fact, they opened the channels to various social groups through *bhakti*, which emerged as a dominant ideology of these new religious sects. The *bhakti* ideology with its messianic appeal integrated new values of devotion, loyalty and complete surrender towards the deity. Further, by drawing paralleism to the deity and king, *bhakti* acted as an important ideology of the ruling elites for legitimation.

Further, Vaiṣṇavism and Śaivism emerged as temple based cults acculturating within their fold various tribal cults such as the cult of *Saptamātrikas*.

In this phase, the data revealed that the ruling elites of both main family and minor families accepted Śaivism as the dominant religious ideology. This is inferred from the patronization of *Kālāmukha* sects of Śaivism by donating land for temple repairs, religious teachers, construction of temples at various Śaivite centres such as Drākshārāmam, Beemēśvaram, Vijayawāda etc, and above all, assumption of titles such as *Paramamahēśvara, Paramēśvara* etc.

An important aspect of religious domination noted in our study was the attempts made by the main ruling elites of Chālukyas of Vengi to seek affiliation with a deity or a sacred centre. We argued that this process of identifying with a deity or a sacred centre provided legitimation to the royal authority and consolidated their power.

On the other hand, these new religious sects also encouraged social mobility. Thus, in this phase, the Eastern Chālukyan rules consciously encouraged the process of social mobility of other *varṇas* especially the *sūdras* by conferring material incentives in the form of military chiefs or position in the army. Also the data revealed that an important phenomenon of proliferation of *jātis* or sub-castes among various caste groups was taking place. The formation of these sub-castes was based on the occuption and regional identities.

Patronization of such varied social groups in Phase II was necessary as this period witnessed constant political threats to the stability of the Chālukyan power from both within and outside the kingdom. Secondly, most of these lower caste groups were rising their status in the religious hieracy through *bhakti*. Therefore, their leanings towards the religious sects like Vainavism and Saivism is necessary as this led to control the various social groups through *bhakti* and its ideology of self-surrender to the king/deity.

Thus, from this overall analysis of our study based on the information provided in the inscriptional data, we concluded that as new ruling elites in an alien land, the socio-ideological variables in Chapter III was necessary to assert their position by legitimizing and validating the new form of State which came into existence in the 7th, 8th centuries A.D. This was essential as every new or changed form of State requires its own legitimacy. Similarly, socio-idelogical mechanisms in Chapter V acted as important variables in controlling the society. In between these two, the concrete economic mechanisms through donations of land to various social groups and institutions, and evolving local level village administration integrated the society through economic linkages. Thus, by bringing out the interplay of the various forces, such as economy, society and polity in their totality, we have conceptualized the state formation during the Eastern Chālukyan period as integrative rather than centralized or decentralized state. In this regard of the study of these various processes, we have seen the early medieval as an "intermediate" phase. It has therefore been attempted by us to look at the Eastern Chālukyan rule as signifying the early medieval in terms of socio-economic and cultural transition and its relationship to the polity at the regional level. These changes were similar to those effecting others part of the country and therefore, the study of the region can be put within the framework of pan-Indian changes rather than looking at them in isolation or purely in particularistic dynastic terms. This study was important because it helped us to identify various factors that were instrumental in enabling the Eastern Chālukyan rulers to establish and control not only the micro-region of Vengi, but a large territory that spread over most of the coastal Andhra from 7th century A.D. to the 12th century A.D. and laid foundations for the growth of new identities in the subsequent periods.

BIBLIOGRAPHY

INSCRIPTIONS

Epigraphia Indica : Vol. III to XXXI(ed.), Hultzsh, Keithorn Stenknow, D.C. Circar, V. Venkayya, J.F. Fleet, Archaeological Survey of India, Calcutta, 1898-1963.

Epigraphia Āndhrica : Vol. I to V(ed.) N. Venkataramaṇayya, P.V. Parabhrahma Sastry, N. Mukunda Rao, Director of Archaeology and Museums, Hyderabad, 1969-1988.

Indian Antiquary : Vol. III to XX (ed.), Jas Burgess, Swati Publications, Delhi.

Journal of Andhra Historical Research Society : Vol. V, IX, XI (ed.), by B.R. Subramanyam 1930, 1934, 1936.

Journal of Bihar, Orissa Research Society : Vol. VIII, (ed.), by K.V., Lakshmana Rao, 1922.

South Indian Inscriptions : Vol. I, V, X (ed.), E. Hultzsch, Rao Bahadur, H.H. Krishna Sastry, Madras 1987.

GAZETTEERS

Ramesan, N. : *Andhra Pradesh District Gazetteers, Krishna,* Hyderabad, 1979.

Ramesan, N. : *Andhra Pradesh District Gazetteers, West Godavari,* Hyderabad, 1979.

Ramesan, N. : *Andhra Pradesh District Gazetters, East Godavari,* Hyderabad, 1979.

Ramesan, N. : *Andhra Pradesh District Gazetteers, Guntur,* Hyderabad, 1979.

SELECT BOOKS

Altekar,A.S. : *State and Government in Ancient India,* Motilal Banarasidass, Ist ed, Varanasi, 1949 Reprint-Delhi, 1977.

Appadorai, A. : *Economic Conditions in South India,*

(1000-1500 A.D.), Volume I&II University of Madras, 1936.

Bhandarkar, R.G. : *Early History of the Dekkan*, Asian Education Services, New Delhi, Second edition-1985.

Bhatt, G.P. : *"Vāyu Purānam" in Ancient Indian Tradition and Mythology*, Vol. 38, 1988.

Chattopadhyaya, B.D. : *Coins and Currency System in South India* (C.A.D. 225-1300), Munsiram Manohar Lal, New Delhi, 1977.

Chattopadhyaya, B.D. & Pande, B.M. : *Archaeology and History,* Vol. II. Agamakala Prakashan, Delhi, 1987.

Chattopadhyaya B.D. : *The Making of Early Medieval India,* Oxford University Press, Delhi, 1994.

Chenna Reddy, P. : *Guilds in Medieval Andhra Desa* (A.D. 1000-1500), Sundeep Prakashan, Delhi, 1991

Dikshit, D.P. : *Political History of the Chalukyas of Badami*, Abhinav Publications, New Delhi; Ist ed. 1980.

Eschmann, Anncharlott Kulke, H. & Tripati, G.C. : *The cult of Jagannath and the Regional Tradition of Orissa*, Manohar, Delhi, 1986, Ist ed., 1978.

Gopal, B.R. : *Minor Dynasties of South India,* Vol. I, New Era Publications, Madras, 1982.

Gopal Chary, K. : *Early History of the Andhra Country*, Madras, 1976.

Hanumantha Rao, B.S.L. : *Religion in Andhra*, Guntur, 1973.

_____ : *Social Mobility in Medieval Andhra*, Telugu University, Hyderabad, Ist ed, 1995.

Jawaharlal, G. : *Jainism in Andhra as Depicted in Inscriptions,* Prakrita Bharai Academy, Jaipur & Akhil Bharatiya Sri Suvarna Jain Seva Fund, Hyderabad, 1994.

Jawaharlal, K.P. : *Hindu Polity*, A Constitutional History of India in Hindu Times, Bangalore, 1978, Ist ed., 1924.

Jha, D.N. : *Studies in Early Indian Economic History*, Anupama Publications, 1980.

Jha, D.N. : *Fedual Social Formation in Early India*, Delhi, *Chanakya, 1987.*

Karashima, Noboru : *South Indian History and Society: (Studies from Inscriptions-A.D. 850-1800)*, New Delhi, 1984.

Kosambi, D.D. : *An Introduction to the Study of Indian History,* Popular Prakashan, Bombay, Ist ed., 1956 Reprint, 1990.

——— : *History and Society,* Department of History, University of Bombay, 1985.

Krishna Rao, B.V. : *History of the Eastern Chalukyas of Vengi (610-1210 A.D.),* Andhra Pradesh Sahitya Akademi Kalabhavan, Saifabad Hyderabad, Ist ed., 1973.

Krishna Sastry, V.V. : *The Proto & Early Historical Cultures of Andhra Pradesh*, The Govt. of A.P. Hyderabad, 1983.

Kulke, Hermann : *The State in India, 1000-1700*, Oxford University Press, Delhi, 1995.

Kumari Krishna, M. : *The Rule of the Chalukya-Cholas in Andhra Desa*, B. R. Publishing Corporation, Delhi, 1985.

Marwick, Arthur. : *Nature of History*, London, 1970.

Mill, James. : *The History of British India*, Vol. I, Associated Publishing House, New Delhi, Ist ed., 1817, Re-print 1972.

Nandi, R.N. : *Religious Institutions and Cults in the Deccan (C.A.D. 600-1000)*, Motilal Banarasidas, Delhi, Ist ed., 1973.

Narayanan, M.G.S : *Re-Interpretations in South Indian History*, Trivendrum, 1977.

Nilakanta Sastry, K.A. : *A History of South India*, Oxford University Press, Madras, Ist ed., 1955, Reprint, 1975.

Om Prakash : *Religion and Society in Ancient India*, Bharatiya Vidya Prakashan, Delhi, Ist ed., 1985

Parasher Aloka : *Social and Economic History of Early Deccan-Some Interpretations*, Manohar, New Delhi, 1993.

Pargiter, F.E.	:	*Ancient Indian Historical Tradition*, Motilal Banarasidas, Delhi, Ist ed. 1922, Reprint, 1972.
Parry, Geraint	:	*Political Elites*, George Allen & Unwin Ltd, London, 1969.
Prasad Rajendra, B.	:	*Chalukyan Temples of Andhra Desa*, Abhinav Publication, New Delhi, 1983.
Rama Rao, M.	:	*Early Chalukyan Temples of Andhra-desa*, Government of Andhra Pradesh, Hyderabad, 1970.
Ramesan, N.	:	*Eastern Chalukyas of Vengi*, A. P. Sahitya Academi, Kalabhavan, Saifabad, Hyderabad, Ist ed., 1975.
Ramesh, K.V.	:	*Chalukyas of Vatapi*, Agam Kala Prakashan, Delhi, 1984.
Ray, Amita.	:	*Life and Art of Early Andhradesa*, Agamkala Prakashan, Delhi, 1983.
Sankaranarayana, S	:	*The Vishnukundis and Their Times*, Agam Kala Prakashasn, Delhi, 1977.
Sastry, B.N.	:	*Andhrula Sanghika Charitra (B.C. 400-1100)*, Musi Publications, Lingampally, Hyderabad. Ist ed., 1975 2nd ed., 1991.
Satyanarayana, K.	:	*A study of the History and Culture of the Andhras from Stone Age to Feudalism*, People's Publishing House, New Delhi, 1975.
Sharma, R.S.	:	*Aspects of Political Ideas and Institutions in Ancient India*, Motilal Banarasidass, Delhi, 1959, 3rd revised ed., 1991.
———	:	*Indian Feudalism (C.A.D. 300-1200)*, Macmillan India Ltd., Delhi, Ist ed., 1965, Reprint-1985.
———	:	*Perspectives in Social and Economic History of Early India*, Munshiram Manoharlal Publishers Pvt. Ltd., 1983.
Sircar, D.C.	:	*Indian Epigraphy*, New Delhi, 1965.
Smith, V.A.	:	*The Oxford History of India*, OUP, Delhi, Ist ed., 1919, 4th ed., 1958.

Stein, Burton : *All the Kings Mana Papers on Medieval South Indian History*, New Era Publications, Madras, 1984.

Subba Rao, B. : *Personality of India-Pre and Proto Historic Foundations of India and Pakistan*, Faculty of Arts, Maharaja Sayiairao University of Baroda, 1958.

Sumati Mulay, M. : *Studies in the Historical and Cultural Geography and Ethnography of the Deccan*, Deccan College Post Graduate and Research Institute, Poona, 1972.

Sandaram, K. : *Studies in Economic and Social Conditions of Medieval Andhra (A.D. 1000-1600)*, Triveni Publishers, Machilipatnam, & Madras, Ist ed., 1968.

Suryakumari,A. : *Temples in Andhra Desa*, Gian Publishing, House, Delhi, 1988.

Suryanarayana, K. : *History of the Minor Chalukya Families in Medieval Andhra Desa*, B.R. Publishing House, Delhi, 1987.

——— : *Inscriptions of Minor Chalukyan Dynasties of Andhra Pradesh*, Mittal Publications, Delhi, 1993.

Swarnkar, R.C. : *Political Elite*, Rawat Publications, Jaipur, 1988.

Thapar, Romila. : *A History of India*, Vol. I., Penguin Books, Great Britain, Ist ed., 1966, Reprint, 1983.

——— : *Past and Prejudice*, Publications Division, Ministry of Inforamation & Broadcasting, New Delhi, May,1973.

——— : *Ancient Indian Social History—Some Intrpretations*, Orient Longman, New Delhi, Apr. 1978.

——— : *From Lineage to State*, Oxford University Press, Bombay, 1984.

——— : *Interpreting Early India*, Oxford University Press, Delhi, Ist ed., 1992, 2nd ed., 1994.

Vaidya, C.V. : *History of Medieval Hindu India*, Vol. II, Cosmo Publications, New Delhi, Ist ed., 1924, Reprint, 1979.

Tomory, Edith : *History of Fine Arts: India and the West*, Orient Longman, Bombay, 1982.

Vaidehi Krishna Murthy, : *Social and Economic Conditions in Eastern Deccan. (A. D. 1000-1250)*, Kabeer Printing Press, Madras, Ist ed., March, 1970.

Veluthat, Kesavan. : *The Political Structure of Early Medieval South India*, Orient Longman Ltd., New Delhi, 1993.

Venkataramanyya, N. : *The Eastern Chalukyas of Vengi*, Vedam Venkataraya Sastry & Bros. Madras, 1950.

——— : *The Chalukyas of V(L)emulavada*, The Archaeological Department, Government of Hyderabad, 1953.

Yadava, B.N.S. : *Society and Culture in Northern India in the 12th Century A.D.*, Central Book Deport, Allahabad, 1973.

Yazdani, G. : *Early History of Deccan*, Vol. I& II, Oriental Books Reprint Corporation, Ist ed., 1982.

SELECT ARTICLES

Balarama Murthy, Y. : "Social Mobility-Horizontal and Vertical", *PAPHC*, Nagaram, 1987-1988.

Bongard-Levin, G.M. & : "Society and State in Ancient India." *IHR*, Vol. V, 1978-79,

Champaka Lakshmi, R. : "The State in Medieval South India: Emerging Perspectives". Presidental address, *PAPHC*, XIII Session, 1989.

——— : "Urbanization in South India" The role of Ideology and Polity, *PIHC*, 47th ss, Srinagar, 1986.

——— : "Urbanization in Medieval Tamil Nadu" in S. Bhattacharya and Romila Thapar (ed). *Situating Indian History*, OUP, Delhi, 1986.

Chattopadhyaya, B.D. : "Poltical Processes and Structure of Polity in Early Medieval India: Problems and Perspectives." *Social Scientist*, Vol. 13, 1985,

Chattopadhyaya, B.D. : "Origin of the Rajputs : The Poltical Economic and Social Processes in Early Medieval Rajasthan." *IHR*, Vol.3, 1976-77,

Dasarathi, S. : "A Sculptural Representation of Chalukya Bhima I" *PAPHC*, Kurnool, 1985.

Gopal, B.R. : "Presidental Address" *PAPHC*, 1991, Nellore.

Hanumantha Rao, B.S.L. : "Formation of Social Groups and Mutual Relations in Andhra", Presidential Address, *PAPHC*, XIII Session, Srisailam, 1989.

----- : "Bōyas in Medieval Andhra History" *JAHRS*, Vol. 38, Part IV.

Heitzman, James. : "Ritual Polity and Economy : The Transactions Network of An Imperial Temple in Medieval South India" *JESHO*, Vol. XXXV, 1991.

----- : "State Formation in South India, 850-1280", in *THE STATE IN INDIA 1000-1700*, ed. by Hermann Kulke, Oxford University Press, Delhi, 1995.

Inden, Ronald : "Orientalist Construction of India", *MAS*, Vol. 20, No.3, 1986.

Jagadeeswari, R. : "The Home of the Chalukyas" *JAHRS*, Vol. XXXI-I-IV Parts. 1965-66.

Jaiswal, Suvira : 'Studies in Early Indian Social History Trends and Possibilities." *IHR*, Vol. 6, 1979-80,

-------- : "Varna Ideology and Social Change" *Social Scientist*, Vol. 19, 1991.

------- : "Studies in the Social Structure of Early Tamil Nadu" In R.S. Sharma, V.N. Jha (ed.), *Indian Society Historical Probings*.

Jha, D.N. : "Early Indian Feudalism—Historical Critique" Presidental Address, *PIHC*,- 40th ss., Waltaire, 1979.

——— : "Presidential Address , Historiography." *PAPHC*, XI, Nagaram, 1987, pp. 161-165.

Jha, V.N. : "Social Stratification in Ancient India" *Social Scientist*, Vol. 19, 1991.

Kameswara Rao, K.S. : "Was the Political System in Medieval Andhra A Monarchical Absolutism,"? *PAPHC*, 1984, Kakinada.

——— : "Social Formation During Eastern Chalukyan Period", *PAPHC*, 1987-88, Nagaram, pp. 80-83.

——— : "An Exploratory Note on the Writings on Social History of Early and Medieval Andhra (Telugu & English), *PAPHC*. Warangal, 1990, pp. 260-265.

——— : "Social Structure of Medieval Andhra Emergence of New Political Elites." *PAPHC*, Nellore, 1991.

Kameswara Rao, V. : "Presidental Address-Medieval Andhra Session" *PAPHC*, XII Session Srisailam, 1989.

Kanaka Durga, P.S. : "Kings, Temples and Legitimation of Autochthonous Communities—A case Study of a South Indian temple" *JESHO*, Vol. XXXV, 1992.

Kulke, Hermann : "The Early and the Imperial Kingdom: A Processural Model of Integrative State Formation in Early Medieval India," in *"THE STATE IN INDIA 1000-1700"* Ed. by Hermann Kulke, Oxford University Press, Delhi, 1995.

Kumar, Dharma : "Private Property in Asia? The Case of Medieval South India." *CSSH*, Vol. 27, No.2, April, 1985.

Kulke, Hermann : "Fragmentation and Segmentation versus Integration ? Reflections on the Concept of Indian Feudalism and Segmentary State in Indian History."

Kumara Swamy. Y. : "Traces of Feudalism during the Eastern Chalukyan Period." *PAPHC*, Warangal.

——— : "Social Dynamics of the Brahmins of Telugu Country" *PAPHC*, Guntur, 1986.

Murthy, M.L.K. : "Environment, Royal Policy and Social Formation in the Eastern Ghats South India, A.D. 1000-1500", Presidential Address, *PIHC*, 53rd Session, Warangal, 1993.

Nagaraju, S. : "Beginnings of Telugu Literature—A Socio-Historical Approach" Presidential Address, *PAPHC*, Nagaram, 1987-88.

Nandi, R.N. : "Gōtra and Social Mobility in the Deccean", *PIHC*, 1970.

——— : "Client, Ritual and Conflict in Early Brahmanical order" *IHR*, Vol. VI, 1979-1980.

——— : "Growth of Rural Economy in Early Feudal India" Presidential address, *PIHC*, 45th Session, Annamalainagar, 1984.

Narayanan, M.G.S. : "Trends & Prospects ofl Historiography" *PIHC*, 39th Session, Hyderabad, 1978.

Parabrahma Sastry, P.V. : "The Boyas in Andhra History," *PAPHC*, Guntur, 1986,

Parabrahma Sastry,P.V. : "Political System in Early Costal Andhra" in Devendra Handa (ed.), *Ajaya Sri*, Vol. I, Delhi, 1989.

Parasher, Aloka. : "Early Settlement Patterns in the Deccan and the Study of Regional History", *PAPHC*, Warangal, 1983.

——— : "Absences in History Towards Recovering History of the Marginal in Early India." *PIHC*, Symposia Papers, 1992.

——— : "Small Localities and the Writing of Regional History." Presidential Address, *PAPHC*, XX Annual Session, Guntur, 1996.

——— : "Early History of Andhra—Some Interpretations," *PAHPC*, IX Session, Kurnool, 1985, pp. 184-191.

Ramachandra Rao, C.V. : "The Kakatiya Polity, Economy and Society: A few considerations (The Kakatiya State as a Metropolitan State)" Presidental Address, *PAPHC*, Warangal, 1990.

Ramanatham, R. : "Vengi", *JAHRS*, Vol. XX

Reddy, Pattabhirama, M. : "Some Thoughts on Historiography Today: Presidential Address, *PAPHC*, Vijayawada, 1978, pp. 143-156.

Sah Ayodhya Prasad : "Feudatories and Beneficiaries in Medieval Orissa." (Circa A.D.600-1200) *PIHC*, 1968.

Sahu, Bhairabi Prasad : "Social Morphology and Physiology of Early Medieval Orissa" (Circa A.D.400-1000) *PIHC*.

Sarkar, H. : "Growth of Cities in Andhradesa (200 B.C. to A.D. 300)," *PAPHC*, Guntur, 1986.

Satish Chandra : "Writings on Social History of Medieval India : Trends and Prospects," *IHR*, Vol. III, pp. 269-285.

Seneviratna, Sudharshan. : "Kalinga and Andhra: The Process of Secondary State Formation in Early India." *IHR*, Vol.7, No. 1-2, 1980, pp. 54-69.

Settar, S. : "Twentieth Century in Ancient India" Presidential Address, *PIHC*, 43rd Session, Kurukshetra, 1982, pp. 57-94.

Sharma, R.S. : "Decay of Gangetic Towns in Gupta and Post Gupta Times," *PIHC*, 33, Muzafarpur, 1972.

——— : "Indian Feudalism Retouched,"—A Review Article, *IHR*, Vol. I, 1974.

——— : "Problem of Transition from Ancient to Medieval in Indian History," *IHR*, Vol. 1, 1974.

——— : "Raja Sasana : Meaning, Scope and Application," *PIHC*, 37th Session, Calicut, 1976.

——— : "The Segmentary State and the Indian Experience," *IHR*, Vol. XVI, 1989-90.

Shrimali, K.M. : "Some Recent Constructions or Rather "Deconstructions" of Socio-economic and Political Formation of Early Medieval India, *PAPHC*, XVIII Session.

Sinha Surajit : "State Formation and Rajput Myth in Tribal Central India" in *"The State in India (1000-1200 A.D.)"* by Hermann Kulke, Oxford University Press, Delhi, 1995.

Somasekhara Sarma, M. : "The Later Chalukyas of Vengi," *JAHRS*, Vol. XXXII, 1971-72.

Stein, Burton : "The Segmentary State: Interim Reflections," In *"THE STATE IN INDIA 1000-1700"* Ed. by Hermann Kulke, Oxford University Press, Delhi, 1995, pp. 134-161.

Subramanyam, B.R. : "Ancient History and Archaeology" Presidential Address, *PAPHC*, Warangal, 1983.

Sundaram, K. : "Medieval Andhra" Presidential Address *PAPHC*, Kavali, 1978.

Thakur V.K. : "Social Mobility in Early Indian Urban Centres : A Theoretical Perspective" *PIHC*.

Veluthat, Kesavan : "Royalty and Divinity : Legitimization of Monarchical Power in South India," *PIHC*, 1978, 39th Session.

——— : "The Temple Base of the Bhakti Movement in South India," *PIHC*, Session 40, 1979.

——— : "The Status of the Monarch: A Note on the Rituals pertaining to Kingship and their Significance in the Tamil Country (A.D. 600-1200)," *PIHC*, Session 43, Kurukshetra, 1982.

Vijaya, N.R. : "Evolution of Prasasti in the Inscriptions of the Eastern Chalukyas," *PAPHC*, Warangal, 1990.

Yadava, B.N.S. : "Accounts of the Kaliage & The Social Transition from Antiquity to the Middle Ages," *IHR*, Vol. V. 1978-79.

——— : "Problem of the Interaction between Socio-Economic Classes in the Early Medieval Complex" *IHR*, Vol.

——— : "The Problem of the Emergence of Feudal Relations," Presidental Address, *PIHC*, 41st Session, Bombay, 1980.

ENCYCLOPAEDIA/DICTIONARIES/ATLASES/GLOSSARY

James Hastings : *Encyclopaedia of Religion and Ethics*, Vol. VI, 1974.

Brown Lesly : *The New Shorter Oxford English Dictionary*, Vol. I & II, 1993.

Schwartzberg, J.E. : *A Historical Atlas of South Asia*, The University of Chicago Press, Chicago, 1978.

Sircar D.C. : *Indian Epigraphical Glossary*, Motilal Banarsi Dass, Delhi, 1966.

APPENDIX-I

GENEALOGICAL TABLE OF THE EASTERN CHĀLUKYAS OF VENGI

- Kubja Vishnuvardhana (624-641 A.D.)
  - Jayasiṁha Vallabha (641-673 A.D.)
  - Indrabhaṭṭāraka (673 A.D.)
    - Vishnuvardhana II (673-682 A.D.)
      - Mangi Yuvarāja (682-706 A.D.)
        - Jayasiṁha II (706-716 A.D.
        - Vishnuvardhana III (719-755 A.D.) (M) Vijayamahādēvi
          - Vijayāditya I (755-772 A.D.)
            - Visnuvardhana IV (772-808 A.D.
              - Narēndramṛgarāja Vijayāditya I (808-843 A.D.)
              - Bhīma Sāluki
              - Silāmahādēvi (m) Dhruva (or Rāshtrakūta family)
                - Indra
              - Vishnuvardhana V, (Kali) (m) Silamahādēvi (843-844 A.D.) [son of Narēndramṛgarāja Vijayāditya I; Silamahādēvi daughter of Indra]
        - Kokkili Vikramāditya I (718-719 A.D.)
          - (Madhya Kalinga Branch) Mangi Yuvarāja II
        - Pṛthvi Poṛi

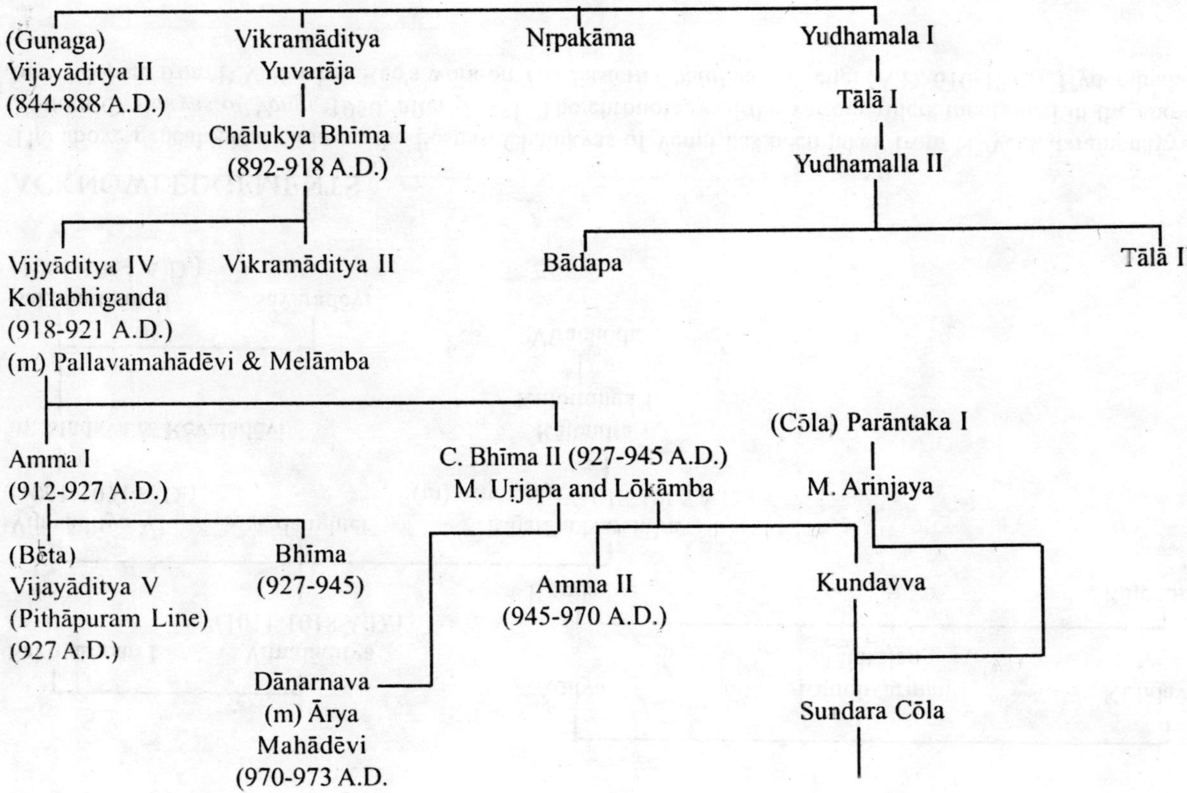
(Guṇaga)
Vijayāditya II
(844-888 A.D.)
Vikramāditya
Yuvarāja
Chālukya Bhīma I
(892-918 A.D.)
Nṛpakāma
Yudhamala I
Tālā I
Yudhamalla II
Vijyāditya IV
Kollabhiganda
(918-921 A.D.)
(m) Pallavamahādēvi & Melāmba
Vikramāditya II
Bādapa
Tālā II
Amma I
(912-927 A.D.)
C. Bhīma II (927-945 A.D.)
M. Uṛjapa and Lōkāmba
(Cōla) Parāntaka I
M. Arinjaya
(Bēta)
Vijayāditya V
(Pithāpuram Line)
(927 A.D.)
Bhīma
(927-945)
Amma II
(945-970 A.D.)
Kundavva
Dānarnava
(m) Ārya
Mahādēvi
(970-973 A.D.
Sundara Cōla

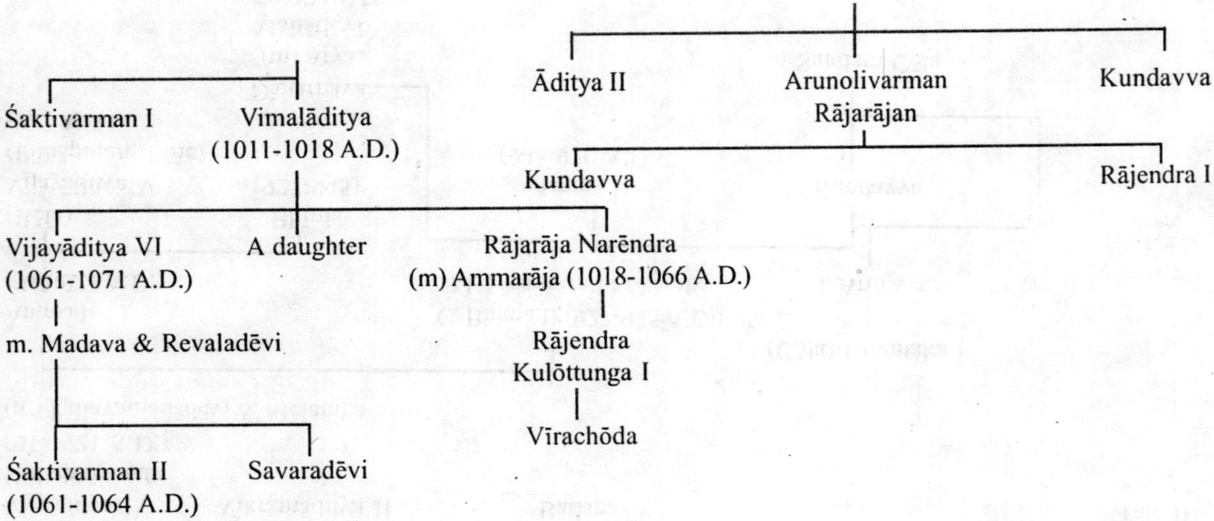

ACKNOWLEDGEMENTS

The above genealogical table on the Eastern Chālukyas of Vengi has been taken from N. Venkataramanayya's book on *Eastern Chalukyas of Vengi*, 1950, after p. 351. The chronology of the various rulers mentioned in the above table has been adopted from B.V. Krishna Rao's work on *The Eastern Chalukyas* of vengi (A.D. 610-1210), Hyderabad, 1973.

APPENDIX - IIA

GENEALOGICAL TABLE OF CHĀLUKYAS OF MUDIGONDA

- Kokkirāja
- Ranamarda
  - Kusumāyudha I (A.D. 870-895)
    - Goṇaga or Vijayāditya (A.D. 895-910)
      - Baddega (A.D. 935-941)
    - Nirāvadya (A.D. 910-935)
      - Kusumāyudha II (A.D. 935-960)
        - Vijayāditya II (A.D. 960-980)
          - Kusumāyudha II I(A.D. 980-1000)
            - Goṇga (A.D. 1000-1025)
            - Nijjayarāja (A.D. 1025-1050)
              - Kusumāyudha IV (A.D. 1050-1075)
              - Bētarāja (A.D. 1075-1100)
              - Kusumāyudha V (A.D. 1100-1125)
              - Batubēta (A.d. 1125-1150)
            - Mallapa
            - Dobhachalata

APPENDIX-IIB

GENEALOGICAL TABLE OF CHĀLUKYAS OF JANANĀTHAPURAM

- Vijayāditya I (A.D. 1118-1124)
  - Vishnuvardhana (A.D. 1124-1151)
  - Mallappa I (A.D. 1151-1158)
    - Vijayāditya II (A.D. 1158-1173)
      - Mallappa II (A.D. 1173-1205)
      - Vīranarēndra (A.D. 1177-1179)
      - Mallapa III or Goṇaga (A.D. 1202-1241)
        - Udayachandra (A.D. 1223-1225)
        - Chandraśēkhara or Vijayāditya III (A.D. 1225-1255)
  - Somidēva
- Vimalā-ditya
- Vikramā-dityr
- Vishnu-vardhana
- Mallapa
- Karṇa
- Rājamārtānda

APPENDIX - IIC
GENEALOGICAL TABLE OF CHĀLUKYAS OF NIDADAVŌLU

Vēngīśvara I (A.D. 1078-1129)

Malla (A.D. 1129-1150) | Vēngi Ayyapa I | (Daughter name not known)

Vēngi Goṇika I (A.D. 1150-1196)

Ayyapa II (A.D. 1193) | Mahādēvi I (A.D. 1196-1235) (alias Vishnuvardhana)

Ganapati (A.D. 1193-1212) | Mannagoṇka (II) (A.D. 1212-1230) | Vēngīśvara II (A.D. 1233-1250) | Induśēkhara I (A.D. 1238-1255)

Mahādēva II | Vīrabhadra (A.D. 1250-66) (m) Rudrama of the Kākatiyas (D) Mummadamma Ruyyamma & Rudrama | Ānyamahādēvi (D)

Virayadēva (A.D. 1266-79) | Induśēkhara II (A.D. 1279-97) | Prithivi Vallabha II (A.D. 1297-99) | Induśēkhara II (A.D. 1300) | Odayamathādēvi (D)

Rudramadēvi (A.D. 1199-1211)

ACKNOWLEDGEMENTS:

The above genealogical tables belonging to the Minor Chalukyan families of Mudigonda, Jannathapuram and Nidadavolu were taken from K. Suryanarayana's *Inscriptions of the Minor Chālukyan Dynasties* of *Andhra Pradesh*, New Delhi 1993, pp. 28,42 & 118

APPENDIX-III

MYTHICAL GENEALOGY OF THE CAṄDRAVAṂŚA LINEAGE

1. Nārāyana (i.e. Vishṇu)
2. Svaymbhūḥ (i.e. Brahmā, the creator)
3. Ātri (born of Brahmā's mind)
4. Sōma (i.e. the Moon)
5. Budha
6. Purūravas (a Chakravartin)
7. Āyuḥ
8. Nahushaḥ
9. Yayātiḥ (A Chakravarthin)
10. Puruḥ (a Chakravartin)
11. Janamējaya (I) (Performer of three aśvamēdhas)
12. Prāchīśan
13. Sainyayātiḥ
14. Hayapatiḥ
15. Sārvabhaumaḥ
16. Jayasēnaḥ
17. Mahābhunaḥ
18. Aiśānakaḥ
19. Krōdhānanaḥ
20. Dēvakiḥ
21. Ṛibhukaḥ
22. Ṛikshakaḥ
23. Mativaraḥ (performer of sasśtras and yāgas)
24. Kātyāyanaḥ
25. Nīlaḥ
26. Dushyantaḥ
27. Bharata (A Chakravartin who performed aśvamēdha on the banks of the Gaṅgā and Yamunā)
28. Bhūmanyuḥ
29. Suhōtaḥ
30. Hasti
31. Virōchanaḥ
32. Ajamīlaḥ

33. Saṁvaraṇaḥ (married Tapatyā, daughter of Tapana)
34. Sudhavāna
35. Parīkshit (I)
36. Bhimasēna (I)
37. Paradīpanaḥ
38. Śantanuḥ
39. Vichitravīryaḥ
40. Pāṇḍurājaḥ
41. Yudhisṭhiraḥ
42. Bhīma (II)
43. Arjuna
44. Nakula
45. Sahadēva
46. Abhimanyu
47. Parīkshit (II)
48. Janamējaya (II)
49. Ksēmukaḥ
50. Naravāhanaḥ
51. Śatānikaḥ
52. Udayanaḥ

ACKNOWLEDGEMENTS

This genealogical table bas been adopted by us from K.V. Ramesh's *Chālukyas of Vātāpi*, Delhi, 1984, pp. 16-18.

INDEX

A

B

C

D

J

K

L

R

S

T